TRADE MARK

Regal Musical Instruments 1895 - 1955

by Bob Carlin

ISBN 978-1-57424-273-7
SAN 683-8022

Cover by James Creative Group

All Illustrations the collection of the author unless otherwise noted.

Photographs by Amanda Kowalski except as noted. Images prepared by Steve Terrill.

CENTERSTREAM®

P.O. Box 17878 - Anaheim Hills, CA 92817

www.centerstream-usa.com

Photograph by Jim Bollman, courtesy Stu Cohen.

Table of Contents

Thanks! And Sources 4

Regal-Made Instruments:
An Introduction 5

Chapter One:
The Birth of Regal 7

Chapter Two:
Regal in Chicago 23

Chapter Three:
Mandolins 37

Chapter Four:
Harp Guitars 95

Chapter Five:
Banjos 103

Chapter Six:
"Four Strings, No Waiting": The "Original" Tenor Guitar 121

Chapter Seven:
Flattop Guitars 125

Chapter Eight:
Archtop Guitars 229

Chapter Nine:
"Four Strings, No Waiting": Ukuleles 255

Chapter Ten:
Octofone, Hawyofone and Basso Guitar 304

A Regal Timeline 314

Regal Labels 315

Regal Advertisements 316

Thanks! And Sources

By no means is this a complete list of all my sources for this work and for the folks that helped me out. I've tried to "hit the highlights," so, I apologize if I've left you off the list.

My "Rabbis" for this project were:

Ron Middlebrook of Centerstream, who, in addition to publishing this book, provided catalogues, photographs and the patience to allow me to follow my instincts.

Stan Werbin/Elderly Instruments, for catalogues, photographs and advice.

Dennis Buchholz/Leaning Dog Guitars, for catalogues, photographs and hooking me up with other Regal collectors.

Rabbinette Arian Sheets, Curator of Stringed Instruments at the National Music Museum (aka: "The Shrine to Music"), for all her hospitality and access to periodicals, catalogues and instruments in their collection, as well as networking with other researchers.

Hubert Pleijsier, the author of Washburn: Prewar Instrument Styles, for providing his unpublished research.

Jim Bollman, for banjo history, catalogues, photography, accommodations and fine dining.

Ed Britt, for information and perspectives on the Bacon Company.

Wil Bremer and Julie Luther/Spruce Tree Music, for introducing me to Larry Phetteplace, instrument photography and going "above and beyond."

The Guitarded Society of Middle North Carolina Lynn Michael, Aaron Morris, Tom Mylet, and honorary chapter president Roy Bookbinder, for support and advice.

And, in no specific order:

Tom Walsh and the late John King for ukuleleinfo; Tony Klassen/New Era Guitars for guitar photography; Stu Cohen/The Music Emporium for use of his rare catalogues and instruments; Ryan Fitzsimmons/The Music Emporium for instrument photography; Larry Phetteplace for access to his father's oral history and inlay work; harpguitars.net/Gregg Miner for information and photographs of Wulschner/Regal Instruments; the Indiana State Archives for Regal and Wulschner Incorporation documents; the Indiana State Library for maps, newspapers and city directories; the Indiana Historical Society for local history on the Wulschner-Stewarts; Warren Dovell /the Guitar and Amp Center and Randy Klimpert for access to their remarkable collections; John and Julie Bernunzio/Bernunzio Uptown Music for sharing their archive of Regals they've sold; Acousticmusic.org for photos of Bacon instruments; www.arcade-museum.com and NARAS for the Music Trade Review; Buzzy Levine/Lark Street Guitars for his collection of Regal and Bacon guitars; Steve Terrell for prepping images; Jim Garber for research on Samuel Siegel; David Portman for catalogues; the Newberry Library for Montgomery Ward catalogues, Chicago City Directories and newspaper databases and the Chicago Museum of History for Montgomery Ward catalogues.

AND:

The descendants of Wulschner-Stewart families, Dave and Carolyn Martin, Tom Benson, Dave Matchette, Mark Demaray, Newspaperarchive.com, Gary Selufsky, Eugene Braig, Kailo Schlegel, Jeffrey Noonan/The Guitar in America, Richard Johnson and Frank Ford/Gryphon Stringed Instruments, Leo Coulson and Kennard Machol/Intermountain Guitar and Banjo, www.guitar-museum.com, www.lapsteelguitar.com, George Gruhn and Walter Carter/Gruhn Guitars, Ebay, Lynn Wheelwright, Andy Fitzgibbons, Gerry Clarke, Ken Lelen, Greg Sadowski, Scott Freilich/Top Shelf Music, Steve Uhrik/Musurgia and Retrofret, the Illinois State Archives, Jake Murrow/Antebellum Instruments, Tony Marcus, Ancestry.com, Scott Huffman, Gary Melnyk, Steve Kovacik/Kovacik Guitars, The Unofficial Martin Guitar Forum (www.umgf.org), Dream Guitars, Neil Harpe/Stellaguitars.com, Tim Kummer/Kummer's Vintage Instruments, Wes Langlois, Richard Carlin, John Schwab, Mark Zimin, Karleen Tyksinski, Atomic Guitars, The Larsons' Creations/Robert Carl Hartman, http://ukediner.ukulele.org and Jim Beloff/Flea Market Music.

THANKS!

Regal-Made Instruments

1895-1955, an Introduction

What are the three most important pieces of information that a vintage instrument enthusiast wants to know? The answer (no, this isn't another guitarded joke) is, "who made my instrument," "what model is it," and "what year was my instrument made?" (The fourth would be, "what is my guitar worth?" but, that is beyond the scope of this book) Some companies, for example C. F. Martin, labeled their products with model designations and, for the last hundred plus years, inscribed a serial number within the instrument as well. Additionally, Martin has only ever moved twice, once within the same small town, still owns their original factory and is still in business after almost 180 years controlled by the same family. Luckily, no company records ever seem to have been thrown away and, so, with a bit of detective work, almost any Martin made instrument can be reasonably identified. The work of other instrument manufacturers is a bit harder to unravel. After bankruptcies, multiple changes of ownership and many moves, company records are just as likely to end up in a dumpster as stay within the current business (such as is the case with Gibson).

Unfortunately, the historian attempting to answer the questions posed above regarding the Regal Musical Instrument Company as opposed to Martin or Gibson suffers from additional problems. First off, no Regal company has operated out of one of their four manufacturing locations since the mid-1950s and their successors have been gone for about forty years. Secondly, Regal-made instruments were sold under a myriad of names, and all but a few of their higher grade pieces lacked serial or model number designations. Thirdly, original Regal catalogues are amazingly scarce considering how successful a business was Regal and distributor catalogues featuring Regal-made guitars, mandolins, tenor guitars and ukuleles aren't much more common. Even when one is lucky enough to find a catalogue, the descriptions of instruments are sketchy at best and filled with hyperbole. Lastly, the pursuit of descendants of various company executives by this researcher has yet to yield positive results.

To further confuse attempts at identifying the "who made my instrument" part of the equation, all of Regal's manufacturing peers utilized the same suppliers, outsourcing various bits such as decals, paint treatments, silkscreen decorations, plastic fingerboards and headstocks, and, later on, engraving and pearl cutting to the same companies or individuals. Especially within the various Chicago makers, everyone made parts and/or completed instruments for everyone else. One musical instrument company might make guitars or ukuleles or mandolins for a wholesaler's "house brand" one year, and a different manufacturer would make them the next. The silkscreened decorations remained the same; the outsourced paint job was consistent between the two years, and construction details for the instruments varied only slightly (such as a different headstock or bridge shape, or a larger versus smaller dowel joining the neck of a ukulele to its body). No wonder it's hard to tell their instruments apart! So, much continues to be unknown or conjecture about the maker of supposed Regal instruments, along with their model and the year of their manufacture.

In the sections on the actual instruments made by Regal, I have attempted to gather the best information possible from period catalogues, along with a wide variety of sources and experts, listed in the <u>Thanks! and Sources</u> section of this work. Additionally, I've tried to examine as many of the higher grade Regal-made instruments as possible, either in person, or, when that proved impossible or impractical, through photographs. This provided difficult for Regals made before 1925, as those identifiable as "Regal-made" have not survived in large numbers. Curiously, this pre-1925 period coincides with a lack of coverage of Regal's activities in trade magazines such as <u>The Music Trade Review</u>. Considering the company's supposed output, the only conclusion that can be drawn besides the improbable destruction of thousands of pieces is that Regal was mainly if not exclusively making instruments for sale under other names, and, according to information set out in the history of the company elsewhere in this book, this included some or all small stringed instruments marketed under the Lyon & Healy moniker.

To completely cover Regal's entire sixty year output would be impossible within one book, as they manufactured thousands and thousands of low-grade guitars, mandolins and ukuleles. Granted, I have allowed my own subjective interests to determine what is included here. And, I can only write about an instrument when I've gathered enough information to do so. Therefore, I focused my attentions on those instruments that will have the greatest importance to today's musician/collector as playable in a modern setting, or, alternately, on those strange and wonderful pieces that only could have been dreamed up at Regal. Additionally, I've intentionally avoided repeating information about the Regal-made Washburns sold in the 1930s by Tonk Bros. except where it was essential in discussing Regal's history and other Regal-made products. That part of the company's story has already been covered within Hubert Pleijsier's admirable book, Washburn Prewar Instrument Styles, also published by Centerstream. And, I've steered clear of the resophonic instruments that resulted from Regal's licensing agreement with the Dobro Company. Those in themselves could fill a whole book, which I hope another author that knows and loves them will undertake in the near future. Likewise, Regal's classical and twelve-string guitars, experiments with electronic versions of their acoustic offerings, along with totally electric solid-body instruments, will have to be covered in a future work.

So, here is my first attempt at making sense out of the Regal story. I take full responsibility for the information contained within these pages. I hope you'll find it to be useful, entertaining and fun.—Bob Carlin, Lexington, NC, December, 2010.

About the Author

Bob Carlin is well-known as an author, record and radio producer, musician and guitar accumulator. He has a particular interest in the history of musical instrument manufactory, with previous writings focused on American banjo manufactory. This is his second book for Centerstream.

Chapter One
The Birth of Regal

Guitars Made in Indianapolis

The Regal Manufacturing Company was one of the many musical instrument concerns clustered around the Chicago area before World War II. Although we tend to associate Regal with the Windy City (and most of this book will deal with the instruments made there), the manufacturer was originally located to the south in Indianapolis, Indiana. The original Regal was the creation of a German band master and his spouse, a member of one of Indianapolis' founding families.

It all began when William Sullivan (1803-1886), lawyer and justice of the peace, came to Indianapolis from Maryland, where he was born of Irish parentage. By marrying Clarissa Tomlinson (1812-1895) of the McCartney (from Pennsylvania) and Tomlinson (out of Ohio) families in 1835, William established a union between two of Indiana's early clans. One side of the family could even claim ancestors that had fought in the American Revolution.

William's daughter Flora McCartney Sullivan, named for Clarissa's sister Florinda, was born in 1847 at the confluence of Maryland and Pennsylvania Streets. When Flora was eight, the family moved to a newly constructed home at the outskirts of the metropolis on a corner lot located at Meridian and St. Clair.

Around 1866, Flora Sullivan married Robert R. Stewart of Terre Haute, Indiana and relocated to that city. Robert had served in the Eleventh Indiana Cavalry, first as a lieutenant during the Mexican War (1846-1848) and then again as a colonel during the Civil War. After the Civil War, Stewart worked as a deputy sheriff. The couple had one child, Alexander (middle name possibly McCartney or MacGregor) in 1867. Unfortunately, a stint during the War Between the States in the infamous Confederate Libby Prison located in Richmond, Virginia left Robert in a weakened state of health, and he died soon after the birth of his son.

Emil Wulschner, Music Trade Review, June 23, 1894, courtesy of NARAS.

By 1873, Flora and Alex had moved back to the Sullivan home on North Meridian. Flora Stewart had musical aspirations dating back to before her first marriage, and she took advantage of her recently widowed status to study in Europe, including a prolonged stay in Germany. While there, she met and married a dashing young army bandmaster named Emil Wulschner.

Born March 27, 1847 near Weissenfels in Saxony, Wulschner showed musical talent from an early age. After studying in Leipzig and Dresden, Emil joined the military, which supported high-quality musical ensembles. During his eleven years in the army, Emil Wulschner served in the Austrian-German war of 1867 and the Franco-Prussian War of 1870-1871. At the age of twenty-four, Emil won a competition to become Kapellmeister of the Bavarian army. Wulschner's duties included the directorship of all Bavarian military musical organizations, as well as performing in the King of Bavaria's own band in Munich. Family lore places Emil's meeting with Flora Stewart, possibly through Wulschner's music teacher Carl H. Weegman, in Munich during 1875, with the couple marrying that year and returning together to Indianapolis.

But, another scenario is possible. Independent of Emil and Flora's supposed meeting in Germany, Wulschner could have either followed Flora back from Munich or emigrated on his own, encountering her in Indiana. There appears a cryptic listing in the 1876/1877 Indianapolis City Directory for "Wm. E. Wulschner, teacher of German" living independently of the William Sullivan family that could indicate the real truth in the matter.

Regardless of why Emil Wulschner came to Indiana, he picked a good time to relocate to America. Partially fueled by the growing German-American immigrant population, the country was enjoying a rapid growth in musical organizations and activities. Through private pupils and an association with choral and instrumental groups, European music masters such as Wulschner could manage a good living in the new world. And Flora, with her own musical skills as a composer and performer, along with some organizational abilities and business smarts, proved a good partner for Emil in his endeavors.

Emil Wulschner first took a position on North Pennsylvania Street with the music publisher Henry L. Benham. Benham had dissolved his partnership with a Mr. Howland at the end of 1876, and begun printing a magazine, Benham's Musical Review, the following year. In 1877/1878, for approximately a year, Wulschner clerked for Benham and also served as the musical director for the Choral Union (known as the Lyra Society). Emil succeeded founder James S. Black in the conductor's position, crowning the season with a joint concert by the five hundred-member Union and the Harmonic Society of Haydn's First Mass at Roberts Park Church on June 28th, 1878.

In February of 1878, Emil Wulschner left Henry Benham's employ, moving up the street to open his own store at 44 North Penn, selling "pianos, organs, [and] music merchandise." Wulschner was later to proclaim that he was the "oldest resident music dealer in Indianapolis." In just five years, Emil Wulschner's business was successful enough that he was able to expand into the building next door. In 1883, Emil stated publicly that "We have a complete assortment of everything in the Music Line—Sheet Music, Band Instruments, Accordeons [sic], Harps, Guitars, [and] Zithers." Growing responsibilities with his own business had caused Wulschner to give up the directorship of the Choral Union in 1881.

A twelve page tabloid catalogue in newspaper format published sometime between 1883 and the early 1890s shows the extent of Wulschner's growing business. The Musical Startler ("warranted to 'startle' everybody as to lowness of [prices]") showed cornets, piston valve brasses, 'Clarionets,' band supplies, music stands, mutes, cymbals, drums, basses, cellos, flutes and piccolos. There were pages devoted to "Spanish" mandolins from $5.00 to $12.00 ("imitation rosewood" with geared tuners), "Imported and American guitars" from $3.50 in red maple to "fine hand-made, equal to the best celebrated makes, $25.00." Undoubtedly, some of their stock was domestically made and some imported from Europe. For example, Emil Wulschner became the sole agent in the United States for Boosey & Company's brass instruments, and he also imported brasses from Austria.

By the mid-1890s, Wulschner's business had grown to the extent that he utilized fifty-six employees. The Indianapolis store, occupying two retail and two wholesale floors at 78-80 North Pennsylvania Street, was joined by branches in Louisville, Kentucky, and Terre Haute, Richmond, Muncie and Brazil, Indiana. The success of his business allowed Emil to sponsor many local musical events, including the Annual May Music Festival, begun in 1889, and the Indianapolis Mannerchor concerts. He also founded and led the Robert Park Church Choral Society, where he was a member.

The Regal Manufacturing Company, Indianapolis, IN, 1901. Music Trade Review, April 6, 1901, courtesy of NARAS.

The next logical step for the Wulschner concern was to produce its own musical paraphernalia. By 1883, Emil was publishing his own line of sheet music that included the range of compositions popular in the last decades of the 19th century. This included dance pieces, minstrel numbers, sentimental and topical songs, as well as light classical music. Not surprisingly, Emil Wulschner specialized in Indiana musicians and his composers included Emil's wife Flora, Sue Ingersoll McWilliams, Barclay Walker (1859-1927), Beardsley Woods (later to become a publisher himself) and one of his own piano salesmen, Roy L. Burtch. Although Flora Wulschner wrote, arranged and translated many pieces, she is best remembered for her song "Forgotten." Published anonymously as a poem by Leslie's Illustrated Weekly in 1892, "Forgotten" was set to music by Eugene Cowles in the year before Flora's death.

Although keyboard and band instruments were the basis for his business, the growing popularity of both the guitar and the mandolin (and possibly their high cost from his suppliers) pushed Emil Wulschner to begin their manufacture. It is unclear the exact date for the start of Wulschner's instrument building. When Lyon & Healy registered the Regal trademark in 1906, the application claimed the name had been in use for musical instruments since 1895. Local lore has Wulschner making guitars in a loft above the store by 1896, and moving the lutherie to 24-28 South Capitol Avenue when work outgrew the original space. The first definitive mention of Wulschner-made instruments dates to an 1896/1897 catalogue. This also seems to be the first appearance of the Regal "crown" logo, which Wulschner used to brand his products and stayed the company's logo throughout its changes in ownership. In May of 1897, Emil advertised "Manufacturers of the celebrated 'Regal' mandolins, violins, guitars, strings, etc. which are 'perfection—musically and mechanically." By 1899, Regal instruments were being advertised in the Cadenza magazine and distributed as far afield as Hawaii, Canada and Mexico. The Baroness Hengelmuller, a member of one of the Royal Austrian families, even chose to purchase a Regal mandolin for her daughter.

By the beginning of 1898, John W. Keyes was brought in to manage the stringed instrument factory. Born in 1870, John Keyes was the son of a well-to-do physician. Prior to coming to Indianapolis, Keyes had been involved with the making of musical instruments in Louisville, Kentucky, first as secretary/treasurer with the J. P. Simmons Company in 1896 and the next year as president of the Keyes-Gallrein Music Company. John Keyes probably supervised the preparations of the South Capitol Avenue location and oversaw the move into the new factory in September of 1898. Subsequently, J.W. Keyes represented Wulschner in the Sheet Music Dealers' Association and worked with his publishing and piano departments.

But, Emil was not destined to enjoy his successes. With his health in decline, Wulschner was forced to retire from the music business. After several years of illness, Emil spent two months in California in an effort to regain his strength. Unfortunately, upon returning home, Emil Wulschner died suddenly from heart failure on April 8, 1900. He was 53 years old.

Wulschner-Stewart

Luckily for the Wulschner Company, Flora had helped to run the business from the beginning and her son Alexander Stewart had followed his mother into music retail. Alex began clerking for the store in 1882 around the age of fifteen. Three years later, Alexander Stewart became Wulschner's bookkeeper and, in late 1891, Emil changed the business' name to "Wulschner & Son" to reflect his stepson's growing involvement. Alex Stewart celebrated his success in the music business by marrying in 1893. Two surviving sons were born to the couple, George Edmond, named for his mother Georgia, in 1894 and James T., in 1899.

After Emil's death, Alex Stewart and his mother reorganized the wholesale/retail business under the Wulschner Music Company name. At the same time as incorporating with Flora as president and Alex as vice president, they took on William E. Ludlow as secretary. The name of the store was changed to Wulschner-Stewart in a move to more adequately reflect the owners of the business. The change was announced at the end of April of 1903, and made legal in September of that year.

At the same time the Stewarts set up the Wulschner Company, they also incorporated their instrument manufactory. In May of 1900, the Regal Manufacturing Company was established with Alex, Flora and Ludlow at the helm. The Wulschner business continued to expand, with Regal instruments becoming available in the Argentine Republic. And, although his name is not listed on the incorporation papers, John Keyes was still a valued Wulschner employee, spending his summer traveling the country visiting dealers. The factory had a large enough workforce for the instrument makers to organize a union, and label their products as "union made."

Inside View of Regal Factory, Indianapolis, IN, 'A Section of the Finishing Department,' with a harp guitar and guitar-mandolin in the foreground. Music Trade Review, April 6, 1901, courtesy of NARAS.

Inside View of Regal Factory, Indianapolis, IN, 'A Section of the "20th Century" Department.' Music Trade Review, April 6, 1901, courtesy of NARAS.

Inside View of Regal Factory, Indianapolis, IN, 'A Section of the "University" Department.' Music Trade Review, April 6, 1901, courtesy of NARAS.

By 1901, the Regal side of the business had grown large and profitable enough that Alex Stewart and Flora Wulschner decided to divest themselves of the Manufacturing Company. Their first step was separating the factory in April from the main Wulschner-Stewart Corporation. By August, Regal had been sold to a group of prominent local businessmen, who retained John Keyes as "secretary" as well as to run the day-to-day affairs of Regal.

Fortunately, The Music Trade Review, an industry publication, visited the Regal Manufacturing Company in the spring of 1901, and provided an inside view of the company through words and photographs. The article discusses the separation on April 1, 1901 of the factory from the Wulschner wholesale department. With the creation of the Regal Manufacturing Company, the maker of the instruments would thereafter deal directly with Wulschner's wholesale accounts, saving stores a hopeful twenty percent plus. There would be three grades of Regal instruments: the top-of-the-line to be called "Regal," the second tier described as the "high-grade machine-made" Universal" brand and finally a low-price/low quality "Twentieth Century" brand. The Regal factory was ready to turn out thousands of instruments annually. Photographs show several views of the outside and inside of the fifty by one-hundred fifty foot factory building, with table saws powered by belts and piles of guitars possibly being

Inside View of Regal Factory, Indianapolis, IN, 'A Section of one of the Polishing Rooms' with bowl back mandolins in the foreground. <u>*Music Trade Review*</u>*, April 6, 1901, courtesy of NARAS..*

Inside View of Regal Factory, Indianapolis, IN, 'Two Sections of the Machine Room.' <u>*Music Trade Review*</u>*, April 6, 1901, courtesy of NARAS.*

Inside View of Regal Factory, Indianapolis, IN, 'Sections of Two Polishing Rooms.' Music Trade Review, April 6, 1901, courtesy of NARAS.

assembled or finished. Mandolins, guitars and harp guitars are all clearly visible. In September, the new owners enlarged Regal, upgrading the quality of the Twentieth Century line of instruments and introducing the new Regal wood rim "art" banjo. In their 1901 catalog, the Regal owners would boast they were "the largest makers of Mandolins, Guitars and Banjos." By the beginning of 1902, there were mandolin and guitar models available for $15.00 each.

The owners of Regal continued their aggressive expansion throughout the 1901-1903 period. Keyes, called the "general manager," traveled the country, opening dealerships in Pennsylvania, Delaware, Connecticut, Rhode Island, Massachusetts, Maine and New York. Regal instruments were also available in England.

Endorsees

Almost immediately, Regal instruments drew the attention of a number of professional musicians. Ads placed in upscale magazines featured artists such as mandolin virtuosos Hilda Hempel, Samuel Siegel and the Young Sisters; guitar and mandolin composer C. E. Pomeroy of Salt Lake City; the Asetceam Trio featuring mandolinist and banjoist Arthur Wells; as well as guitar soloist Johnson Bane. In February of 1902, the duo of Lemont & Zell wrote that they "are using your new Regal banjo and mandolin in a tour of South Africa and find they stand the climate fine," and the local San Francisco

The Young Sisters, advertisement, Munsey's Magazine.

Hilda Hempel, advertisement, McClure's Magazine.

dealer remarked that Regal banjos were being used by the Banjo and Mandolin Club of UC-Berkeley. That month, Regal also announced that they would promote concert tours by Regal endorsees Samuel Siegel, Hilda Hempel, Johnson Bane, and the Young Sisters.

Hilda A. Hempel

Richard Hempel, a German "Professor" of the zither, mandolin, guitar and banjo, raised his daughters to be musicians, expecting them to practice six hours a day. By 1899, when Hilda was thirteen years old and her sister Elsie was sixteen, they had joined their father in concert as "The Boston Trio." A strange name for a group based in Atlantic City, N. J., where Richard Hempel taught and led the local Guitar and Mandolin, and Zither Clubs.

Samuel Siegel

Samuel Siegel, America's first "mandolin virtuoso," was born in Des Moines, Iowa on March 17, 1875. His parents, David and Rachel Siegel, came from Baden, Germany, the descendants of Polish-Russian Jews. Along with three of Samuel's older siblings, the couple had immigrated several years before Sam's birth, dividing their time between Des Moines proper and Marshalltown some fifty miles to the northeast. Typical of new arrivals, the Siegel family attempted a number of related businesses, running a grocery and a restaurant before settling into the new and used furniture business.

Sam Siegel began concertizing around the age of eighteen. Siegel led the Des Moines Mandolin Club for 1894, at the same time giving local solo concerts and competing in regional competitions during 1894 and 1895. In this same time period, he attended Cornell College in Mount Vernon, Iowa outside Cedar Rapids, and made his first attempts at assembling a touring variety company made up of local performers.

By 1898, Samuel Siegel was working out of Chicago, no surprise as the city dominated the upper Midwest. As a member of the ten musician strong Maeldoft Imperial Mandolin Orchestra, Siegel was on their spring tour of small concert halls in Northeast Iowa, accompanied by a Mr. Wolfe on the guitar. Sam Siegel is credited with being the first American mandolinist to appear in England, as he played the St. James Hall in London during the late fall of 1899.

Luckily for Siegel, America's infant recording industry was looking for talent. Along with the proximity to better engagements, the presence of record labels such as Berliner, Columbia and Edison around New York City might have drawn Samuel Siegel to the area. Or, New York might have just provided a good "way-stop" between England and Chicago. Regardless, Siegel was recording and performing in the New York area by 1899, with his first concert appearance at Chickering Hall on March 2nd. Sam Siegel was living on the lower west side of the New York City by the following year. His recordings probably reflected Siegel's concert repertoire, and included popular songs, light classical music and his own compositions for solo mandolin.

Samuel Siegel, advertisement, Munsey's Magazine, 1901.

Samuel Siegel's involvement with the Regal Company dates to November of 1900. Siegel had in the 1890s begun playing mandolins made by Lyon & Healy of Chicago and marketed under their Washburn brand name, but simultaneously endorsed and publicized Regal instruments as well. In January of 1901, Sam Siegel wrote Wulschner that "the Regal mandolin only has the perfection of tone and scale I find necessary for success in my concert work. I use it exclusively." When John Sunier and Son, a music dealer located in Iowa City, sponsored Samuel Siegel's appearance on April 1, 1902, they gave away a $30.00 Regal mandolin to the person selling the most concert tickets. To further demonstrate his ties to Regal, the following week, Siegel shared a concert stage with fellow Regal endorsees the Young Sisters.

Samuel Siegel spent the first years of the new century touring America, making a cross country tour in early 1901. About half the dates were promoted by Regal through their network of dealers, in exchange for Siegel's endorsement of Regal mandolins. Beginning on January 14, 1901 in Knoxville, TN, Siegel played Chattanooga, Louisville, Cincinnati, Fargo, Anaconda, Butte, Spokane, Portland, San Francisco, Los Angeles, San Diego, Salt Lake City, Denver, Omaha, Chicago, Minneapolis, Milwaukee, Detroit, Pittsburgh, Baltimore and Washington, before ending up in New York City on March 22, 1901. His appearance in Montana prompted the local media to write that Siegel's "Magnificent Recital Charms a Large Audience. Siegel's A Master Hand. Magic Touch of the Fingers Causes Mandolin to Speak in Tones That Sink Deeper Than Ever Words Can." The tour was so successful that it was repeated the following year.

On Friday, March 15, 1901, as a part of the first Regal promotional tour, the Wulschner Music Company brought Siegel to Indianapolis to participate in a large mandolin, guitar and banjo festival at Tomlinson Hall. This engagement was a follow-up to Siegel's recital the previous winter. Siegel, with "an orchestra of one hundred members" made up of local music students on mandolin, guitar, banjo, violin, cello, flute, harp and viol, was the featured soloist. Johnson Bane, also a Regal endorsee (see below), appeared on the program as well.

Sam Siegel was active in the early days of the American Guild of Banjoists, Mandolinists and Guitarists (known as the "BMG."). By 1903, he was appearing at their conventions and at meetings of local chapters, and served on the executive committee from at least 1902-1906. He was still performing and lecturing at Guild meets in May of 1922, when Siegel was elected director of the organization.

Like many musicians, Siegel gleaned a portion of his living from teaching. He was publishing instruction manuals by at least 1901 and teaching classes through local stringed instrument teachers as a part of his national touring. In 1903, Sam Siegel joined with violinist Arthur Heft to found the Siegel-Myers Correspondence School of Music. When Siegel married Anna Saperstein in June of 1909, the headquarters for the school moved from Iowa to Chicago, Anna's hometown.

By 1918, Samuel Siegel was back in New York City, living on West 144th Street. The Siegels appeared to stay in New York and Sam continued to tour and teach, replacing recording with radio work. He received several patents for inventions geared toward making keyboard instruments more accessible to children and non-musicians, and appeared in the mid-1920s at several all-star evenings of music held in

The Deseret Mandolin Club, advertisement, Munsey's Magazine, 1900.

conjunction with the meetings of musical instrument manufacturers. As his style of mandolin playing became passé, Samuel Siegel's career declined, ending with his death in 1948.

Siegel pointed to his exclusivity as a mandolinist as the reason behind his success, and also for his belief in developing a new repertoire limited to the instrument. Unlike many mandolinists of the time, Sam began on the instrument (he was self-taught) rather then switching over from the violin after learning the fingering common to both. Samuel specialized in playing multiple lines simultaneously, with a heavy use of harmonics, left hand pizzicato and arpeggios on pieces such as "Cavaleria Rusticana," Bizet's "Carmen," the "Medley in F" by Rubinstein, as well as his own "Spring Flower Gavotte."

C. E. Pomeroy

The son of a physician, Charles Enos Pomeroy was born in Genesco, Illinois on February 26, 1843, showing a proclivity toward music at an early age. Pomeroy began his professional life as an operator/manager with the Western Union Telegraph Company. By 1867, C. E. Pomeroy was stationed in Salt Lake City, where he married Christiana Monroe Stuart (1851-1923) and began raising a family. After switching careers to banking in 1868, he made a further sideways move into real estate and loans five years later. While continuing to make music as an avocation, C. E. began studying the mandolin and guitar in 1890, teaching himself to both play and compose on those two instruments.

Arthur Wells

Banjo virtuoso James Arthur Wells of the Asetceam Trio was another endorsee of Regal instruments. Born on a farm outside of Indianola, Illinois on May 2, 1869, Arthur's father James moved the family north into the town of Danville by the time Arthur was eleven years old. By his thirtieth birthday in 1899, Arthur Wells was making his living as a musician.

Although the Asetceam Trio, as Wells' group was named, was billed as being from Chicago, all three members came out of the farm country along Illinois's eastern border due south of the City. Besides Arthur on mandolin and banjo, there was mandolinist and banjoist Henry Sulcer (later replaced by Arthur Wells' relative Robert Wells on mandolin), and the Wells' neighbor Hayes Greenawalt on banjo, guitar and harp-guitar.

Hayes James Greenawalt was born between Harrisburg and Hersey, in Dauphin County, Pennsylvania in October of 1872. Sometime between the birth of his last sibling in 1886 and 1900, Hayes' parents Samuel and Ella moved the family to Danville, Illinois. Although his musical compatriot Arthur Wells was confident enough to tell the 1900 census taker that he was working as a musician, Hayes was still holding down his full-time job as a printer while performing with the Asetceam's.

THE ASETCEAM TRIO.

The Asetceam Trio, Cadenza, May/June, 1899. Courtesy Jim Bollman/Eli Kaufman

Arthur Wells was actually performing with a version of the Trio, billed as the Asetceam Mandolin and Guitar Club, as early as 1893, when the group shared the stage in Danville on Thanksgiving night with the renowned banjoist Parke Hunter. After the group endorsed Regal instruments in 1899, they combined with (or took on the roll as) the Johnson Swiss Bell Ringers and featured a program similar in nature to Wells' later touring groups. In addition to selections on banjo, mandolin, guitar and harp guitar, aluminum chimes, sleigh bells and saxophone were employed, with dramatic readings by Hayes Greenawalt being cited by some critics as the most enjoyable part of the evening. At one time during their existence, the Asetceam's included Hayes' younger brother Clarence on mandolin and banjo and Arthur's future wife and performing partner Alta R. Smith on piano.

The Asetceam/Bell Ringers Company made it as far as New York State before disbanding. Hayes Greenawalt went on to pursue an acting career and was married briefly to another thespian. By 1920, Greenawalt had moved back to Danville, where he returned to the printing profession, working at the local newspaper. By the time Wells had reorganized the group as the Apollo Concert Company sometime prior to 1908, Arthur and Alta had become man and wife.

Alta R. Smith was born June 9, 1880 in Battleground, Indiana. Her father Erastus was a farmer, but this did not stop Alta's older brother Ward from becoming a physician. In 1900, Alta was living with Ward and his wife of five years in the nearby town of Bolivar, where she taught music.

It is unclear how Smith and Wells met. They were a study in physical contrasts. Wells, over six feet tall, was fair haired with a light complexion and billed as tipping the scales at three hundred pounds. Smith was only five feet four inches in height, with dark hair and coloring. But, they seemed to have made a good match. As musicians and performers, they were together traveling the world for over thirty years.

Arthur and Alta formed the Apollo Concert Company as a quintet late in the first decade of the twentieth century. There prospects must have been great, as they attracted first-rate musicians to their band. Along to present numbers such as "The Scottish Chimes" and "The Wayside Chapel" on the bells and "Hungarian Rhapsodies" on saxes was reader/mezzo-soprano Margaret Puckett, a native of Kentucky (soon replaced by Coyla M. Spring of Chicago), composer and arranger Guy E. Holmes on flute and cornet, as well as trombonist and harp guitarist Charles W. "Clay" Smith, Jr. Arthur did his "trick" banjo playing and offered up "Humoresque" by Dvorak, Smith played "Annie Laurie," Spring read "A Little Boy's Naughty Day," and Holmes brought out his cornet for "The Searchlight." In 1913, Arthur Wells spent over $1000.00 on the acquisition of new eighteen (or twenty-two or twenty-four, depending on which newspaper article you read) carat gold saxophones and his biggest novelty, the "Apollophone," a giant keyed sixteen foot instrument played with mallets that supposedly combined "the tone qualities" of a xylophone and marimba "and has all the musical possibilities of the Steinway grand piano." This group primarily worked the lyceum circuit during the cold months and toured Chautauquas under canvas during the summer.

Coyla May Spring was born in Chicago to railroad engineer Joe and his wife Celena/Selena November 4, 1889. Celena was of English descent, which may or may not have contributed to her artistic naming of her daughters. Unfortunately for the Wells', Spring had aspirations toward leading her own ensemble. At the end of 1913, as soon as her sister, cellist Lotus Flower (born June 23, 1894) had come of age, Coyla formed a trio with Lotus and began touring the Midwest. Two years later, the Apollo's had two more defections to the Spring Company. Whether fueled by music, love or both, Clay Smith and G. E. Holmes followed the Spring sisters to make this rival act a quintet. Eventually, Coyla became Mrs. Clay Smith and Lotus married Guy Holmes.

Before Arthur and Alta were scrambling to fill the vacancies created by departing ensemble members, the Wells' were sent in the spring of 1913 by the United States government to perform in the Panama Canal Zone. Later on, the Ellison-White Chautauqua System dispatched the Apollo's to Australia and

New Zealand for the 1918-1919 season. Until disbanding the Apollo Concert Company ten years later, Arthur and Alta continued to present programs utilizing a variety of musicians.

But, as the nature of touring changed, Arthur and Alta were forced to disband their group. For another seventeen years, the Wells' soldiered on as a duo. Initially, the character of their engagements showed little change from the heyday of the Apollo Concert Company. Entertainment continued to be a strong feature of their presentations. For a 1929 performance in Wisconsin:

"Most unusual of the numbers was the selection in which each artist played two instruments at the same time, Mrs. Wells playing the piano and soprano saxophone and Mr. Wells manipulating two saxophones simultaneously. Negro spirituals, during which the artists were costumed, was [sic] another feature of the varied program which the duo offered. . . . Delightful costumes worn by Mrs. Wells enhanced the entertainment, especially the dress depicting the girl of the Civil War days. Mrs. Wells, gifted with unusual poise, presented a piano reading, 'Black and White,' as her feature number. . . . A banjo number by Mr. Wells while he sang without piano accompaniment gave a colorful close to the program."

In Ohio the following year:

"the banjo solos seemed to please the audience more than anything else. A most unusual feature was the 'Second Hungarian Rhapsody' played by Mr. Wells on a tenor banjo. Another feature of the program in which 'Art' offered a selection on the banjo, throwing it over his head, under his legs, and twisting and turning it every way, was received by the students with much applause."

More and more, the Wells' presented their programs in association with local schools, filling auditoriums with students. Although there were a few trips outside the United States proper, by and large, they traveled the States by automobile, delivering a string of one-nighters all year long.

The Apollo Duo, as they billed themselves, came to a close with Arthur's death in 1940. Mid-tour, Wells died suddenly in Tremonton, Utah, on January 15, just before a scheduled appearance at a local high school.

Johnson C. Bane

The Regal endorsee who has left the largest historical trail is the guitarist Johnson C. Bane. According to a Wulschner advertisement from the Crescendo, Bane was born March 7, 1861 in Waynesburg, Pennsylvania, fifty miles south of Pittsburgh proper. He was the son of farmer William and Phebe Bane. Johnson Bane began studying the guitar at the age of eleven. According to Jeffrey Noonan's analysis of Banjo, Mandolin and Guitar magazine, Bane spent the bulk of his career touring as a solo performer. Johnson Bane traveled the country as a guitarist at a time when the profession was still being established.

The best documentation of his career comes from those decades around Bane's association with Regal instruments. Newspaper advertisements and magazine articles intimate that Bane began performing around 1881. He appears to have been based in Pittsburgh during this time period, although one report mentions his membership in a theatrical troupe, traveling for three years between Chicago and Boston. Johnson Bane married in 1884, thereby for the next five years trading in the traveling life of a performer for that of a music teacher. Bane presumably missed the stage, and resumed a schedule of recitals in churches and other non-traditional venues in 1889.

At the end of 1892, Bane (described as "a guitar virtuoso") played a Christmas week concert in Tyrone, Pennsylvania, northeast of Pittsburgh. Billed as "Professor," Bane was in Cortland, outside of Syracuse, New York in September of 1893, performing Chopin's "Nocturne" and Willard's operatic selections. In March of 1896, Johnson Bane joined forces with the Uniontown, Pennsylvania Mandolin, Banjo and Guitar Club to perform south of Pittsburgh. Proclaimed as "then the world's greatest guitarist," Bane performed a "Spanish Dance," among other pieces. June, 1897 took Bane to Newark, outside Columbus,

Ohio, where his concert was supported by a collection rather then an admission price. He came back through the area in July, when he played for a private party at the Underwood home in Zanesville. The Times-Record wrote that:

"Mr. Bane is a composer of wonderful ability. His 'overture pathetique' suggested Mendelssohn strongly, and a Spanish dance of his own creation struck one as being equal to Mozsskowi's [sic] best works in that line. Besides these, Mr. Bane revels in Nocturnes, Sonatas, and selections from the Standard Operas. In his hands the guitar becomes a solo instrument of wonderful power and sweetness."

For a joint Steubenville, eastern Ohio concert with the Star Mandolin Club in April of 1898, Bane was described in the local newspaper as "a master of the instrument, indeed he was the best guitarist heard in this city for some time past." In September of 1898, Bane was performing at the YMCA Hall in New Castle, PA (he appears to have favored churches and YMCAs as performing venues). "A guitar in his hands becomes a grand concert instrument, a wonder and delight to all" crowed the local publicity.

Johnson Bane, Frets, September, 1925. Courtesy The National Music Museum.

Bane performed in Iowa City during September of 1900 and in Cedar Rapids, Iowa in November, where he was billed "of New York City" and using "the celebrated Regal Guitar in his recitals." "Guitar music is generally of a very simple order," wrote an unknown reporter for the Connellsville, Pennsylvania newspaper on the occasion of a 1909 appearance, "but Mr. Bane plays the best class of compositions in all their beauty, with delightful expression and remarkable technical execution. This artistic playing upon such an instrument as the guitar excited the enthusiasm of Mr. Bane's auditors." Johnson Bane continued to travel and perform throughout the east and Midwest at least through 1930.

Bane's recital programs appeared frequently in the BMG magazine and confirm that he seldom played any of the standard guitar literature, preferring instead a nearly unchanging repertoire of arranged light classics by Ethelbert Nevin and Moritz Moszkowski as well as his own compositions. This unique repertoire grew out of Bane's almost exclusive use of an open-string tuning system that he promoted as the "Saxton System." Johnson Bane began publishing music for guitar, including his own compositions, as early as 1885. Bane's affiliation with Wulschner and Regal dates to at least 1899, when Emil's company published two of Bane's most popular concert pieces. Frederic Chopin's "Nocturne Op. 9, No. 2" and the Polish/German composer Moszkowski's (1854-1925) "Spanish Dance No. 2," a piano piece popular in this period, dominated Johnson Bane's performances throughout his documented career. Eventually Wulschner published at least fifteen compositions and/or arrangements by Bane for the guitar. Although Johnson Bane continued to publish and perform throughout the 19-teens and twenties, his use of the "Saxton System" restricted his long-term popularity and effect on the history of American guitar.

The End of an Era

Regal was able to attract top endorsees and to turn out an attractive and functional product. John W. Keyes put all of his energies into the production and promotion of Regal instruments. Ultimately, it wasn't enough to ensure long term success for the company. By fall of 1903, Keyes had left Regal, taking a variety of positions with various piano concerns over the next couple of years. In the beginning of 1904, the Regal Manufacturing Company went out of business. At the directors' meeting held in February, all stock was "redeemed," effectively closing their factory.

As early as April of 1904, and as late as June 4, W. M. Richards, the secretary of the Regal Company, advertised that the factory was for sale. "An opportunity is offered to secure the controlling interest in the capitol stock of the Regal mfg. Co. The Regal guitars, mandolins and banjos are conceded to be the leading ones made in America. This is an unsurpassed opportunity to engage in the manufacture of instruments of admitted worth and wide sale, and every facility for their manufacture." Unable to sell the business intact, by September, the company was liquidated, and by November, Lyon & Healy had bought all of the company's remaining assets.

In his book on one of Regal's competitors, Hubert Pleijsier discusses economic downturns during the first decade of the twentieth century as affecting the musical instrument business, and it is possible that it had an effect on Regal as well. Regardless of the reason for the company's failure, no Regal instruments were made in Indianapolis after 1904. Regal would reemerge under new ownership in Chicago, the story of which will be told in the next chapter.

Following the death of her husband, Flora Wulschner's health went steadily downhill. In 1908, after a stay in an Atlantic City, NJ sanatorium, Flora's doctor sent her to Italy in hopes that the climate would improve her constitution. Unfortunately, the change did nothing to improve her strength and, in April of 1909, she passed away.

Alex Stewart continued running Wulschner-Stewart with great success. His first wife had died in 1906, and Stewart remarried in 1911, fathering two additional sons, one whom died as a youngster. The music store moved at the end of 1909 to 229-231 North Pennsylvania and Stewart entered the real estate business in September of 1910. With real estate occupying more and more of his time, Stewart engineered a trade combining property and cash for Wulschner-Stewart. William T. Woodley of Chicago became the new owner in May of 1912. Unfortunately, by the beginning of the New Year, Stewart and Woodley were deep in litigation, countersuing each other for violation of their agreement. Ultimately, William Woodley would destroy the Wulschner-Stewart business, closing all of their branch stores, selling off the stock, fixtures and real estate and moving what remained to Chicago. Two years after the sale to Woodley, Wulschner-Stewart Chicago was out of business.

The assets of the retail store passed to a group of investors from Chicago, who dissolved the corporation in January of 1916. By that time, Alexander's business interests had fully diverted into real estate and phonographs. The "Stewart Talking Machine Company" opened near the location of the Wulschner music store, first at 110 and then a year later at 221 North Penn. In time, Stewart became the only Victor dealer in Indiana. For a time, Alex's son George worked as a salesman in the talking machine store. George then acquired the Indiana Avenue Music Shop, a record and phonograph shop. Alexander Stewart Sr. died in 1932 at the age of sixty-five.

Headstock inlay By Joe Phetteplace, photograph/courtesy Spruce Tree Music.

Chapter Two
Regal in Chicago

By the time the Regal Manufacturing Company in Indianapolis met its demise, Chicago had emerged as the Midwest's, if not the nation's, center for musical instrument manufacturing. By 1910, half of American-made pianos came out of Chicago. Additionally, two prominent mail-order companies, Montgomery Ward & Company and Sears, Roebuck & Company, operated out of the windy city and featured full lines of musical merchandise aimed at rural America.

Under the leadership of Patrick Healy, the firm of Lyon & Healy had grown to dominate the field of musical instrument manufacturing in Chicago. So, it came as no surprise when, in November of 1904, Lyon & Healy purchased the remaining assets of the Regal Company. This included the Regal trade name, completed instruments unsold when the Indianapolis facility closed, as well as various parts and raw materials. In the coming months, L&H sold off their heavily discounted Regal inventory to dealers. By the end of July, 1905, Lyon & Healy announced that on September 1, it would bring out "a new line of Regal mandolins and guitars made in the Lyon & Healy factory here in Chicago. . . . The new Regal mandolins and guitars will include the same styles as formerly, but with considerable improvement in tonal qualities and finish." Toward that goal, L&H re-registered the "Regal" trademark in 1906. Possibly, the Lyon & Healy employee placed in charge of the reactivated Regal line was Frank Kordick.

Frank Kordick was born in the small Bohemian (Austrian) town of Meuern on February 3, 1872. In 1878, his father, Mathias/Matthew, brought the family to America, settling in Chicago in 1880. The elder Kordick was first a wagon maker and later the operator of flour mills. In 1886, at the age of fourteen, Frank Kordick left public school to apprentice at the Joseph Bohmann Musical Instrument Company, a notable early Chicago manufacturer, continuing his education at night. Two years later, in 1888, Kordick was hired by Lyon & Healy, where he received another several years of training. In 1890, the year of his father's death, Frank was placed in charge of the fifteen man contract work department at L&H. As an indication of his success in America, at the end of 1893, Frank Kordick became a naturalized citizen of the United States.

In 1897, Kordick married Alma A. Smith (ne: Schmitz, born December 8, 1877); their one daughter, Helen M., was born two years later. By 1900, Frank Kordick was a foreman in the "polishing" department at the Lyon & Healy factory. Eventually, Kordick would run four different departments simultaneously, becoming especially expert in the manufacturing of "small goods," i.e.: guitars, mandolins, etc.

In the meantime, Pat Healy had died. The resulting changes in leadership, the movement of the company toward harp production, or the depressions of the first decade of the twentieth century, any or all could have resulted in the manufacturer divesting itself of some divisions. However, there is evidence that, while spinning off parts of their manufactory, Lyon & Healy still maintained partial control over these new entities.

That Lyon & Healy kept a business interest in the new Regal Company can be derived from several facts. First off, the "Regal" trademark, registered by Lyon & Healy in November 1906 for use with guitars and mandolins, was not transferred to the Regal Musical Instrument Co. until 1924. Additionally, the Cratty Brothers law firm, who counted Lyon & Healy among their clients, was involved in the incorporation of Regal in March, 1908. Part of the corporate legal documents were printed on the law firm's stationary, and Josiah Cratty was appointed as one of the commissioners entrusted with making all necessary preparations for the actual incorporation of the new company. During the same year, Josiah's brother and law partner Thomas Cratty became one of the directors of Lyon & Healy. Within six months he was made treasurer of the company, a position he held until his death in 1913. Lastly, Regal made some or all Lyon & Healy branded stringed instruments through the 1920s.

Lyon & Healy's first divestiture occurred in 1907, when the company "sold" their drum department to L&H employee Tom Wilson. Like Kordick, Wilson was a twenty-year veteran of Lyon & Healy. The Wilson & Jacobs Drum Manufacturing Company was still located within the L&H factory when, in February of 1908, Frank Kordick led a group of four "investors" to form a "separate" Regal Musical Instrument Company that also worked out of the Lyon & Healy facility at Randolph Street and Ogden Avenue. Reports from the period indicate that all "small" stringed instrument manufacturing was transferred from Lyon & Healy to Regal, leaving L&H to concentrate on the building of pianos and harps. Two Hundred and fifty shares of capitol stock valued at $35,000.00 were issued to fund the manufacture of guitars, mandolins and zithers. According to Hubert Pleijsier, author of Washburn: Prewar Instrument Styles (Centerstream Publishing, 2008), "the shares were paid up by the founders with an inventory of musical instruments worth $13,000.00." Could those instruments have been completed Washburn branded goods?

Besides Kordick as president, Regal was to be run by A. M. Nelson/treasurer and Herman Joseph Schlitt/secretary. Anton Nelson was, like Kordick, an immigrant from Western Europe, born in Norway on December 29, 1866. Nelson came to the United States at the age of twenty through New York City. Within two years, Anton Nelson had made his way to Chicago, where he first worked as a laborer, and, by the time he met Kordick in 1888, as an instrument maker for Lyon & Healy. The college-educated Schlitt, who appears to have had no prior experience working in musical instrument manufacturing but in the somewhat related wholesale lumber company of March-Hathaway, had previous employment as a clerk, but, as Kordick's brother-in-law by marriage (Alma Kordick and Clara Schlitt were sisters), was probably recruited as someone Frank Kordick could trust to help with the business side of the new company. Herman was born in Dehrn, Germany on March 14, 1874, and had immigrated in 1881, living in Rochester, NY, where he became a naturalized citizen in the late 1890s. Herman Schlitt settled in Chicago by the turn of the century. These three would steer Regal Musical Instruments through 1927, Kordick remaining president until his death in 1940 and Schlitt staying on in management through the demise of Regal as an independent entity in the mid-1950s.

Their fourth partner, pearl cutter Marselius "Martin" Danielson, played a key role in the actual day-to-day running of the Regal factory. Danielson, who is remembered by Regal employee Joe Phetteplace (see below) as a foreman in the late 1920s, may have been in Chicago as early as 1891. Marselius Danielson was born in Norway in August of 1869. Marselius came to the United States in 1887, married around 1892 and was naturalized in October of 1894.

Regal initially concentrated on making instruments for other concerns, including former "owner" Lyon & Healy. And Frank Kordick was the engine that pulled the new Regal Company forward. As Josiah Currey reports in Manufacturing and Wholesale Industries of Chicago:

"For the first two years the manufacturing activities of the new company were continued at the extensive Lyon & Healy plant, where was utilized sixteen thousand four hundred square feet of floor space, comprising three floors of one of the principal buildings of the plant. In assuming control of the business the new company retained twenty-five of the most skilled and expert instrument makers formerly in the employ of Lyon & Healy, and during the first twelve months the sales aggregated forty thousand dollars. The policy of the company from the beginning has been to sell its products exclusively to wholesale and jobbing dealers in musical instruments, and the general supervision of the business has been effectively placed under the administration of the president, Mr. Kordick, who is himself a recognized expert in the manufacturing of high-grade musical instruments.

"In 1911, in order to provide the larger accommodations demanded by the constantly expanding business, the company purchased five city lots with a frontage of one hundred and twenty-five feet [at 3211] West Grand avenue with a depth of one hundred and fifty-five feet. On this site was at once instituted the erection of a modern brick industrial building specially designed for the purpose for which it was to be placed in commission. The foundations were laid for the erection of a four-story structure with a seventy-five foot frontage, and in a preliminary way the building was carried to a height of two stories, the building as thus formed giving for factory and office purposes a total floor space of about twenty thousand square feet.

The Home of Regal Instruments

"At the time of this writing, in the summer of 1917, plans are being perfected for adding the other two stories for which the original design of the building calls, and this will, as a matter of course, double the area of available floor space and make the plant the largest in the world as devoted to the manufacturing of the smaller types of stringed musical instruments. Under vigorous and progressive policies and careful management the business of the company has shown a steady and normal growth, the force of employees varies from seventy-five to one hundred, and the annual business for the fiscal year 1916 attained to the noteworthy aggregate of one hundred and fifty thousand dollars.... In the manufacturing of a diversified line of stringed musical instruments, with special attention given to mandolins and guitars, this company has attained large success and high reputation, and the products of its extensive manufactory have disseminated the fame of Chicago as a distributing center, as the fine instruments manufactured by the company find sale in all sections of the Union, besides which an appreciable export trade has been developed, especially in England and the Hawaiian Islands."

Regal Musical Instrument Co., Chicago factory, from the 1934 catalogue, courtesy Ron Middlebrook.

Ten years after Regal separated from parent business Lyon & Healy, the manufacturer was coming into its own. The principals of the company bought their own homes, and President Kordick began taking long business and pleasure trips around the world that reflected Regal's affluence. Frank and Alma Kordick became patrons of the arts and supported local cultural institutions such as the Art Institute of Chicago. As in the rest of the country, the 1920s were boom times and Regal did well.

Like the majority of musical instrument manufacturers of the 1920s, Regal sold their products through several large distributors rather then directly to music stores or to the consumer. These included

Wurlitzer of Cincinnati, New York and Chicago, Jenkins of Kansas City, Tonk Bros. of Chicago, H. C. Schultz of Detroit and Cleveland, Ohio, Ditson of Boston and New York, Carl Fisher and B&J in New York City, and E. A. Sutphin of Philadelphia, PA, among others.

The 1920s were a good time to be in the music business. Multiple local, regional and national organizations were founded toward the purpose of promoting business. A side effect was the promotion of a spirit of cooperation between the different instrument makers. If one company prospered, so would all the others. Perhaps it was this cooperative spirit that resulted in friendships, which led to joint agreements between the various firms. It isn't much of a leap from being golf partners or vacationing together to instruments made by one company for another or the sharing of parts and like. After all, there was plenty of business to go around. One can just picture Kordick fielding a phone call from Henry Kuhrmeyer, the head of Kay or Jay Kraus of Harmony, requesting help in filling a rush order or a box of bridges or tuners to substitute for those that hadn't yet arrived.

With success, however, came change. With the company growing and Kordick away for longer periods of time for both business and pleasure trips, more management was needed. And so, once again, the president of Regal turned to someone he already knew, salesman Albert Hunter, and recruited him into the company.

Albert Edward Hunter was born February 14, 1890, in Muskegon, Michigan. His father, Edward, had migrated from England three years before Albert's birth. The elder Hunter had moved his family from Muskegon to Chicago sometime between 1900 and 1910, where Albert met Frank Kordick (they were neighbors in the building where Edward worked as a janitor). By the time Albert Hunter came to Regal, and Hunter was definitely working for Kordick by June of 1924, he had sold biscuits and paper, but not musical instruments. Hunter must have been a quick study, for in the next couple of years he was ubiquitous in the business, serving on the boards of various trade groups and rising to general manager of Regal Musical Instrument. When, in 1927, Anton Nelson, one of the original partners in Regal, moved to the West Coast for health reasons, Hunter took over his position as vice president and treasurer.

Regal: Inside the Factory

We are fortunate that one employee left behind an oral history of his years making musical instruments in Chicago. Joseph A. (possibly Arms) Phetteplace was born March 28, 1906, the son of Wilson and Estella Arms Phetteplace, in Auburn, Nebraska, although he soon returned to the Wauzeka, Wisconsin home of his mother. After finishing his schooling, he worked in construction, and then moved to Chicago at the end of August of 1927 when recruited by Regal.

"Upon arriving at the factory the next morning, I was introduced to the foreman, Mr. Martin [sic] Danielson, in charge of the inlay department and also the entire first floor of the factory. I had hired out as a full-fledged inlay artist. It became quite obvious to Mr. Danielson in about ten minutes that I was not. A consultation between the general manager, Mr. Hunter, Mr. Danielson and myself was then in order. At the end of the meeting between the three of us, I had two choices: either learn the trade as an apprentice under the direction of Mr. Danielson or be retired before I had really started. They were willing to give me enough money for my board and room plus two dollars a week for two years, the board and room not to exceed twelve dollars. After considerable thought of about ten minutes, I decided 'what have I got to lose?' On many occasions in the next six months I wished that I hadn't stayed, as Mr. Danielson was a perfectionist and what I thought was near perfect was considered pure junk to be thrown in the waste basket.

"My first job was cutting out small block type pearl letters from mother of pearl with a small hand jewelry saw. The blades on this saw were so small you could hardly see the teeth. The pearl was in small thin pieces, three being glued together so when you cut one letter you really were cutting out three letters, which were then separated by boiling the glue out in water. If you did not hold the saw perfectly straight up and down, the bottom two letters were ruined by either being too small or too big.

"Each evening, Mr. Danielson would pick my work up, look at it very closely, and then throw it in the waste basket. Needless to say, I was a very discouraged young man. The small saw blades I was using were so fine that sometimes I would break two or three blades before I got a letter cut out. My issue of about four dozen blades a day could be gone before the first hour was up if I wasn't extremely careful. After finding out where these blades were purchased, I would buy extra ones out of my two dollars a week. They cost about two dollars a gross at that time and were made in Germany.

"Mr. Danielson was very kind in many ways now that I look back at the end results. Many days he would pat me on the back and say, 'You're making progress. It won't be long before we can use some of your work.' At the end of approximately six weeks, he said, 'here is a letter we can use. Keep it up and we can soon use all of them.' As the days went by, he selected more and more of my work as usable.

"Now, this was only the first phase of learning inlay work, as I had to then start sawing veneers nailed together six to a bunch with the print 'Regal' on them. After the veneers were sawed and separated, you had to fit the pearl letters into them, and filler was used to hold them in place. If the pearl letters and the veneers were not perfectly cut, the pearl would not fit in the veneers. The trick was to cut the pearl letters perfectly and the opening in the veneer just slightly larger. If they did not fit, you had to use a sharp knife and cut out a little of the veneer, or file the letters down. The pearl letters and veneers were both about the thickness of a thin piece of cardboard. I broke many a pearl letter by trying to file the edges smaller to fit the veneer opening. If I tried cutting out the edges of the hole in the veneer, I would ruin the veneer. At the end of about nine months, however, I was doing Regal head plates, as they were called, that could be glued onto the necks of guitars.

"When the Christmas season arrived, we were all given a week's vacation without pay. When I arrived back for the first day of work in January [1928], my work at Regal as an apprentice had progressed to the point where the factory was again able to produce high grade instruments with pearl designs on the head pieces, fingerboards and around the sound holes. Later I was inlaying pearl around the entire body of the instruments.

"After learning this part of the trade, it became necessary to learn how to cut the shells up into pieces and grind them flat on both sides to a uniform thickness. Here again was a job which took a considerable amount of patience and quite a little teaching before I was able to do it and hold the pearl to the thickness it should be.

"During this time, there was an employee by the name of Bill. Every piece of wood that came into the factory first had to go through Old Bill's hands to decide what instrument could be made from it. We were making guitars, banjos and a few bass fiddles, ukuleles and some mandolins. Well, one day Old Bill asked for a raise. Now, this man was on a salary. Most of the rest of the people in the factory were on piece work; you were paid so much for each piece of work that you did. Old Bill asked for a raise and they decided not to give him one, so he left.

"After he had gone, they decided they had better hire a new man. The first man they hired brought in, before the day was half over, a barrel full of scrap lumber. Now, Old Bill would go a whole week and hardly ever have a complete barrel of scrap lumber to throw away. When you stop to think that rosewood, ebony and mahogany cost a terrific amount of money, why, this made quite a bill for the factory. Before the day was out, he had at least two barrels or maybe more. So, the next day they fired him and they hired another man. And the same thing happened: three to four barrels of scrap in one day. So they got rid of him after two days. They hired a third man and they had the same problem. So much wood was thrown into the barrel and this, in turn, into the furnace and burned up that there was no profit. About the fourth or fifth day, they decided to hunt Old Bill up. Well, he'd already got another job, so in order to get him back, they had to double his salary!

"During this particular time (it was probably about a year after I had been to work and learning the trade of inlay), the men in the office decided that I should have a little more rounded education. Unbeknownst to me, they decided I should learn everything there was to know about making guitars, banjos, etc, so I was sent around to different parts of the factory.

"The first department I was sent to was gluing. I worked in that department off and on for the next year and I did commendable work. After about a day or two I made very few mistakes. Then a little later on it was decided that I should go up into the paint department and help up there. I had to do a little spraying of paint, had to put on a little by hand, and also had to put on some stain. In other words, you had to take birch and when you got through, it had to look like mahogany with a little sort of wavy effect to it. Well, this again took a little conceit out of me because I was up there, probably, two days before I was of any value to them at all.

"One day they sent me over to help make some wood inlays. You've seen it on some of the older furniture, little pieces of wood that's inlaid: diamond shaped, little squares, alternating colors, and maybe a little strip of different wood along each side. It's called marquetry. A little later I was sent into the packing department.

"By this time, I had pretty well gotten over most of the jobs in making guitars and banjos. There were, however, a few little things that I didn't know, and one of them was stringing guitars. I learned stringing but the one thing that I never was too good at was putting the bindings on guitars. This was a little celluloid strip that goes around the edge of the guitar. They used a tape that was probably about a half inch wide and about fifty feet long. I would judge it was made out of linen because it felt like that. A piece of this would be for binding each guitar.

"After learning all the jobs in the plant, I had been there about two years and my inlay work had improved to the place where I was doing the most complicated inlay and doing a very good job of it.

"Mr. Danielson said, 'Do you know what day it is?'

"'No,' I answered.

"'Today is just two years from the day you walked into this place. Come with me.' He took me into the office.

"I didn't know what was going to happen and all the management was there and he said to them, 'Gentlemen, Joe has just completed his apprenticeship. I would say today that he is the best inlay craftsman in the United States, as of now. He's even got me beat because he's got steadier nerves than I have. I think now we ought to begin to pay him a decent wage.'

"They discussed it there in front of me and so they decided I could start at the same wage the other fellows were getting, which meant about thirty dollars a week, which was pretty good, considering I was getting only about fourteen. So, that ended my apprenticeship. They put me on the regular payroll then and I was quite thankful about it.

"I continued to work there for quite some time and now I don't recall exactly how long it was but I think I went there in about '27 and this was '29."

Phetteplace was employed by Regal at least through the spring of 1930.

"Now, about this time work began to slack off at the factory. Every so often one or two fellows would be laid off. Eventually it got down to where one-fourth of the crew was laid off. One day the bookkeeper from the office, a fellow named Frank, came out and he came over and said, 'Joe, we're having a little problem. We've got to lay off one more man this coming week and as far as we can figure it has to be between you and the Polish gentleman back there. Now, we would rather keep you because you know more about everything in the factory than he does. He only knows one job. But it has to be one of the two of you because you're the latest ones put on the payroll.'

"I told him, 'Frank, I don't think there should be any question here who should be laid off because, after all, he has five or six children. I'm single and just have myself to support and I certainly can find something to do, so I think you'd better lay me off.'

"Well, that's what they did. They gave me one week's work. Well, during the week's work, I went in and saw the president of the factory and was talking with him. He wanted to know what I was going to do. I told him, 'Well, I'll start out first by asking you if I can buy a bunch of ukuleles that you have upstairs. They are all mahogany. They've been lying up there ever since I came here, on a rack, and I would like to buy them as cheaply as possible and take them out as I sell them because I have an idea I can sell those.'

"He said, 'You surely can buy them at cost if you want them, but I don't know how you're going to sell them. We haven't been able to.'

"'I have an idea,' I said, 'so I'll take twelve of them and pay you for them as they are sold.'

"So, a deal was made then and I took out twelve of these ukuleles. I had bought myself a little saw and a bunch of wood carving chisels. All I needed was some pearl, so I bought some from the Regal Company. This was stuff that they would normally call scrap. It was hardly big enough for most of the work. But I took this pearl and sawed out names, such as Bob, Jim, Betty, etc., and I'd inlay one pearl name on each of these ukuleles. When I had finished twelve of them, I went to stores that handled music and put these in the stores. The ukuleles were costing me around seventy cents apiece and I offered to inlay anyone's name up to five letters and furnish the ukulele for two and one half dollars. The store could sell it for five dollars. They jumped at that chance because that was a bigger profit than they were making on anything else. They were only making about ten to fifteen per cent profit at that time.

"So, I managed to plant these ukuleles around and I left a phone number. Sure enough, I began to get calls for them. Now, anything over five letters I charged a quarter for each letter. So, when these names came in, I'd sit down, draw them up, cut them out of pearl and proceeded to inlay their names. I delivered the ukuleles and, of course, streetcar fare was only a nickel, so it wasn't too much of a problem to get back and forth.

"Eventually, I cleaned the factory of all these ukuleles. I think there were around five hundred of them. In the process of doing this, I had made myself a little extra money. I was able to pay my room and board and lay a little bit of money aside.

During the fall of 1933, Joe Phetteplace moved to the West Side of Chicago.

"The flat included a place I could use as a shop. I set up my jigsaw on a bench and put my hand tools on another bench and was back in business without any work. Having kept contact with the Regal Company all of this time, it did not surprise me when they called a week later and wanted to see me. The cheap guitars they were forced to make to stay in business needed the jobber's [i.e.: the wholesale distributor's 'house brand'] name on the head of each instrument.

"To do this, you used a silk screen, which was very slow work, or a thin piece of metal with the name cut out which you laid on the wood and sprayed the color of paint through the name. They asked me to cut out the name 'Le Domino.' In discussing this project with the paint foreman upstairs, I had a chance to look at this type of work. It was so smeared that you could hardly read the name. The next morning I took up my finished piece of metal with 'Le Domino' cut out. They wanted to know what it cost and I told them five dollars. They nearly blew their top at that price because the poor ones they had upstairs only cost fifty cents each, so I told them they could use the piece I had made for one day free of charge;

I'd be up and get it the next day. I went home rather discouraged. In the afternoon they called and wanted me to come back up. They handed me five dollars and gave me an order for twenty more names to be cut out.

"About two weeks later I again got a call from Regal. They were in a bind, so to speak. They had a contract with a California company by the name of Dobro to make all of their guitars sold east of the Rocky Mountains. The Roosevelt N. R. A. had come into effect and they had to pay their workmen forty cents an hour, which was double what they had been paying. There was one job which caused them to lose money on each guitar made, and that was cutting the 'F' holes and a large round hole about one foot in diameter in each top panel.

"Old Martin, my former boss, had tried a dozen men on this job and none of them could make

Inlay by Joe Phetteplace for Washburn Model 5257 made by Regal. Photograph/courtesy Spruce Tree Music.

Headstock overlay awaiting inlay, by Joe Phetteplace. Courtesy Larry Phetteplace.

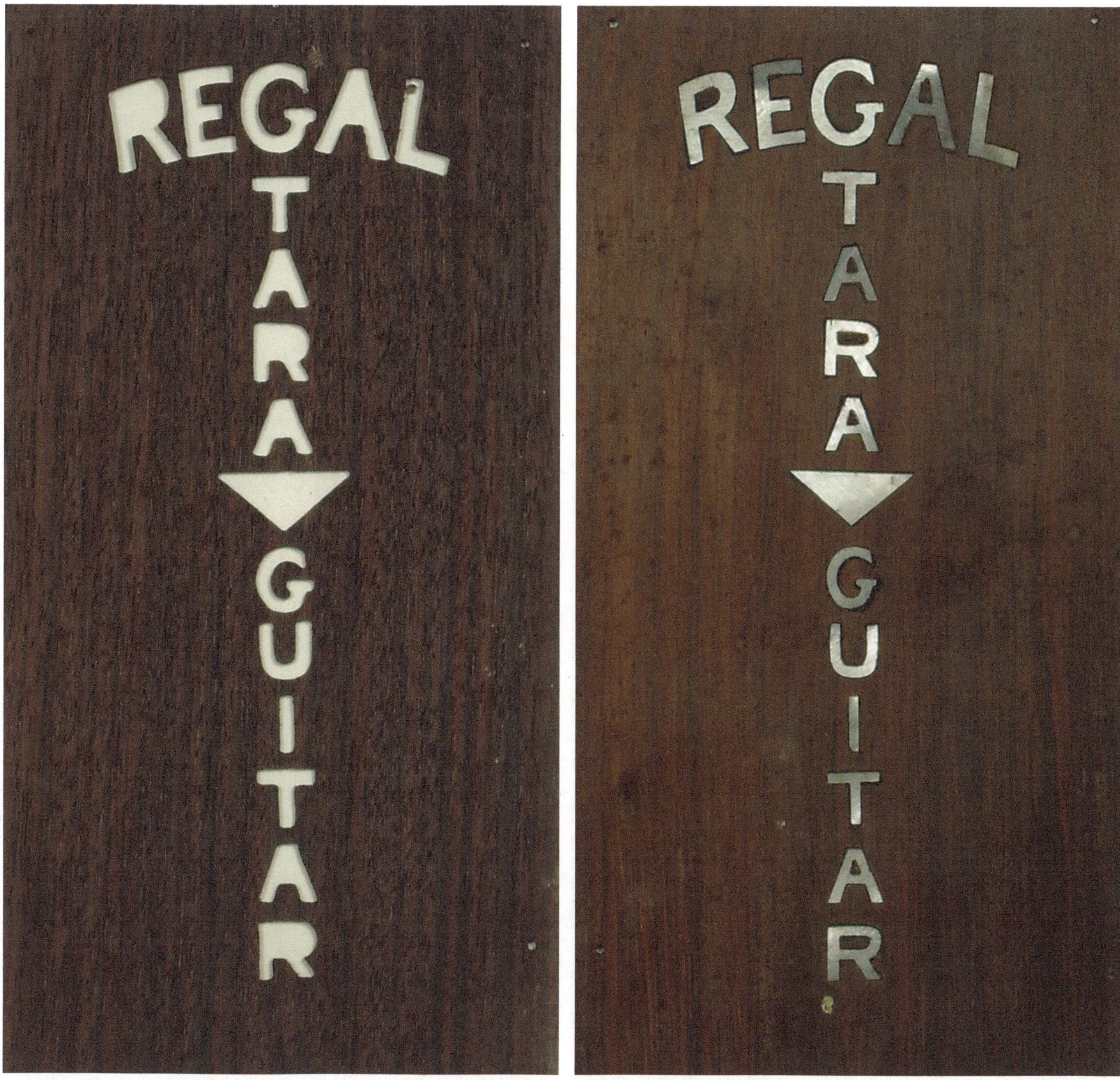

Headstock overlay without and with inlay, 'Regal Tara Guitar,' by Joe Phetteplace. Photograph/courtesy Spruce Tree Music."

over fifteen cents an hour doing the work, so he suggested they get me. When I got to the factory, the president, Mr. Kordick, vice-president, Mr. Schlitt and the general manager, Mr. Hunter, all went back where Mr. Martin was and they told me their problem. I asked what the mill rate was on this job. I made bargain with them at the same mill rate providing they would never cut the price and let me work when I wanted to. Man, did they all smile and really figured they had made a good deal.

"At the end of the first week my check was over a hundred and thirty dollars. If you have never heard any bellyaching, you should have been there. First the bookkeeper came out and tried to get me to lower my price. He said the general manager didn't make that much. Eventually Mr. Hunter and Mr. Schlitt came out and tried to argue me out of the price that was set. I guess I was stubborn or bull headed about lowering my prices. That $130.00 looked like gold to me and I wanted more of it. A little later Mr. Kordick, the president, came out. I thought, 'Oh, oh, here it comes. I've lost my job.'

"Instead, he slapped me on the back and said, 'I'm sure glad you didn't back down for those other fellows in the office. You made us a good deal and you're going to get your money. I hope you make two hundred dollars next week. You've got it coming. Any person who would spend two years of his life learning a trade deserves a break.'

"By fall the people I rented from lost their building, so I moved. I rented a vacant store on Fifth Avenue a short distance from where I was. It had a small apartment in the back. By this time I had quite a little money stacked in the bank so I bought more power equipment to work with. I was still working for Regal. One day I offered to make them some new pearl inlays free to put on guitars if they would show them at the musical conventions. They agreed, so I spend quite a bit of time designing and inlaying samples for the convention, which was held in Chicago. Later I found out they only did this because I had asked

Headstock overlay, 'Regal Fandango,' by Joe Phetteplace. Photograph/courtesy Spruce Tree Music.

"Washburn" headstock logo and overlay, used by Regal throughout the 1930s. Photograph/courtesy Spruce Tree Music.

them to. They had no hopes of selling any. The convention was a huge success for Regal. They were the only ones there with inlaid instruments and they got some big orders for them. So, at last, I am in the inlay business, my chosen profession. The first big order was from a jobber who wanted the name 'Orpheum' on the head of the guitar. Also, many orders came in for Regal inlaid guitars. I was treated like a king whenever I went up to Regal with an order done. They were making money, I was making money and their old employees were being called back to work.

"Washburn" headstock logo and overlay, unknown model, by Joe Phetteplace. Photograph/courtesy Spruce Tree Music.

"Along about this time I began to be caught up on my inlay work for Regal, so they suggested I go down and see Dobro, who now had a small factory in Chicago. Soon I had orders from them to inlay in pearl the name 'National.' One day Mr. Hunter at Regal suggested I go over to see Kay Musical Company. They were a coming concern and might be able to use some inlay work. I spent about an hour in their office talking pearl inlay to them. Well, they had tried to use some pearl inlay another person had furnished and it all cracked up. I showed them my work and told them that I was doing the work for Regal and for National/Dobro and I gave them a guarantee that any piece of pearl work of mine that would crack I'd replace free. So, right away I got an order from them, a small order to start with. Kay Musical became one of the largest companies I worked for for a long time.

"Shortly later I contacted the Harmony Company that was also in Chicago and got them as a customer. Now, between the four factories, I was kept fairly busy. As time went on, whenever they would have a musical convention in Chicago, which was about every second or third year, I would be invited to come down by one of these four companies and I'd roam around and meet different people that would be interested in pearl work. Eventually, I got to be quite well known by all of the musical factories."

The Depression of the 1930s and Its Effect on Regal

As the decade of the 1920s wound down, the members of Regal's top management continued to travel the world on combined business and pleasure trips. They all lived a comfortable lifestyle. The company was so successful that Regal could proclaim, "Take Heed! Certain Manufacturers concede the popularity and the superiority of 'Regal' Instruments by copying them. We caution you against cheaper and inferior imitations of our products. Let REPUTATION be your GUIDE and QUALITY your CHOICE. 'Regal" Tenor Guitars and Tiples like all instruments with the 'Regal' label, stand unchallenged and supreme."

By 1930, the lead up to the Depression had bankrupted Washburn and J. R. Stewart, two of the major brands in the national music business and both located in Chicago. However, as many companies struggled, Regal continued to thrive. In October of 1930, Regal advertised "our factory has operated almost to capacity during the past twelve months while some of our competitors have been facing disaster or even been compelled to liquidate." This success was achieved while "stay[ing] aloof from the price-slashing tactics resorted to by certain manufacturers." It is a good indictor of the continued success of Regal that all the principals in the company's management owned their own homes and continued to extensively travel.

Back in 1927, Lyon & Healy had a change of management, which led to the sale of what was left of their manufacturing arm to J. R. Stewart, with the intention of shifting Lyon & Healy into retail sales. Unfortunately, the move couldn't save Lyon & Healy wholesale distributor, which the parent company

Regal Musical Instrument Co, work force outside of the Chicago factory, November 5, 1934. Notice there are only forty-five workers including management. Joe Phetteplace is fifth from the left sitting in the front row. My guess is that the two men in suits standing sixth and eighth from the left in the back row are Herman Schlitt and Frank Kordick. Courtesy Larry Phetteplace.

sold to Tonk Bros. in November of 1928. Less then two years later, Stewart's assets passed to Tonk, who chose to keep ownership and distribution rights to Lyon & Healy's Washburn brand. Paul Monnig, president of Tonk Bros. and Al Hunter's old golfing partner, decided to sell Regal both the trademarks "Le Domino" and "Stewart," along with the right to manufacture Washburn instruments for Tonk. In 1924, Lyon & Healy had already begun the transfer of the "Regal" trademark to the namesake company, a process which was completed in 1929.

Unfortunately, the worsening depression eventually caught up to Regal as well. As many wholesale distributors failed in the early 1930s, an association of Chicago manufacturers created their own wholesaler and the so-called Chicago Musical Instrument Company began distributing Regal. In another depression era move, Regal joined forces with Harmony and Globe to offer discounted instruments in a national ukulele campaign. As industry consolidation continued, Regal licensed the use of the Dobro name for resophonic guitars sold east of the Mississippi, building bodies utilizing Dobro-made metal parts. In 1937, after the Dobro Company moved their factory from California to Chicago, the manufacturing of their resonator instruments passed exclusively to Regal.

Finally, in 1938, possibly in an attempt to increase profits, Regal began selling directly to dealers, forgoing distributors such as CMI. In a form letter titled "Regal Goes Direct" and signed by the three company principals, the Regal Musical Instrument Co., "Manufacturers of Plectrum Instruments," announced "An Invitation to Get Acquainted With Regal:"

"After 30 years of distributing our products through the wholesale trade, we have decided that we can give you a much better service by going direct from our factory to you with our splendid lines of Regal Instruments and Dobro Amplified Instruments.

"This should be of great interest to you, as it means a direct factory contact on two great lines of Fretted Instruments. It assures you of fresh factory merchandise at all times, correctly styled and correctly priced, in a great range from the cheapest that is good up to the very finest that skill and experience can produce. . . .

"This direct contact with the Regal Factory means bigger and better profits for you. Your customers will be better satisfied for Regal Instruments represent the greatest dollar for dollar value in any price range.

"Look for the 'Regal' name and learn that it stands for the BEST to be had in plectrumland.

"You and your customer MUST BE SATISFIED and that is the guarantee of the Regal Musical Instrument Co., an independent corporation thirty years old, owned and managed by its officers."

Frank Kordick, founder and guiding light of Regal, had spent most of the 1930s traveling to promote the company, although more and more, he left the day to day affairs of the company to others. On November 16, 1940, Kordick died of heart disease. Presidency of the company and leadership of Regal then passed to Frank Kordick's protégé Al Hunter, who continued along with Herman Schlitt and his son Arthur to pilot Regal for the remainder of its existence.

Unfortunately, the passing of Frank Kordick was the beginning of the end for Regal. Although the company was to exist for another 15 years, its successful days were over. As Hubert Pleijsier, author of Washburn: Prewar Instrument Styles, wrote in an unpublished article:

"In the years after the Second World War Regal started to lose ground to the other big Chicago based budget instrument manufacturers, Kay and Harmony. The company's management failed to come up with an adequate response to the increasing competition, and a long decline began which eventually led to the liquidation of the Regal Musical Instrument Co. on November 28, 1955. The Grand Ave factory was sold at an auction to the Michael Lewis Co., an Illinois-based airline supplier."

Harmony, one of the other Chicago makers of stringed instruments, took over the Regal trademark, and used for a line of instruments that said "Regal" on the headstocks, but looked, for all intensive purposes, like other Harmony products. In the late 1950s, the Regal name was used for a series of acoustic guitars made for Fender, an arrangement that continued into the 1960s. After the demise of Harmony as an American company, the Regal trademark passed into disuse. In 1987, Saga Musical Instruments revived the Regal name for a line of resonator guitars made overseas, which continues to this day.

Regal Musical Instruments catalogue cover, 1934, courtesy Ron Middlebrook.

Chapter Three

Mandolins

Bowl Back Mandolins

Summary

Instrument: Mandolin.

Model: Bowl back, "Neapolitan," or "Tater-Bug."

Years Made: 1896-1934.

Brand(s): Wulschner, Regal, 20th Century, University, Sterling, Concertone, Perfacktone, Columbia.

Quality: Low to high grade.

Special Features: Tuners covered by metal plate on back of headstock on high grade models.

Woods: Various, see below.

Measurements: N/A.

Logos Used: "The Wulschner" paper soundhole label, Regal Crown in pearl in headstock, "Regal Mfg Co." soundhole medallion, "Regal" oval paper soundhole label.

Known Original List Price: $1.98-$75.00 retail, $7.70-$35.00 wholesale.

When Wulschner listed Regal brand instruments in their 1896/1987 catalogue, the mandolin was enjoying its first period of popularity here in the United States. At that time, all mandolins were built with a bowl-shaped body formed from multiple strips of wood. This construction method originated in Naples, Italy, and was therefore known as the "Neapolitan" style of mandolin. Brought to the United States by Italian immigrants, the instrument became known as the "Tater-Bug" because (according to Wikipedia) its body resembled not just the shape of the "Leptinotarsa decemlineata" (i.e.: Colorado potato beetle) but, its vertically striped markings as well. Neapolitan mandolins dominated the market into the first decades of the twentieth century, when the new "flat back" style came to prominence.

Because so few early examples of Indianapolis Regal mandolins have surfaced, and due to the rarity of Wulschner/Regal catalogues, I've reproduced here both Emil Wulschner & Son's Regal-brand mandolin listings for 1896/1897, as well as their "20th Century" and "University" lines from 1901.

In 1896, Wulschner sold eleven bowl back mandolins and one mandola under their Regal name. The mandolins ranged from the $23.75 Style 2, which featured nine "ribs" (i.e.: the pieces that formed the instrument's body) of mahogany and birds-eye maple, through various bodies of rosewood and birds-eye maple or mahogany, to the Style 18. Selling for $75.00, the No. 18 was built with forty-two rosewood ribs with inlay between them, a real tortoise shell pickguard, and finished in a French polish. An extant instrument features a pearl Lyre inlaid into the headstock, fancy fingerboard markers, white celluloid bound top, fingerboard, headstock and soundhole with added wood marquetry surrounding the top and soundhole as well as high-end Handel-made inlaid tuner buttons and engraved tuner covers. All models of Regal mandolins featured natural finished spruce tops, mahogany necks and ebony fingerboards. Although Emil wanted the world to believe that the Wulschner concern was making instruments in a loft above his store, the lack of evidence to support this contention leads one to conclude that these mandolins were made for Regal by an outside firm.

MANDOLINS.

The "Regal."

Emil Wulschner & Son:

The Regal Mandolin came yesterday. We were delighted and happily surprised with it, as it far surpassed anything we had anticipated, both in beauty and in tone. There is no mandolin equal to the Regal that I have ever heard.

Very sincerely yours,

MUNCIE, IND. **DEMAINE WOOD,**
Teacher of Mandolin and Guitar.

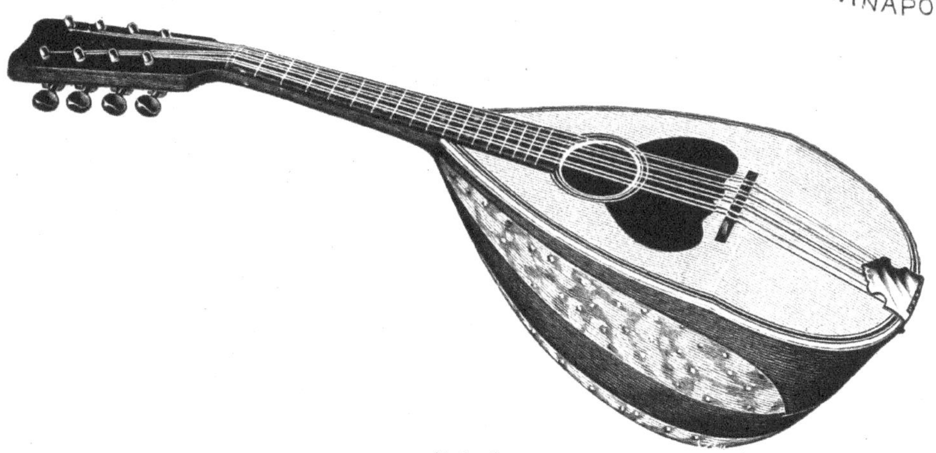

Style 2.

Style 2. Mahogany and Birds-eye Maple, 9 Ribs, Guard Plate, Soundhole and Top Inlaid with colored woods and Celluloid Bound, Mahogany Neck, Oval Ebony Fingerboard, Pearl Position Dots, Finely Polished, Nickel Plated Patent Head and Tailpiece............Each, $23.75

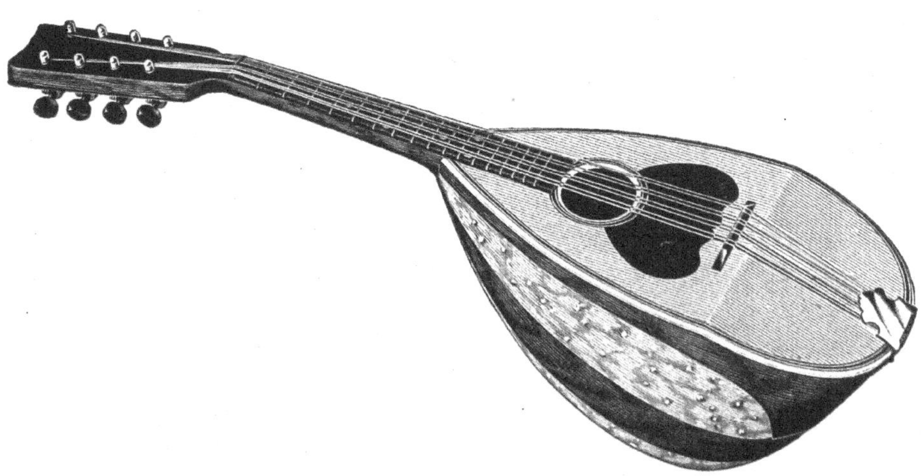

Style 4

Style 4. Rosewood and Birds-eye Maple, 9 Ribs, Soundhole and Top Inlaid with fancy colored woods and Celluloid Bound, Mahogany Neck, Oval Ebony Fingerboard with Pearl Position Dots, Finely Polished, Nickel Plated Patent Head and Tailpiece...... .....Each, $26.25

Emil Wulschner & Son, Indianapolis, IND., The "Regal" mandolins, 1896-1897 catalogue, p182-187. Photographs by Jim Bollman, courtesy Stu Cohen.

MANDOLINS.

The "Regal."

WULSCHNER & SON,
TRADE MARK
Regal
INDIANAPOLIS, IND.

Emil Wulschner & Son:

DEAR SIRS:—I am using in my work, as Teacher and Concert Soloist, the "Regal" Mandolins and Guitars. I have found them superior in *tone*, true to the last fret and free from that woody tone so common to most mandolins.

Yours truly,

COLUMBUS, IND. A. E. BUTLER,
Teacher Mandolin and Guitar.

Style 5.

Style 5. Rosewood, 18 Ribs, with White Inlay between, Soundhole and Top neatly inlaid with fancy colored woods and Celluloid Bound, Mahogany Neck, Oval Ebony Fingerboard with Pearl Position Dots, Finely Polished, Nickel Plated Patent Head and Tailpiece .... Each, $28.75

Style 6.

Style 6. Rosewood and Mahogany, 15 Ribs with White Inlay between, Inlaid Guardplate, Soundhole and Edges neatly inlaid with fancy woods and Celluloid Bound, Mahogany Neck, Veneered Headpiece, Oval Ebony Fingerboard with Pearl Position Dots, French Polished, Nickel Plated Patent Head and Tailpiece .... Each, $31.25

MANDOLINS.

"The Regal."

Emil Wulschner & Son,
Indianapolis, Ind.

GENTLEMEN: I consider the "Regal" Mandolin I purchased of you the very best in quality and volume of tone that I have ever heard. In my opinion it is the very best mandolin in the world.

Most respectfully,

BEAVER FALLS, PA. J. A. WALLACE.

Director of Mandolin and Guitar Orchestras.

WULSCHNER & SON,
TRADE MARK
Regal
INDIANAPOLIS, IND.

Style 8

Style 8. Rose-wood and Birds-eye Maple Stained an Orange Tint, 15 Ribs, Inlay between, Mahogany Neck, Veneered Headpieee, Oval Ebony Fingerboard with Pearl Position Dots, Soundhole and Edges Elaborately Inlaid with colored woods and Celluloid, Inlaid Guard Plate, French Polished, Nickel Plated Patent Head and Tailpiece ....Each, $35.00

Style 10

Style 10. Rosewood and Birds-eye Maple, 15 Ribs with Inlay between, Inlaid Guard Plate, Mahogany Neck, Oval Ebony Fingerboard with Pearl Position Dots, Veneered Headpiece, elaborate colored wood and Celluloid Inlay around Soundhole and Edges, French Polished, Nickel Plated Patent Head and Tailpiece .... Each, $36.25

MANDOLINS.

The "Regal."

Emil Wulschner & Son:

DEAR SIRS: I regard the Regal Mandolin as having the sweetest tone and best carrying power of any mandolin I have ever used.

GEORGIA WHITTIER.

ATTICA, IND.

Style 12

Style 12. Rosewood and Birds-eye Maple Stained a beautiful Silver Gray, 15 Ribs with white Inlay between, Ebony Fingerboard with Pearl Position Dots, Mahogany Neck, Veneered Headpiece, Inlaid Guard Plate, Soundhole and Edges elaborately Inlaid with fancy colored woods and Celluloid Bound, Elegantly French Polished, Fine Patent Head, Nickel Plated Tailpiece. A superb instrument throughout and spec ally designed for the use of artists and Teachers .... Each, $38.75

Style 14

Style 14. Rosewood, 15 Ribs with white Inlay between, Mahogany Neck, Veneered Headpiece, Oval Ebony Fingerboard with Pearl Position Dots, handsome Inlay of Celluloid and colored woods around Soundhole and Edges, Inlaid Guard Plate, Elegantly French Polished, Nickel Plated Patent Head and Tailpiece .... Each, $41.25

MANDOLINS.

The "Regal."

Emil Wulschner & Son:

GENTLEMEN: I can, with pleasure, recommend the "**Regal**" Mandolins. They give perfect satisfaction in every respect. I find that they are far above any I ever used in concert work (and I have tried all of the best makes). Their sweet tone cannot be excelled.

Sincerely,

HOOPESTON, ILLS. MARION R. CLEMENTS,
Leader of Greer College Mandolin Orchestra.

WULSCHNER & SON, TRADE MARK Regal INDIANAPOLIS, IND.

Style 15.

Style 15. Tulip and Rosewood, 21 Ribs with white inlay between, Mahogany Neck, Veneered Headpiece, Oval Ebony Fingerboard with Fancy Pearl Position Dots, inlaid Celluloid Guard Plate, Soundhole and Edges elaborately inlaid with fancy colored woods, Pearl inlay in Headpiece, Fingerboard and Edges Celluloid Bound, elegantly French Polished, Nickel Plated Patent Heads and Tailpiece..Each, $50.00

Style 16.

Style 16. Rosewood, 21 Ribs with white inlay between, Mahogany Neck, Oval Ebony Fingerboard inlaid with Pearl Position Ornaments, Veneered Headpiece, Pearl inlaid, elaborate inlayings of colored woods, and Celluloid around Soundhole and Edges, inlaid Celluloid Guard Plate, elegantly French Polished ....Each, $55.00

MANDOLINS.

The "Regal."

NEW ORLEANS, LA., Aug. 18, 1895.

Emil Wulschner & Son:

DEAR SIRS—I have given the Regal Mandolin a thorough test and am more than pleased with the result. It is by far the best I have ever played. It has a fine, clear tone, the fingerboard is perfect, and is well made and beautifully finished. I advise anyone wishing a first-class instrument to purchase a Regal.

Yours truly, CARL CAMERON,
Trombonist with Bellstedt-Ballenberg Band.

WULSCHNER & SON, TRADE MARK, Regal, INDIANAPOLIS, IND.

Style 18

Style 18. Rosewood, 42 Ribs with white Inlay between, Tortoise Shell Guard Plate, Mahogany Neck, Pearl inlaid Headpiece, Oval Ebony Fingerboard with beautiful Pearl Inlayings, Soundhole and Edges elaborately Inlaid with Celluloid and fancy colored woods, Headpiece, Fingerboard, Apron and Edges Celluloid Bound, Elegantly French Polished. For quality and volume of tone this instrument **can not be equalled** .. Each, $75.00

"REGAL" MANDOLA.

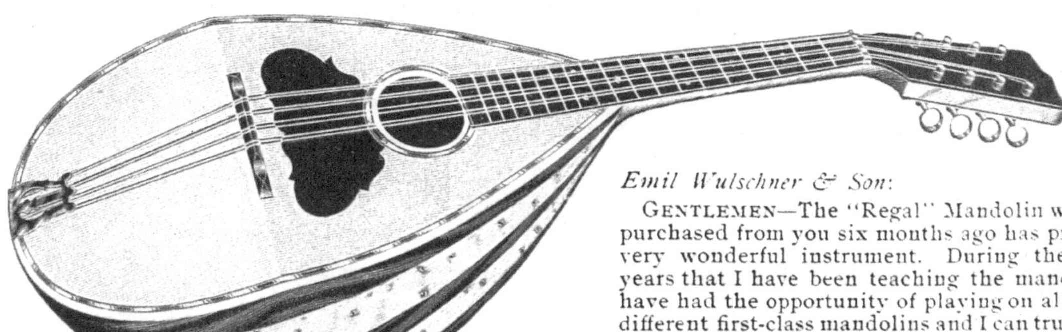

No. 25

Emil Wulschner & Son:

GENTLEMEN—The "Regal" Mandolin which I purchased from you six months ago has proven a very wonderful instrument. During the many years that I have been teaching the mandolin I have had the opportunity of playing on all of the different first-class mandolins and I can truthfully say that the "Regal" is superior to all in neatness, workmanship, durability and quality of tone. I cheerfully recommend the "Regal" Mandolin to all players who wish a first-class instrument.

Respectfully, A. G. RINKLE,
Teacher Mandolin and Guitar.

No. 25. Rosewood and Birds-eye Maple Stained a beautiful Silver Gray, 15 Ribs with white Inlay between, Oval Ebony Fingerboard with Pearl Position Dots, Mahogany Neck, Veneered Headpiece, Inlaid Guard Plate, Soundhole and Edges elaborately Inlaid with fancy colored woods and Celluloid Bound, Elegantly French Polished .... Each, $55.00

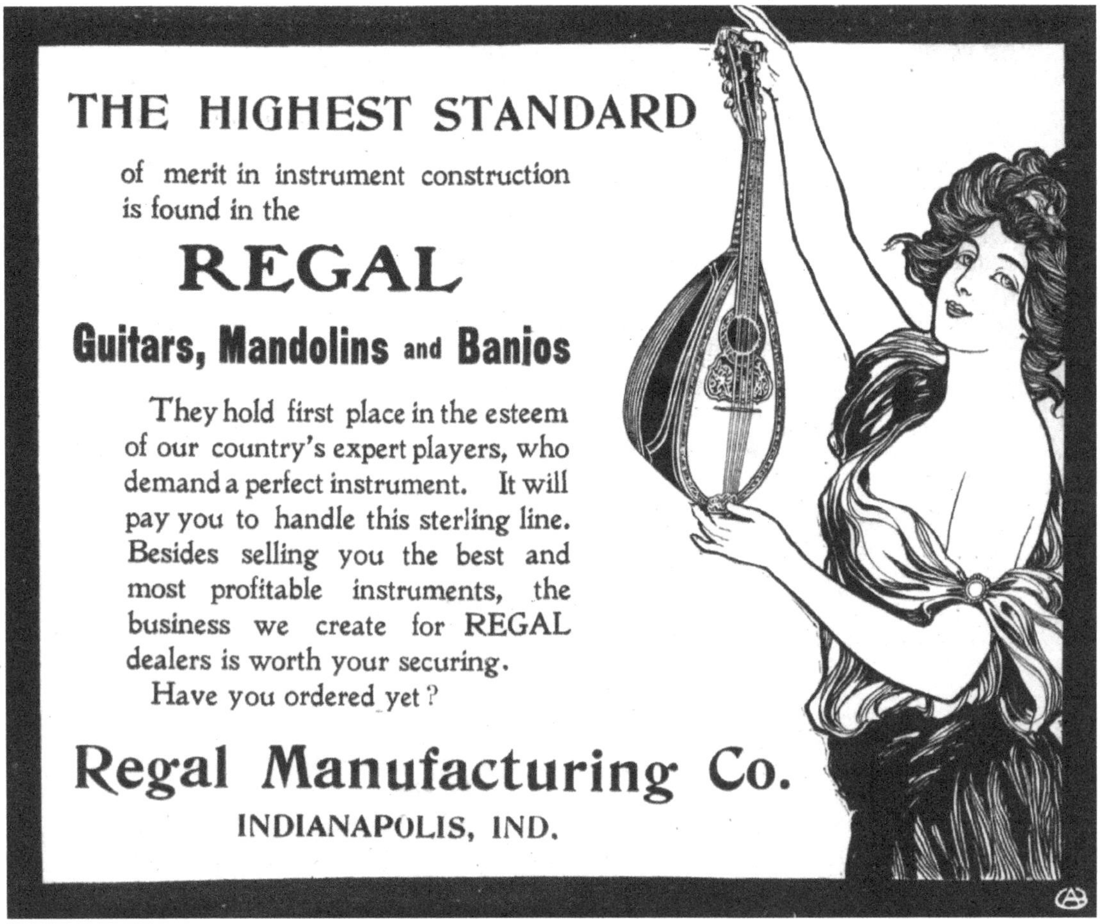

Advertisement, "The Highest Standard," Music Trade Review, January 25, 1902. Courtesy NARAS.

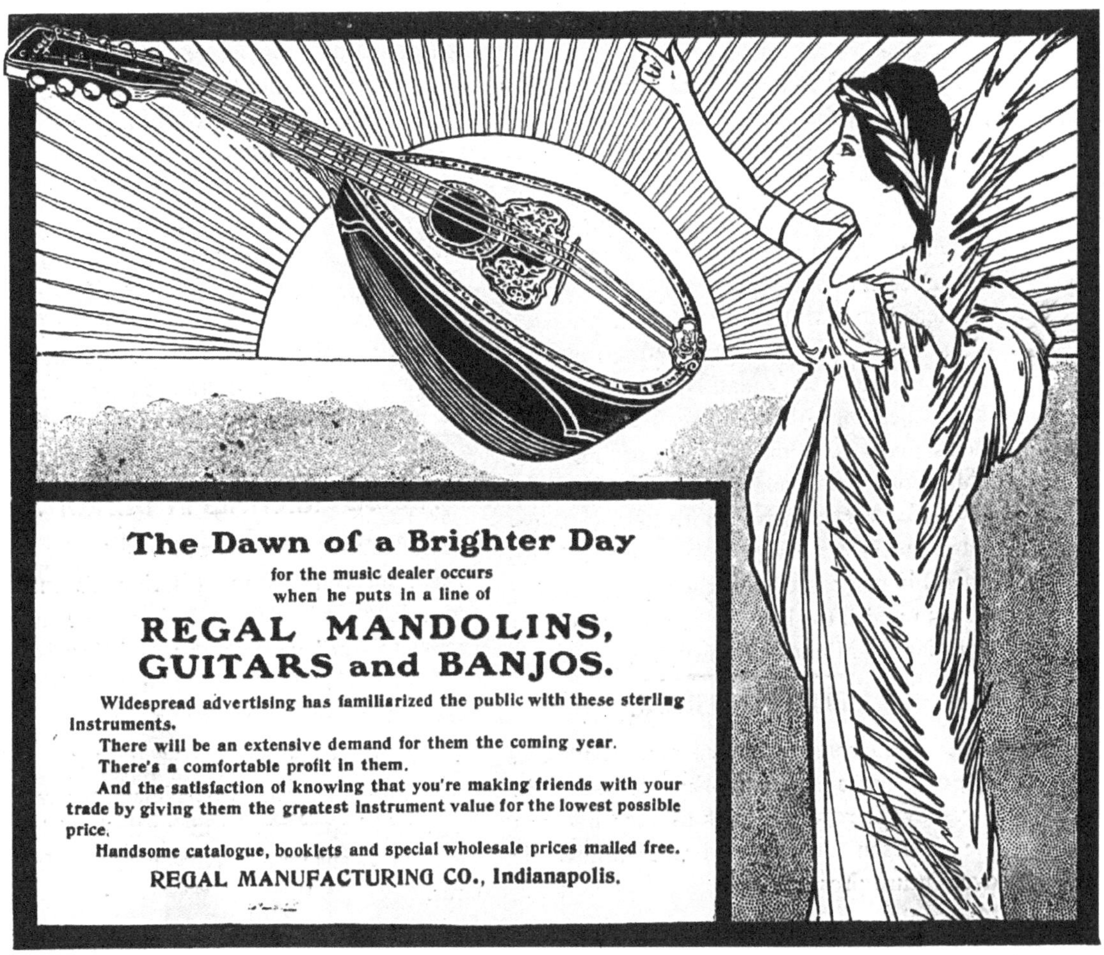

Advertisement, "The Dawn of a Brighter Day," Music Trade Review, February 8, 1902. Courtesy NARAS.

20TH CENTURY MANDOLIN

STYLE 200

Nine Maple Ribs, inlaid strips between each rib, Mahogany finished neck, ebonized finger-board and bridge, pearl positions, celluloid guard plate, sound hole inlaid and bevelled, bevelled edge. **American patent heads.** Hand polished.

Price, $5.00.

Regal Manufacturing Co., Indianapolis, "University" and "20th Century" mandolins, 1901 catalogue, p8-12 and p15-20. Photographs by Jim Bollman, courtesy Stu Cohen.

20TH CENTURY MANDOLIN

STYLE 202

Nine Mahogany Ribs, inlaid strips between each rib, mahogany finished neck, ebonized finger-board and bridge, pearl positions, celluloid guard plate, sound hole inlaid and bevelled, edges inlaid and bound with celluloid, American patent heads, hand polished.

Price, $6.25.

20TH CENTURY MANDOLIN

STYLE 204

Eleven Maple and Rosewood Ribs, inlaid strips between each rib, mahogany finished neck, ebonized finger-board and bridge, pearl position, celluloid guard plate, sound hole inlaid and bevelled, edges inlaid and bound with celluloid, American patent heads, hand polished.

Price, $8.13.

20TH CENTURY MANDOLIN

STYLE 206

Nine Rosewood Ribs, inlaid strips between each rib, mahogany finished neck, ebonized finger-board and bridge, pearl positions, celluloid guard plate, sound hole fancily inlaid and bevelled, edges fancily inlaid and bound with celluloid, American patent heads, finely hand polished.

Price, $9.38.

20TH CENTURY MANDOLIN

STYLE 208

Fifteen Rosewood and Mahogany Ribs, inlaid strips between each rib, mahogany finished **neck, ebonized** finger-board and bridge, pearl positions, celluloid guard plate, sound hole fancily inlaid **and bevelled, edges** fancily inlaid and bound with celluloid, American patent heads, finely hand polished.

Price, $10.00.

University Mandolins
ARE STRICTLY HIGH GRADE

The materials are all of the very best, and the workmanship superb We offer them in competition with any of the extensively advertised instruments, and claim them superior in tone to many makes that are listed at much higher prices.

All University Instruments Are Fully Warranted

THE UNIVERSITY MANDOLIN

STYLE 400

Eleven Rosewood Ribs, inlaid strips between each rib, Spanish cedar neck, ebony finger-board and bridge, pearl positions, ebony veneered head-piece, sound hole and edges inlaid and celluloid bound, celluloid guard plate, nickel plated American patent heads, French polished.

Price, $15.00.

THE UNIVERSITY MANDOLIN

STYLE 402

Fifteen Rosewood Ribs, inlaid strips between each rib, Spanish cedar neck, ebony finger-board and bridge, positions pearl ornamented, ebony veneered head-piece, sound hold and edges fancily inlaid and celluloid bound, celluloid guard plate, nickel plated American patent heads, French polished.

Price, $18.13.

The University Mandolin

STYLE 404

Twenty-four Rosewood Ribs, inlaid strips between each rib, Spanish cedar neck, ebony finger-board and bridge, positions fancily ornamented with pearl designs, ebony veneered head-piece, pearl inlaid, sound hole and edges fancily inlaid and celluloid bound, pearl inlaid guard plate, nickel plated covered machine heads, French polished.

Price, $23.75.

THE UNIVERSITY MANDOLIN

STYLE 406

Thirty Rosewood Ribs, inlaid strips between each rib, Spanish cedar neck, ebony finger-board, celluloid bound with positions fancily pearl inlaid, ebony veneered head-piece, pearl inlaid, edges and sound hole fancily inlaid and celluloid bound, pearl inlaid guard plate, nickel plated covered machine heads, French polished.

Price, $31.50.

THE UNIVERSITY MANDOLIN

STYLE 408

Thirty-eight Rosewood Ribs, inlaid strips between each rib, Spanish cedar neck, ebony finger-board, celluloid bound and fancily pearl inlaid in the positions, ebony veneered head-piece, pearl inlaid, sound hole and edges fancily inlaid and celluloid bound, fancily inlaid pearl guard plate, nickel plated covered machine heads, French polished.

Price, $39.38.

The University Mandolin

STYLE 410

Forty-two Rosewood Ribs, inlaid strips between each rib, Spanish cedar neck, ebony finger-board, elaborately inlaid with a handsome pearl flower design and celluloid bound, ebony veneered headpiece ornamented with pearl designs, sound hole and edges celluloid bound and elaborately inlaid, elaborately pearl inlaid guard plate, gold plated covered machine heads, French polished.

Price, $53.75.

Regal Manufacturing Company bowl back mandolin, "122-72" (model and serial number?) incised in top of headstock, made between August, 1901 and January, 1904. Full front.

Bowl Back Mandolin, full back.

Close up headstock serial and model number.

Close-up Handel tuner buttons.

Headstock logo.

Close up of top.

Four views of a high end Regal bowl back mandolin serial number 1076 from circa 1900. Photographs by Matthew Spencer.

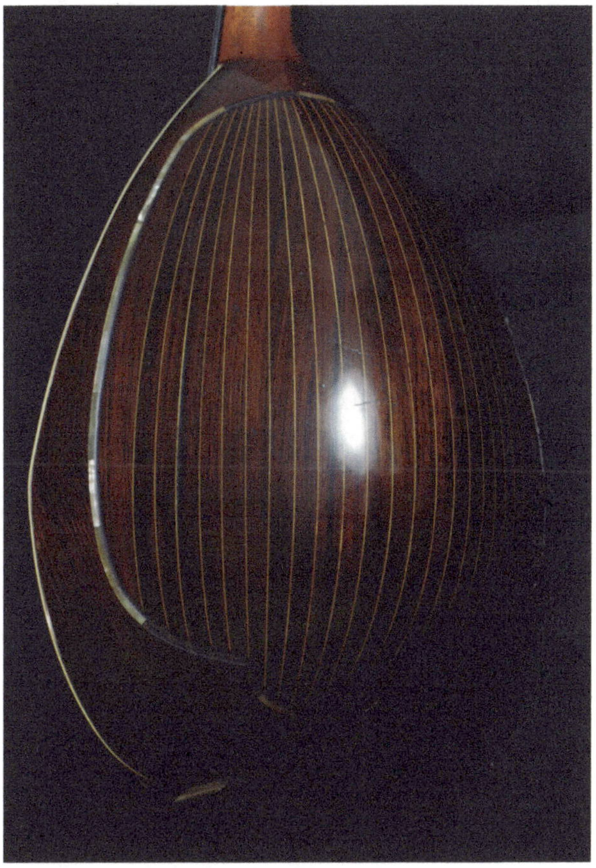

By September of 1898, soon after the catalogue shown here, Wulschner had moved into his own Indianapolis factory. Renamed the "Regal Manufacturing Company" in 1900, a catalogue from the next year showed off two of their three instrument "lines." The top grade would continue to be labeled "Regal," the second tier bore the "University" brand and the low-price group were named "20th Century." The six "University" models began with the Style 400, priced at $15.00, which had a neck of "Spanish" cedar, body of eleven rosewood ribs, ebony fingerboard, bridge and headstock overlay, and a top and soundhole bound in white celluloid. The top grade "University" mandolin went for three and half times that price. Its forty-two ribs supported a heavily pearl inlaid pickguard, while the ebony fingerboard had fancy pearl flowers up and down its length. The instrument was topped off with gold plated tuning gear covers. The five "20th Century" models, as might be expected, were plainer and more utilitarian then their higher-priced "University" cousins. They ranged from $5.00 to $10.00, had nine to fifteen ribs in combinations of maple, mahogany and rosewood, ebonized (dyed wood) instead of ebony fingerboards, necks of lesser grade woods, and little to no extraneous decoration. The 1901 catalogue either did not include the Regal line, or that part went missing years ago. The few surviving Regal-labeled bowl back mandolins from that period show a continuation of the instruments advertised in the 1896/7 catalogue, the addition being an inlaid pearl crown with "Regal" in the headstock, as well as a rectangular paper label and wooden medallion in the soundhole (see photographs. Soundhole labeling is discussed in more depth in Chapter Seven, the Flattop Guitar section of this book).

After the Regal company was moved to Chicago, the best evidence of Regal Neapolitan mandolins is contained within the pages of the Montgomery Ward catalogues. For the ten year period beginning in 1914, at least some Montgomery Ward mandolins look to be Regal made. Under Ward's "Concertone" house brand, four catalogues have at least eight models of Regal bowl backs, one has seven models, one has six and another, eleven mandolins by Regal (not all models were offered in every catalogue). Models by Regal include:

No. 6501/6506 the "Maywood" with nine maple and black walnut ribs for $1.98-$3.89 (prices fluctuated, but generally went up in later years),

No. 6503 the "Clifton" featuring 18 birch ribs for $2.95-$8.95,

No. 6505/6508 the "Victor/Superba" with twenty ribs of rosewood for $4.65-10.79,

No. 6507/6516 the "Waverly" included twenty ribs of rosewood and holly for $6.90,

No. 6517 the "Linden" with twenty-nine rosewood ribs for $6.95-9.45,

No. 6509/6510 the "Lakeside" $7.35-$14.98 for 42 rosewood and holly ribs,

No. 6511/6518 the "Belcanto" with 52 rosewood ribs at a price of $8.95-20.90,

No. 6513 the "Ardale/Belmont" for $12.75-19.25 with 52 rosewood/celluloid ribs and

No. 6515/6520 the "Windsor/Artist" (a fancier version of the Belmont) for $19.00-34.75.

For the remainder of the 1920s, Regal supplied their own branded mandolins to the wholesalers Schultz of Detroit and Cleveland and Progressive (aka: PMI) in New York City. Their catalogues are indicative of what Regal was making until they discontinued bowl backs in 1934 and are shown here. Five "Sterling" house brand models probably made by Regal were offered through Tonk Bros., and, as late as 1934, Regal still offered four models of bowl backs in their own catalogue.

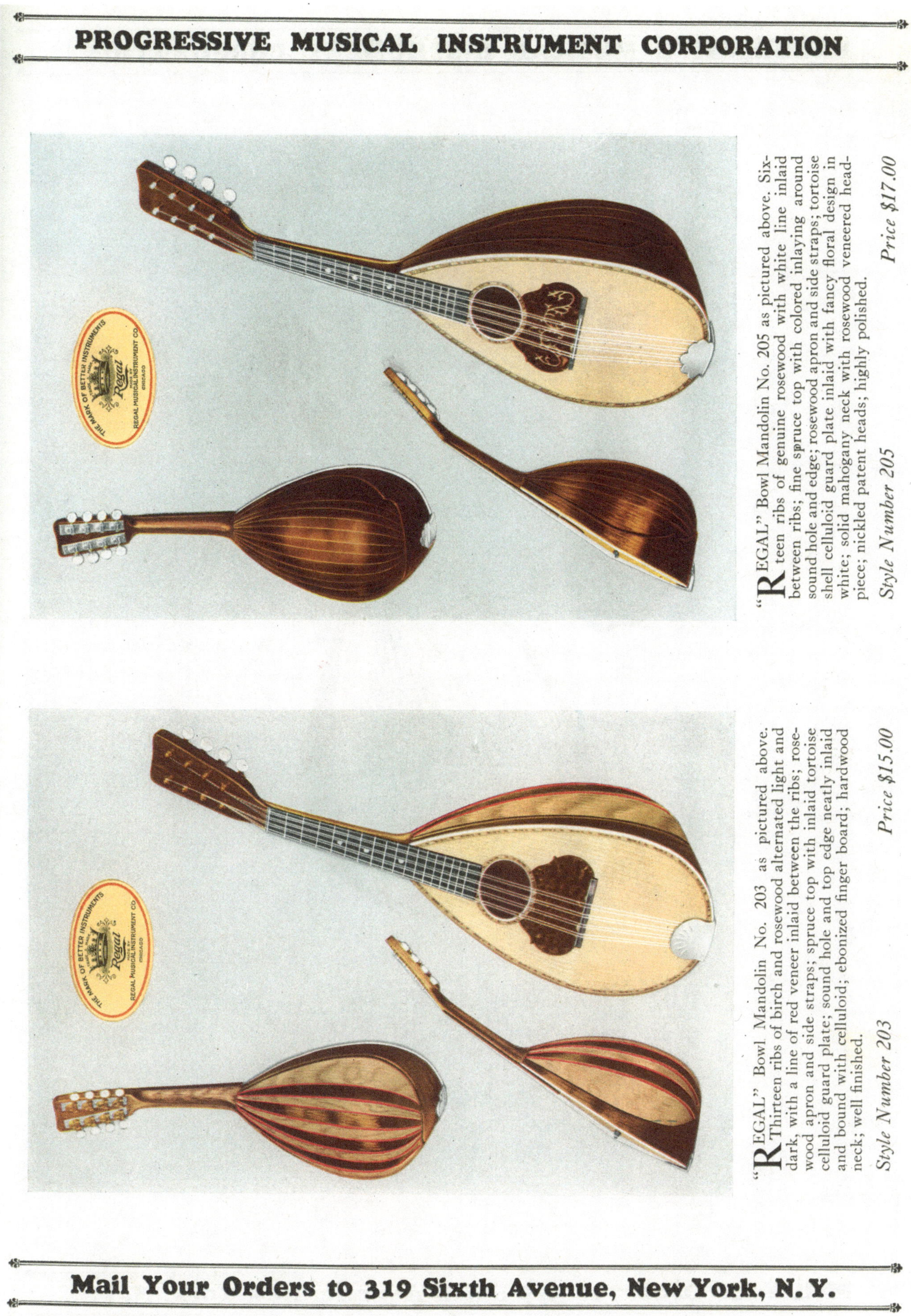
PROGRESSIVE MUSICAL INSTRUMENT CORPORATION

"REGAL" Bowl Mandolin No. 205 as pictured above. Sixteen ribs of genuine rosewood with white line inlaid between ribs; fine spruce top with colored inlaying around sound hole and edge; rosewood apron and side straps; tortoise shell celluloid guard plate inlaid with fancy floral design in white; solid mahogany neck with rosewood veneered headpiece; nickled patent heads; highly polished.

Style Number 205 *Price $17.00*

"REGAL" Bowl Mandolin No. 203 as pictured above. Thirteen ribs of birch and rosewood alternated light and dark, with a line of red veneer inlaid between the ribs; rosewood apron and side straps; spruce top with inlaid tortoise celluloid guard plate; sound hole and top edge neatly inlaid and bound with celluloid; ebonized finger board; hardwood neck; well finished.

Style Number 203 *Price $15.00*

Mail Your Orders to 319 Sixth Avenue, New York, N. Y.

"Bowl Mandolin No. 203" and "Bowl Mandolin No. 205," PMI catalogue, circa 1928. Courtesy the National Music Museum.

PROGRESSIVE MUSICAL INSTRUMENT CORPORATION

"REGAL" Bowl Mandolin No. 209 as pictured above. Fifty-two rosewood ribs separated by an inlaid strip of white celluloid; selected spruce top with a genuine pearl inlaid tortoise celluloid guard plate; wide band of inlay around sound hole, edge and side of body; white celluloid binding around cap; mahogany neck; extension finger board with fancy positions and white binding; covered patent heads. Strictly high grade instrument well finished and carefully adjusted.

Style Number 209 *Price $35.00*

Mail Your Orders to 319 Sixth Avenue, New York, N. Y.

"Bowl Mandolin No. 209," Progressive Musical Instrument Corporation (PMI) catalogue, circa 1928. Courtesy the National Music Museum.

Flat Back Mandolins

Kordick Design

Instrument: Mandolin

Model: Kordick patent design reverse scroll.

Years Made: 1914-1935.

Brand(s): Regal, Guydyu, Lyon & Healy, Washington, Concertone, Victoria, Howard, Sterling, Arcadia, Lyra, Marlboro.

Quality: Low grade.

Special Features: Kordick single piece neck/neck block, reverse bass scroll and stocking "Fender" headstock, Bell brand tailpiece. "MOTS" fingerboard and headstock overlays on some models.

Woods: All birch or spruce over birch body, birch or poplar/basswood neck.

Measurements: 10" wide, 13 ¼" long, 2 ½" deep, 23 ¾" entire length.

Logos Used: Oval paper soundhole label, Regal medallion headstock decal, Sterling triangle headstock decal.

Known Original List Price: $5.00-13.25 retail, $8.00-$14.00 wholesale.

Once the mandolin gained popularity among the American public, various makers began to tinker with its construction. Some were motivated to attempt to "improve" the tone of the instrument, some wanted to streamline the manufacturing process of the mandolin and others just wanted to make the instrument more comfortable to hold and play. Although he appears to have been experimenting with violin-shaped mandolin bodies as early as the 1880s, Orville Gibson's violin-influenced creations did not begin to reach the market until around 1900. Gibson's mandolins utilized the slightly arched back and teardrop (or "lute") shape that has become the standard for today's instruments.

Possibly inspired by Orville Gibson, but more probably motivated by the challenge of producing a distinctive product for Regal that was easy and cheap to manufacture, President Frank Kordick had begun plans for a low-cost, high profile mandolin by the time his company had moved into their own factory. In October of 1911, Kordick filed a mandolin patent assigned to Regal that "aims to provide an instrument which will be simple in construction, cheap to manufacture and which will have a sweet and pleasing tone." His design combined the neck and the end block into one part, utilized a single piece back and eliminated many of the internal brace supports from the instrument. Frank Kordick further finessed his invention with a second patent filed on July 10, 1914. In what became the model for Regal's first innovative product, Kordick combined the internal construction ideas voiced in his first patent granted in 1913 with the external design elements utilized for the production mandolin. While keeping the floating bridge, tailpiece, four-on-a-plate tuners and oval soundhole from Neapolitan mandolins, the 1914 patent mandolin features a reverse bass scroll, opposing bass and treble upper body points, and, what was later used by Fender, "stocking" shaped headstock, that make this design distinctive. In describing the mandolin's release in 1913, the Montgomery Ward catalogue declared that, "While the shape of this instrument is unusual, it should not be classified as a 'freak' by any means."

While the Kordick mandolin went through some cosmetic "tweaks" during its twenty plus year history, the basic construction remained the same. In order to contain costs, low-grade woods and parts were used for the instrument. The fingerboards and bridges were made of "ebonized" (i.e.: dyed) maple, birch or some other non-descript wood, with a twenty-fret fingerboard that was slightly rounded at the end, making the last two frets partial on the treble side. The necks were of birch, basswood or poplar, the tops were either birch or spruce and the bodies birch stained in various ways ("faux mahogany," "faux rosewood" or "imitation Koa"). Binding was of white paint, colored wood marquetry and/or white or black celluloid. This was topped off with a floating triangular celluloid pickguard. The fancier models (from 1920-1935) sported "MOTS" ("Mother-Of-Toilet-Seat") marbleized plastic fingerboards and headstock overlays. One distributor, Progressive, even offered the Kordick/Regal mandolin with custom, hand painted designs of dancing Poiret figures.

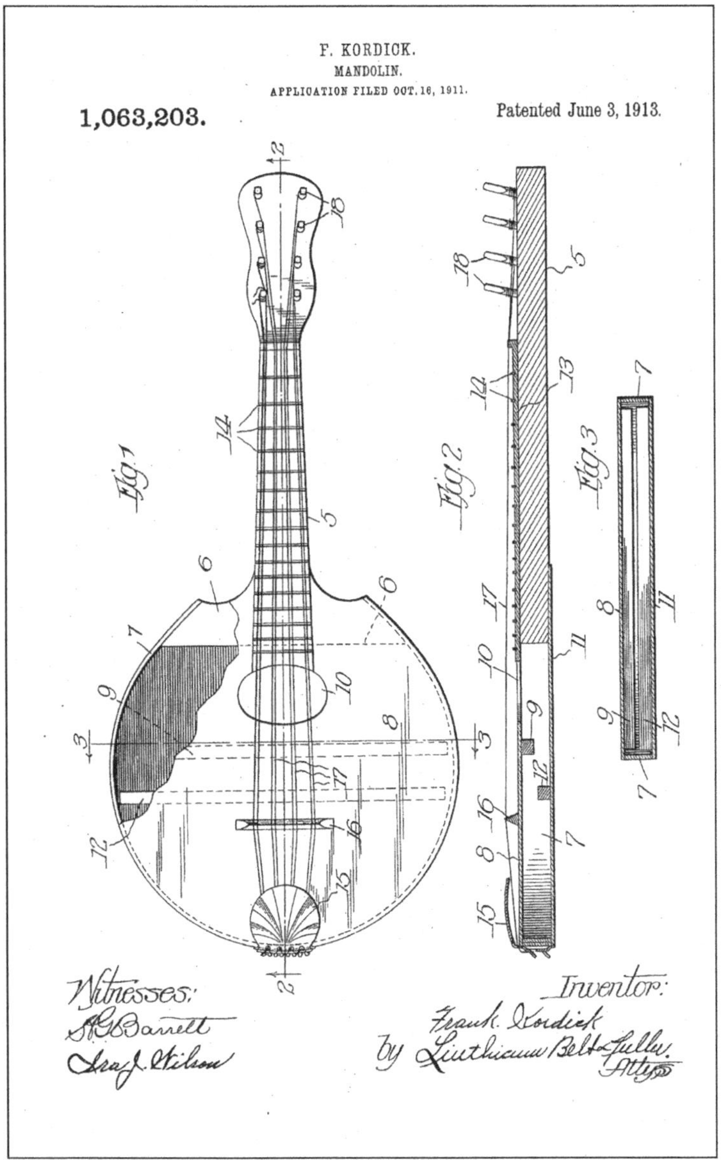

Patent drawing, "F. Kordick, Mandolin. Application Filed Oct. 16, 1911."

Patent drawing, "F. Kordick, Musical Instrument. Application Filed July 10, 1914."

"REGAL" Flat-Back Mandolin No. 107 as pictured above. Back and sides of birch; spruce top; entire body and neck shaded a deep mahogany color; all edges bound with white celluloid; raised pearl celluloid guard plate; rubbed and polished.

Style Number 107 *Price $12.50*

PROGRESSIVE MUSICAL INSTRUMENT CORPORATION

"Flat-Back Mandolin No. 107," Progressive Musical Instrument Corporation (PMI) catalogue, circa 1928. Courtesy the National Music Museum.

Mail Your Orders to 319 Sixth Avenue, New York, N. Y.

"REGAL" Flat-Back Mandolin No. 101 as pictured above. Shaded mahogany colored top, back and sides, hardwood neck; sound hole and top edge bound with white celluloid; shell tailpiece; ebonized bridge; polished finish.

Style Number 101 *Price $7.50*

"Flat-Back Mandolin No. 101," Progressive Musical Instrument Corporation (PMI) catalogue, circa 1928. Courtesy the National Music Museum.

PMI No. 101

Summary

Instrument: Mandolin.

Model: PMI No. 101.

Years Made: 1923-1937.

Brand(s): Regal, Washington, Sterling.

Quality: Low grade.

Special Features: Faux mahogany or walnut finish.

Woods: Birch body, "hardwood" neck.

Measurements: N/A.

Logos Used: Oval paper soundhole label, headstock medallion decal, Regal green headstock decal (1935-1937).

Known Original Wholesale List Price: $6.50-$16.00.

Schultz No. 2216.

Summary

Instrument: Mandolin and Mandola.

Model: Schultz No. 2216.

Years Made: 1923-1937.

Brand(s): Regal, Artex, S. S. Stewart, Sterling.

Quality: Low.

Special Features: Faux mahogany or faux walnut finish.

Woods: Natural finish spruce top over birch back and sides, "hardwood" neck.

Measurements: N/A.

Logos Used: Oval paper soundhole label, "S. S. Stewart" headstock logo, green headstock decal (1937).

Known Original List Price: $10.50-23.50 wholesale, $5.95-$7.45 retail.

Once the transition was made from bowl back to flat back lute shaped mandolins, Regal excelled as a supplier of mandolins to the wholesale trade. Their entry-level instruments featured all birch bodies stained to resemble either mahogany or walnut with or without a spruce top, a neck made of probably poplar, basswood or birch with the Regal "tulip" headstock shape, ebonized fingerboard and little else. Some were bound in celluloid and/or wood marquetry; a 1935 model even featured a "pearlette" "MOTS" fingerboard. However, mostly, these were "no frills" mandolins.

PROGRESSIVE MUSICAL INSTRUMENT CORPORATION

Perfacktone Lute Mandolins

2917

2923

2922

2923—**Perfacktone** mandolin, **genuine rosewood,** hand rubbed and polished **spruce top,** imitation tortoise shell guard plate, extending to inlaid top edge. Heavily inlaid top and bottom edges and soundhole. Ebony extension fingerboard inlaid with position dots. **Shielded cover plate** for patent heads, latest type tailpiece.................Each **$24.00**

2913—**Perfacktone** Mandolin, **genuine mahogany,** top and bottom edge inlaid with fancy wood block and edged with celluloid, soundhole inlaid to match. Spruce top, mahogany neck, ebonized fingerboard, three pearl position dots, nickel-plated ivoroid patent heads ....Each **$15.00**

2917—**Perfacktone** Mandolin, **genuine mahogany** body with finest mahogany top to match. Large inlaid guard plate at soundhole, genuine mahogany neck, ebony extension fingerboard. Top and bottom edges inlaid with neat black and white purfling. Patent heads are **protected with nickel plated shield**.......Each **$19.00**

2918—**Perfacktone** Mandolin, **genuine rosewood** with finest selected **Eastern spruce** top, large guard plate, genuine mahogany neck, extension ebonized fingerboard, accurately fretted. Top and bottom edges trimmed with fine inlaying, finest fittings.........................Each **$24.00**

2922—**Perfacktone** Mandolin, **genuine rosewood body,** highly polished **genuine selected spruce top, both edges** and soundhole bound with black fancy cut alternating inlaying, veneered head piece with full plate nickel patent heads, extension ebony fingerboard with fancy pearl position dots. Beautifully inlaid with fancy design pearl guard plate. Engraved tailpiece and patent head plate.....Each **$29.00**

Mail Your Orders to 319 Sixth Avenue, New York, N. Y.

161

"Perfacktone Lute Mandolins," "No. 2917" and "No. 2922" made by Regal. Progressive Musical Instrument Corporation (PMI) catalogue, circa 1928. Courtesy the National Music Museum.

Perfacktone No. 2917

Summary

Instrument: Mandolin.

Model: Perfacktone No. 2917

Years Made: 1920-1937.

Brand(s): Regal, Howard, Washington, Kleartone, Perfacktone, Artex, Sterling, Marveltone, Orpheus.

Quality: Low to mid-grade.

Special Features: Some instruments have nickel-plated tuner coverplate.

Woods: All mahogany.

Measurements: N/A.

Logos Used: "Washington" headstock decal, medallion headstock decal, oval paper soundhole label.

Known Original Wholesale List Price: $10.00-$21.00.

It was a big step up from a birch mandolin to one made of mahogany. The mahogany model had the same shape and some of the same appointments of the higher-priced spruce-topped instruments. These included celluloid or marquetry binding on the top, back, soundhole and fingerboard; a rosewood veneered headstock; curved fingerboard end; covered Bell Brand tailpiece; and ebony fingerboard and bridge.

Schultz No. 2213, 2361 and PMI No. 114

Summary

Instrument: Mandolin, Mandola.

Model: Regal "Superior," Schultz No. 2213, 2361 and PMI No. 114

Years Made: 1921-1935.

Brand(s): Regal, Washburn, Washington, Sterling, S. S. Stewart, Columbia, Orpheus.

Quality: Good.

Special Features: Some instruments have nickel-plated tuner coverplate.

Woods: Natural finished spruce top, mahogany back and sides, mahogany neck (one Washburn example has a maple neck).

Measurements: N/A.

Logos Used: Oval paper soundhole label, engraved "S. S. Stewart" in script on tuner coverplate.

Known Original Wholesale List Price: $10.50-$30.20.

The classic, mid-price Regal-made lute mandolin shows up in 1921 as the Lyon & Healy Washburn Style 2424. Outside of Lyon & Healy, Regal (and its distributors) thought enough of the instrument to identify the mandolin as a "Regal-made" product. Typically, this mandolin sported the "tulip"

DETROIT H.C. SCHULTZ, INC WHOLESALE EXCLUSIVELY CLEVELAND

Regal Flat-Back Mandolins

Style Number 2213

No. 2213. Venetian Model. Back and sides of genuine mahogany; spruce top; inlaid tortoise-celluloid side guard plate; sonndhole and top edge bound with colored inlay and white celluloid; hardwood neck, neatly finished; ebonized fingerboard; nickeled trimmings. Popular everywhere. **Price, each** **$14.00**

"Regal Flat-Back Mandolins" "No. 2213," H. C. Schultz catalogue, 1928. Courtesy Elderly Instruments.

Regal Flat-Back Mandolas

Style Number 2361

No. 2361. "REGAL" SUPERIOR MANDOLA. Figured mahogany back and sides; fine spruce top; inlaid tortoise-celluloid guard plate; mahogany neck with engraved patent heads, covered with nickled back plate; ebonized fingerboard accurately fretted; top and back edges bound with black celluloid; top edge and soundhole inlaid with lines of thin veneer; highly polished.
Price, each **$30.20**

No. 2365. "REGAL" GUITAR MANDOLA. Made of selected birch, finished in rich shaded mahogany color; front and back edges bound with white celluloid; nickel patent heads; strung with eight steel strings. Tuned exactly like regular mandolin.
Price, each **$10.00**

"Regal Flat-Back Mandolins" "No. 2361," and "No. 2365," H. C. Schultz catalogue, 1928. Courtesy Elderly Instruments.

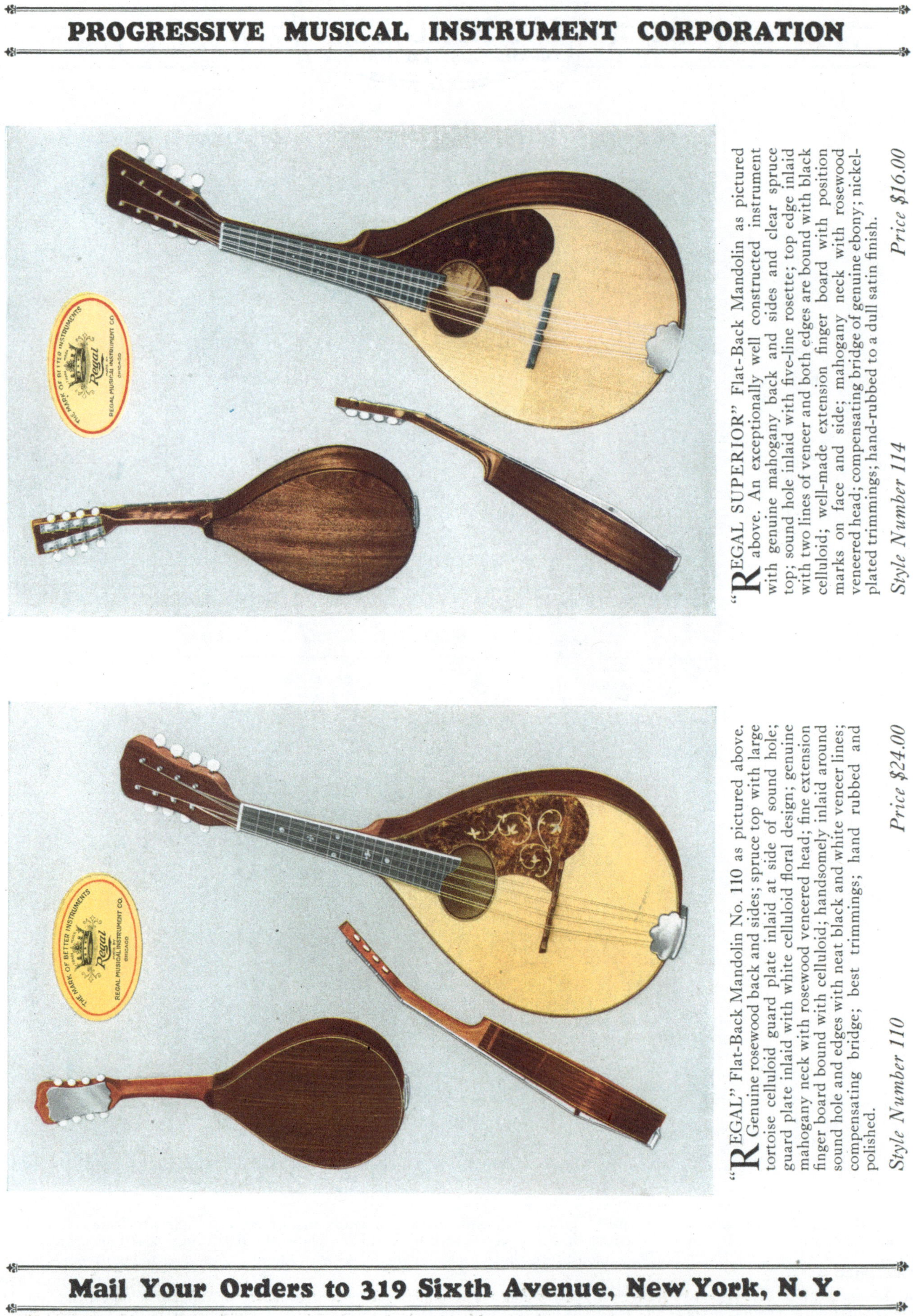

PROGRESSIVE MUSICAL INSTRUMENT CORPORATION

"REGAL SUPERIOR" Flat-Back Mandolin as pictured above. An exceptionally well constructed instrument with genuine mahogany back and sides and clear spruce top; sound hole inlaid with five-line rosette; top edge inlaid with two lines of veneer and both edges are bound with black celluloid; well-made extension finger board with position marks on face and side; mahogany neck with rosewood veneered head; compensating bridge of genuine ebony; nickel-plated trimmings; hand-rubbed to a dull satin finish.

Style Number 114 *Price $16.00*

"REGAL" Flat-Back Mandolin No. 110 as pictured above. Genuine rosewood back and sides; spruce top with large tortoise celluloid guard plate inlaid at side of sound hole; guard plate inlaid with white celluloid floral design; genuine mahogany neck with rosewood veneered head; fine extension finger board bound with celluloid; handsomely inlaid around sound hole and edges with neat black and white veneer lines; compensating bridge; best trimmings; hand rubbed and polished.

Style Number 110 *Price $24.00*

Mail Your Orders to 319 Sixth Avenue, New York, N. Y.

"Flat-Back Mandolin No. 110," and "Number 114," Progressive Musical Instrument Corporation (PMI) catalogue, circa 1928. Courtesy the National Music Museum.

headstock shape (the mandola and S. S. Stewart, Washburn and Columbia-model mandolin had a single-point headstock), four-on-a-plate tuners, celluloid binding and colored wood marquetry or fine lines on the higher priced models, covered tailpiece, oval soundhole, ebonized fingerboard (a few variations had an ebony fingerboard), floating bridge, pickguard that covered the treble side of the top above the bridge and dots on the fingerboard. The Regal and Sterling mandola, as well as the S. S. Stewart (at that time, a "house brand" of B&J wholesalers in New York City) mandolins, sported a nickeled tuner plate that covered the back of the headstock.

PMI No. 110

Summary

Instrument: Mandolin

Model: PMI No. 110, Harwood "Artist," Ditson "Victory."

Years Made: 1920-1934.

Brand(s): Regal, Harwood, Perfacktone, Sterling, Kleartone, S. S. Stewart, Ditson, Stahl, Orpheus.

Quality: High.

Special Features: Tuner coverplate some engraved, higher priced models have pickguards inlaid with celluloid vines.

Woods: Spruce over rosewood, mahogany neck.

Measurements: Overall length is 24", 9 ½" width, and 2 ¼" in depth measured at the side of the body, scale length is 13", width of nut is 1 1/8".

Logos Used: Regal pearl medallion headstock logo, "Harwood" on headstock in pearl, paper soundhole label, "S.S. Stewart, Philadelphia, PA" decal on headstock, engraved "S. S. Stewart" in script on tuner coverplate, engraved "Ditson Victory" in script on tuner coverplate.

Known Original Wholesale List Price: $17.50-$30.00.

We now get into Regal's finest offerings of mandolin models in the 1920s. Rosewood was considered a premium wood, utilized for the top offerings in a maker's line. Regal's entry-level rosewood back and sides mandolin featured black and white binding/purling of celluloid and white holly around the spruce top, rosewood back and oval soundhole; a mahogany neck with a headstock overlay of rosewood; bound ebony fingerboard with rounded extension end; twenty total frets; floating bridge; Bell brand tailpiece with removable cover; and single point Regal headstock shape. The tuners featured a back cover plate, as was common on all Regal rosewood mandolins of this period. The fingerboard marker dots are replaced, in some locations, with diamonds. Some models featured a treble side pickguard inlaid with celluloid in a vine pattern. B&J's "S. S. Stewart" and Ditson's "Victory" models have the added feature of an engraved tuner backplate.

Regal Flat-Back Mandolins

Style Number 2223

No. 2223. "Regal Superior". Venetian Model. A beautiful rosewood instrument heavily inlaid around sound-hole, top and back edges and down center of back with fine cut black and white blocks; tortoise shell celluloid guard plate with inlaid pearl floral design; pearl "Regal" name plate in head; genuine mahogany neck; rosewood-veneered headpiece; fingerboard bound with white celluloid; patent heads covered with nickel-plated, engraved back plate; highly polished finish; carefully adjusted and inspected.
Price, each. **$36.00**

"Regal Flat-Back Mandolins" "No. 2223," H. C. Schultz catalogue, 1928. Courtesy Elderly Instruments.

Schultz No. 2223

Summary

Instrument: Mandolin

Model: Regal "Superior," Schultz No. 2223, Harwood "Artist."

Years Made: 1923-1928.

Brand(s): Regal, Harwood, Kleartone.

Quality: High.

Special Features: Engraved tuner coverplate and tailpiece cover, pickguard inlaid with vines in pearl.

Woods: Spruce over rosewood, mahogany neck.

Measurements: Overall length is 24", 9 ½" wide, and 2 ¼" in depth measured at the side of the body, scale length is 13", width of nut is 1 and 1/8".

Logos Used: Pearl headstock medallion, "Harwood" in pearl in headstock, paper soundhole label.

Known Original Wholesale List Price: $27.50-$40.00.

A fancier version of the rosewood mandolin above. Additional features include wooden marquetry around the top, back, soundhole and for the back centerstripe; pearl replacing celluloid in the pickguard inlay; and an engraved tuner backplate and pickguard cover standard. Models sold under the Regal name featured their "medallion" headstock logo in pearl.

Custom Built

Summary

Instrument: Mandolin.

Model: Custom Built.

Years Made: 1928-1936.

Brand(s): Regal.

Quality: Low to high grade.

Special Features: Tulip/rabbit ears headstock, "bent" top.

Woods: Natural finished spruce over birch, mahogany or rosewood.

Measurements: 14" scale.

Logos Used: Regal oval paper "Custom Built" soundhole label, medallion headstock logo, green headstock decal.

Known Original Wholesale List Price: $10.50, $13.50, $21.00 and $27.00-28.00.

Regal took four of their tulip headstocked lute mandolins made prior to 1928 and relabeled them "Custom Built." The No. 1 was a spruce-topped mahogany-finished birch back and sides instrument, with a bound top and soundhole and back coverplate for the tuners (later just regular four-on-a-plate

Regal Flat-Back Mandolins

Style Number 2224

No. 2224. "Regal Superior". Two-Point Venetian Model. A very popular instrument of unique design; back and sides of selected genuine rosewood; fine-grained spruce top; tortoise celluloid guard plate; both edges bound with white celluloid and top edge and soundhole with inlaid lines of black and white veneer; mahogany neck with rosewood veneered head; "Regal" nameplate inlaid in head; head bound with white celluloid; extension fingerboard, celluloid bound; highly rubbed and polished; carefully adjusted and inspected.
Price, each. **$27.90**

"Regal Flat-Back Mandolins" "No. 2224," H. C. Schultz catalogue, 1928. Courtesy Elderly Instruments.

bottom geared tuners). The No. 2 and No. 3 came with mahogany back and sides, an inlaid pickguard, bound top and soundhole, and back tuner coverplate. The No. 3 added a white celluloid bound ebonized fingerboard, back center stripe and pearl inlay on the headstock. No. 4 was a rosewood model, with a pearl inlaid pickguard, colored marquetry around the top, back and soundhole and pearl on the headstock. All featured a teardrop pickguard with the top cut off and a rounded-end fingerboard with twenty frets.

Two Point

Summary

Instrument: Mandolin.

Model: "Venetian" Flat Back Two Point.

Years Made: 1928-1930.

Brand(s): Sterling.

Quality: Low.

Special Features: None.

Woods: Natural finish spruce over birch or mahogany.

Measurements: N/A.

Logos Used: None.

Known Original List Price: $11.50-$13.00 wholesale, $5.95-$7.25 retail.

Regal's fanciest mandolin of the 1920s utilized a "two point" body shape. It appears that the company also made some low-priced spruce-topped versions in birch and (possibly) mahogany. These came with ebonized fingerboards, white bound oval soundholes, fingerboards and tops, with marquetry around top and soundhole.

Schultz No. 2224

Summary

Instrument: Mandolin.

Model: "Venetian" Flat Back Two Point, Schultz No. 2224.

Years Made: 1915-1932.

Brand(s): Regal "Superior," (1928-1932), Washburn (1917-1925).

Quality: High.

Special Features: Engraved tuner coverplate.

Woods: Natural finish spruce over rosewood, mahogany neck.

Measurements: N/A.

Logos Used: Paper soundhole label, pearl headstock medallion, Washburn paper soundhole label, "Washburn" engraved on tuner backplate.

Known Original List Price: $27.90 wholesale, $7.35-14.75 retail.

DETROIT **H.C. SCHULTZ, INC** WHOLESALE EXCLUSIVELY CLEVELAND

Regal Flat-Back Mandolins

Style Number 2221

No. 2221. "REGAL SUPERIOR." Two-Point Venetian Model. An instrument of charming beauty as well as tone quality. Genuine rosewood back and sides; finest spruce top obtainable; soundhole, guard plate and top edges inlaid with wide band of genuine iridescent pearl, backed up with small black and white wood block inlaying; same block inlaying around sides at top and back, back edge and center of back; edges of body bound with black celluloid; fine extension fingerboard bound with black and white celluloid; genuine mahogany neck with fancy shaped head; artistically finished and highly polished.
Price, each **$54.00**

"Regal Flat-Back Mandolins" "No. 2221," H. C. Schultz catalogue, 1928. Courtesy Elderly Instruments.

A rare offering from Regal's (and Washburn's) high end, this mandolin was the second to the top model made during the 1920s and early 1930s. Utilizing a two point body made of naturally finished spruce over rosewood, its appointments included white celluloid binding with fine lines of black and white veneer, engraved tuner cover plate, a rosewood headstock overlay with the Regal logo in pearl and white celluloid binding.

Schultz No. 2221

Summary

Instrument: Mandolin.

Model: "Venetian" Flat Back Two Point, Schultz No. 2221.

Years Made: 1928-1937.

Brand(s): Regal "Superior."

Quality: High.

Special Features: Fancy engraved tuner and tailpiece coverplates, headstock cut-out on early models, pearl bound body, pearl inlaid pickguard.

Woods: Natural finish spruce over rosewood, mahogany neck.

Measurements: N/A.

Logos Used: Paper soundhole label, green headstock decal.

Known Original Wholesale List Price: $48.00-$54.00.

Here is Regal's top "Venetian" mandolin from the late 1920s/early 1930s. Its spruce top and oval soundhole are heavily decorated with black celluloid, black and white marquetry as well as a band of iridescent pearl. This theme, minus the pearl, is repeated on the rosewood back, with a centerstripe of marquetry. The fingerboard is double-bound in black and white celluloid and the pickguard inlaid with pearl in a vine motif. The mahogany neck features a headstock shape unique to Regal with a cut-out heart at the top (on early versions; later versions have the solid, single point headstock of the less fancy models), somewhat reminiscent of what Martin was using at the time. The tuner backplate is heavily engraved, as is the tailpiece cover.

Two models of Regal-made Bacon mandolins, a "B&D Ramona" and a "B&D Sultana Grand," shown in the 1937 Chicago Musical Instrument (CMI) catalogue. Courtesy the National Music Museum."

Modified Kordick Shape

Summary

Instrument: Mandolin.

Model: Modified Kordick patent shape.

Years Made: 1936-1939.

Brand(s): Regal, B&D, Maurer.

Quality: Low to high grade.

Special Features: Arched top, carved on higher grade instruments, "F" holes on some models.

Woods: Spruce over maple, mahogany neck (B&D).

Measurements: 13 ¾" scale, 1 3/16" nut width ("Ramona" and "Ultra").

Logos Used: Oval paper soundhole label, various Bacon model designations on headstock, Maurer stamp inside, green headstock decal (1939).

Known Original List Price: $12.00-135.00 wholesale, $8.45-13.50 retail.

In 1935, Regal mandolins underwent an overhaul. Although the company would continue to market the models with which they had success in the 1920s, new styles to reflect what other companies were making began to be introduced into the Regal line. This included a number of arched and carved top mandolins and larger bodies overall. "The Country Asked for Bigger Mandolins," said Regal in their 1939 catalogue, and the company answered with larger instruments.

The old standby Kordick patent shape with its reversed bass scroll and two opposing bass/treble body points was retained but given a new arched body design. The stocking headstock shape was initially preserved, but was soon phased out. On the lower end, instruments such as those sold through Montgomery Ward, by the Tonk Bros. and, after 1938, by Regal themselves directly to dealers, featured an ebonized fingerboard, Bell brand tailpiece, fourteen inch scale, and an oval or "F" holes.

Where Regal really excelled were in a line made for the Bacon Banjo Company of Groton, Connecticut. Although Bacon had previously marketed instruments designed for them by prominent mandolinist William Place, Jr., which look like the work of Lyon & Healy (we know that they weren't made by Bacon themselves, although it is unclear who actually did made them), the Bacon Company had not shown mandolins in their catalogues since 1929/1930.

From around 1936 through 1939, Regal, under the "B&D" moniker, built mandolins that were completely different from anything else on the market. The top end instruments were eye-popping in their appointments, art deco to-the-max and more akin to the archtop guitars also being produced by Regal under the Bacon & Day label (see Chapter Eight on Archtop Guitars fmi). In their promotional literature, Bacon poured on the hyperbole. "Bacon & Day Mandolins," stated their catalogue circa 1936, "set new heights of tonal beauty. It is no exaggeration to state that the tone of the new 'Sultana' rivals that of a fine violin, and all models, from the lowest priced up, are characteristic of the fine quality always associated with the names of Bacon and Day."

Their two carved-top models utilizing the modified Kordick patented body shape were the "Ramona" for a $75.00 wholesale list price and the "Sultana" for $135.00.

Regal made "B&D Sultana Grand" mandolin, full front view. Photograph by Ryan Fitzsimmons, courtesy the Music Emporium.

Regal made "B&D Sultana Grand" mandolin, full back view. Photograph by Ryan Fitzsimmons, courtesy the Music Emporium.

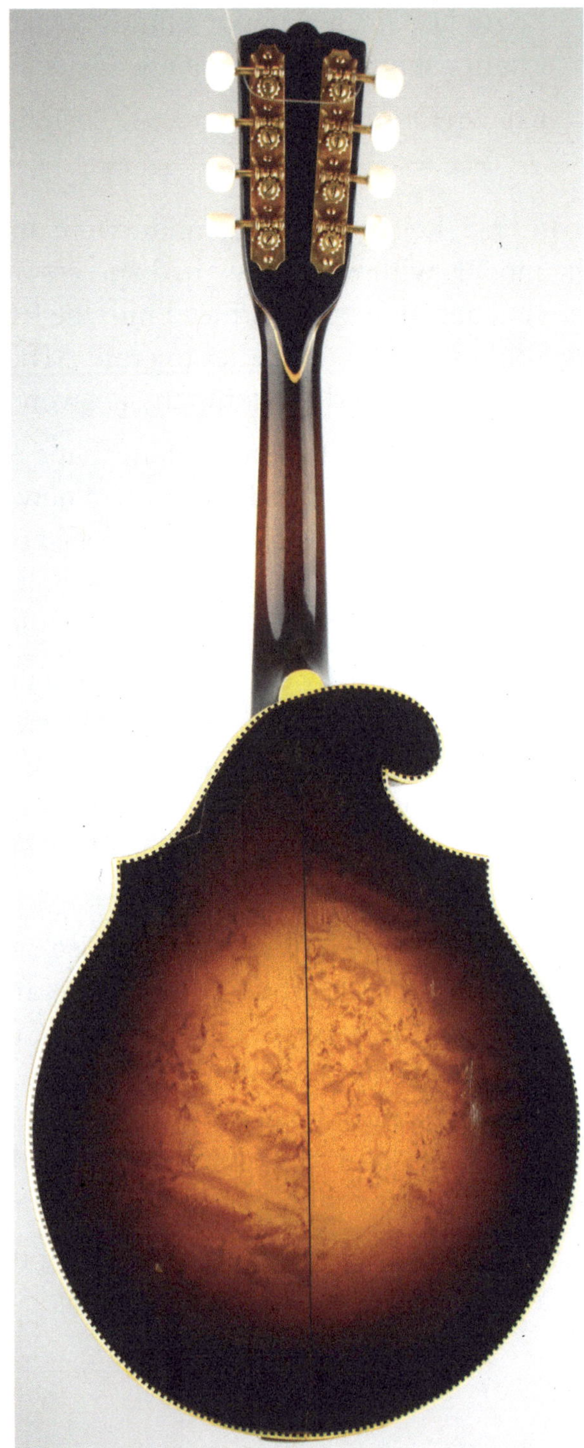

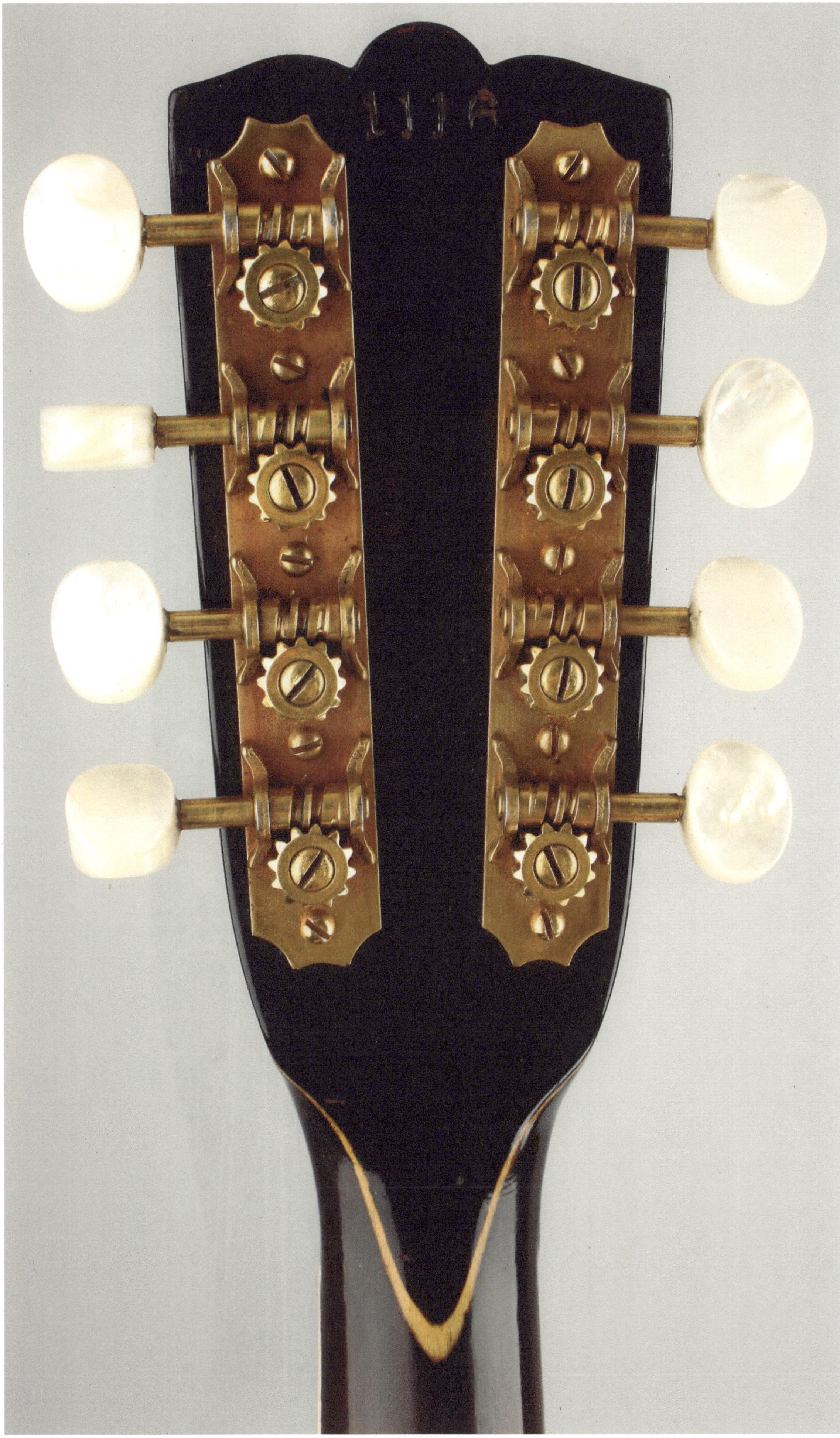

Regal made "B&D Sultana Grand" mandolin, back of headstock close-up with serial number and tuners. Photograph by Ryan Fitzsimmons, courtesy the Music Emporium.

Regal made "B&D Sultana Grand" mandolin, headstock close-up. Photograph by Ryan Fitzsimmons, courtesy the Music Emporium.

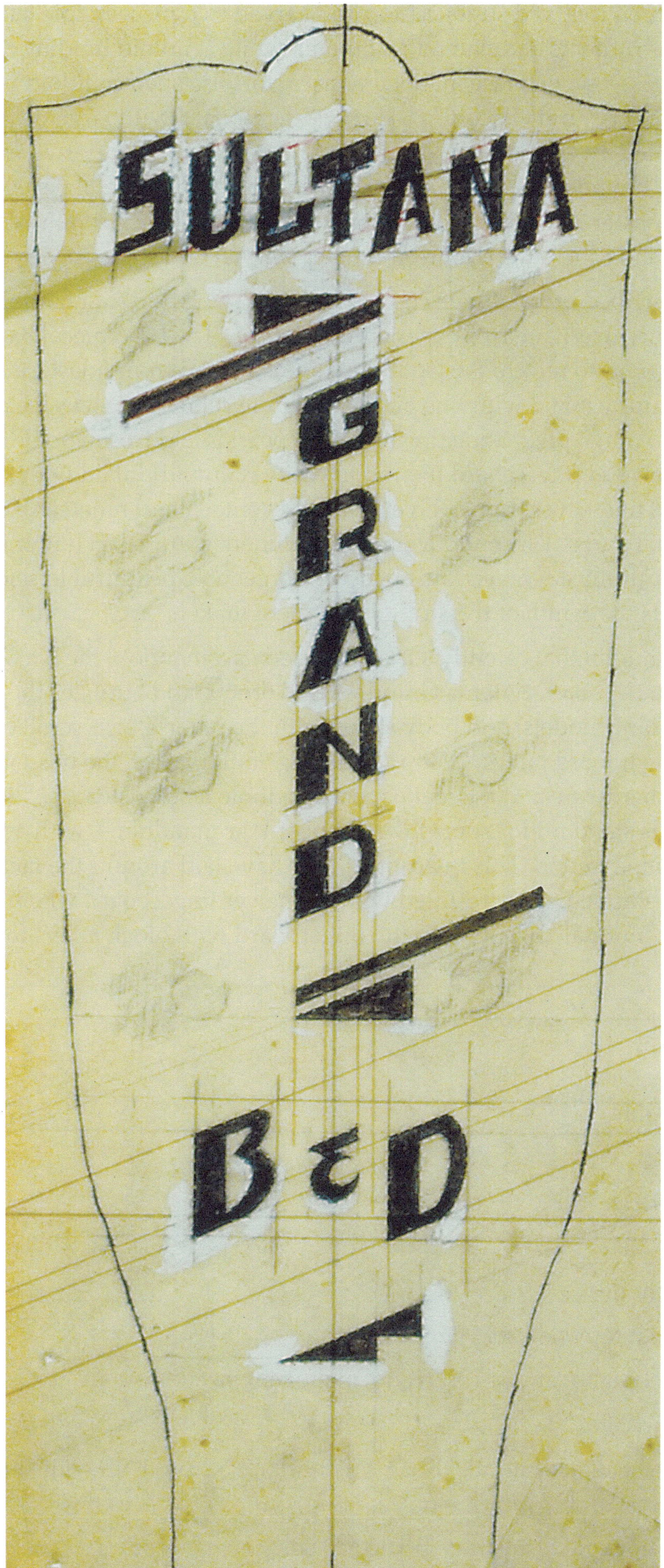

Drawing for headstock inlay by Joe Phetteplace, "B&D Sultana Grand." Photograph/courtesy Spruce Tree Music.

The "Ramona" featured a carved sunburst top and carved two piece maple back with black backstripe (bird's-eye on some instruments and flamed on others); white celluloid binding around the top, back, oval soundhole and neck; a seven piece mahogany neck; tortoise shell celluloid headstock overlay with engraved "B&D," "Ramona" and "Bacon;" rosewood fingerboard with large pearl block inlays at frets one, three, five, seven, ten, twelve, fifteen, seventeen and nineteen; twenty-two frets total with a curved fingerboard end; triple bound pickguard and headstock; gold plated metal parts; rosewood adjustable floating bridge; and "lobster claw" shaped floating pickguard. The serial number was inscribed into the back of the headstock and tuners were four-on-a-plate with tab ends possibly by Kluson.

The "Sultana" is described by catalogue copywriters as "The 'Strad' of mandolins. A tonal quality of such strength and beauty that it amazes experienced soloists. The [two piece] back is carved from choice birds-eye maple, with sides to match; the [sunburst] top is carved from finest eastern spruce; edges [and oval soundhole] beautifully inlaid with fine black and white celluloid blocks [i.e.: "zipper binding"] and bound with white celluloid; 7-ply mahogany neck with pearl inlaid [rosewood] headpiece ["Sultana, " "Grand," "B&D"]; rosewood fingerboard [bound in white celluloid] inlaid with large engraved pearl blocks [frets one, three, five, seven, ten, twelve, fifteen, seventeen and nineteen]; beautiful French polish finish; gold plated metal parts; [Kluson four-on-a-plate tuners with] pearl buttons; new[floating "lobster claw"] guardplate beautifully engraved and shaded. Gorgeously beautiful in selection of woods and trimmings, it represents the zenith of the string instrument makers' art."

One other Regal mandolin that recently surfaced deserves a mention, the No. 255 "Ultra Grand." A scaled down version of the "B&D Sultana Grand," the "Ultra Grand" utilizes the same headstock (a "tulip" headstock on some models) and body shape with the reverse bass scroll eliminated, dots instead of the "scrimshaw" fingerboard inlays, "Ultra" replacing "Sultana" on the headstock, nickel or chrome instead of gold plated hardware and a Regal paper soundhole label instead of "B&D" on the headstock. The dyed fingerboard is standard for some low-end post-War mandolins, with a long "finger extension, making this a twenty-nine fretter! This instrument may have laid around the factory for ten years and then was finished and shipped, or, retro-fitted with the newer fingerboard when the old one wore out, as the catalogue shows a "normal" twenty-two fret fingerboard with block inlays for this model.

Flat Top

Summary

Instrument: Mandolin.

Model: Flat top.

Years Made: 1936-1939.

Brand(s): Regal, "B&D."

Quality: Medium grade.

Special Features: Flat top and back, large body.

Woods: Spruce over mahogany or rosewood, mahogany neck.

Measurements: 14" scale.

Logos Used: Green headstock decal, "B&D," "Senorita," "Groton" in white on black plastic headstock overlay.

Known Original Wholesale List Price: $15.00-$50.00.

Two models of Regal-made Bacon mandolins, a "B&D Senorita 1" and "Senorita 2," shown in the 1937 Chicago Musical Instrument (CMI) catalogue. Courtesy the National Music Museum.

Bacon & Day also marketed two models of "Senorita" flat top and back mandolins made by Regal. The "Senorita 1" featured "mahogany back and sides and fine spruce top, soundhole inlaid with black and white veneer, edges of body bound with heavy white celluloid nicely rounded, fine mahogany neck of 7-ply construction, headpiece of black celluloid neatly engraved, new 14-inch scale, rosewood fingerboard bound with white celluloid, beautifully finished in hand rubbed bound shading, nickel plated patent heads with white buttons, . . . compensated bridge, and tortoise celluloid guardplate." "The Senorita 2" came "with genuine rosewood back and sides . . . . The top is of fine spruce with edges of soundhole and edges of body inlaid with black and white holly bound with white celluloid, 7-ply mahogany neck with black celluloid headpiece neatly engraved, white celluloid heel, rosewood fingerboard with pearl buttons and bound with white celluloid, highly polished finish, chromium plated patent heads with white buttons; chromium plated tailpiece, . . . compensated bridge and tortoise celluloid guardplate." Both models had a sunburst finish; fingerboard position markers at the third, fifth, seventh, tenth, twelfth and fifteenth frets (the "Style 2" also had a seventeenth fret marker); twenty-two frets; a floating bridge and "lobster claw" pickguard. Regal's version of the "Senorita 1," the No. R 116, appeared in their 1937 catalogue and also the Tonk Bros. wholesale catalogue for that year.

Arched Top

Summary

Instrument: Mandolin.

Model: Arched top

Years Made: 1935-1939

Brand(s): Regal, Groton, Rotary.

Quality: Medium grade.

Special Features: Oval or "F" holes, carved top on highest priced.

Woods: Spruce over mahogany, maple or rosewood.

Measurements: 14" scale.

Logos Used: Green headstock decal, "Groton 1, B&D" in white on black plastic headstock overlay, headstock medallion decal.

Known Original Wholesale List Price: $9.50-$50.00.

The arched top mandolins made by Regal in the late 1930s featured either an oval hole or "F" holes. Their best quality offerings included the No. 247, an "F" holed spruce over maple sunburst model; No. 248, an oval holed spruce over mahogany mandolin with a carved top, rosewood fingerboard and deep body, and the No. 155 "Ultra Grand" described above.

Three models of Regal mandolins from their 1939 catalogue.

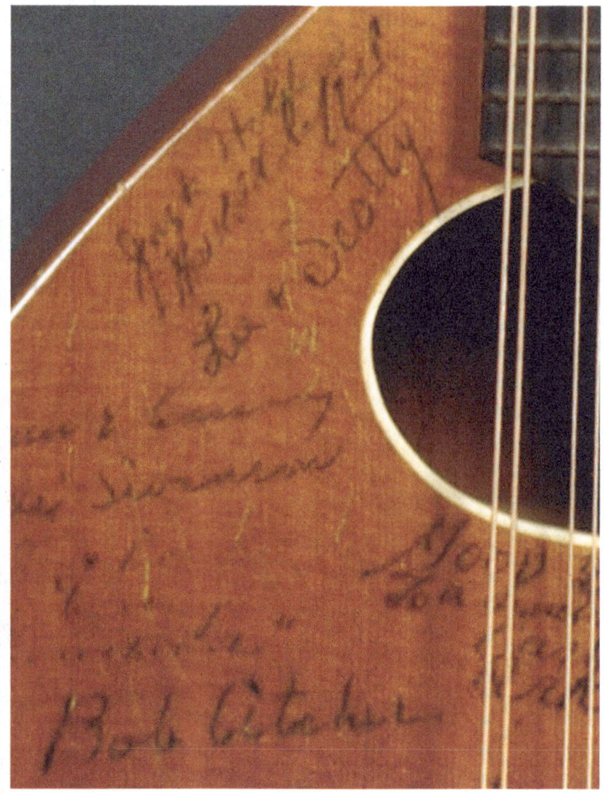

A post-War Regal mandolin presented to Karl Davis from the duo of Karl and Harty upon his retirement from the WLS Barndance in Chicago, signed by members of the cast. Among the recognizable signatures on the face are Lulu Belle and Scotty, and Bob Atcher. Courtesy of Karleen Tyksinski, photograph by Spruce Tree Music.

Teardrop

Summary

Instrument: Mandolin.

Model: Flat back teardrop shaped body.

Years Made: 1945-1955.

Brand(s): Regal.

Quality: Low grade.

Special Features: None.

Woods: Spruce top, mahogany or birch back and sides, probably poplar/basswood neck.

Measurements: "10 ½" by 12 ½" by 3" some models.

Logos Used: Regal light blue background multi-colored headstock decal.

Known Original Wholesale List Price: $13.50-$35.00.

After World War II, Regal's mandolin offerings shrank to just five models in the circa 1949 catalogue. By that time, all mandolins featured an oval soundhole and teardrop lute shaped body. The high end correlated to the pre-War No. 248, but, mostly what survives these days (or at least frequently turns up in online auctions) are the low end models. These feature stained birch back and sides, a sunburst or natural birch top, ebonized or rosewood fingerboard with twelve frets to the body and twenty frets total, tulip-shaped headstock, teardrop pickguard, white painted binding, and a sunburst poplar or basswood neck.

(See Chapter Eight: Flattop Guitars for information on mandolins with vinyl fingerboards and other decorative features common to other Regal-made instruments.)

Guitar Bodied Mandolin

Summary

Instrument: Mandolin.

Model: Guitar-mandola, mandolina, guitar-mandolin, "Serenata," "Royal."

Years Made: 1901-1932.

Brand(s): 20th Century, Regal, Boston, Sterling.

Quality: Low grade.

Special Features: Scaled down guitar body shape, painted body some models.

Woods: Early models maple or sycamore, later all birch, with faux mahogany basswood neck.

Measurements: Overall length is 29 ¼", 10 ½" width, and 3 ¼" in depth at the end block. Scale length is 17", width at nut is 1 and ¼" (post-1932 model).

Logos Used: Rectangular paper soundhole label "Regal Manufacturing Company, Indianapolis."

Known Original List Price: $4.90-$6.50 retail, $8.13-$11.25 wholesale.

The 20th Century Guitar-Mandolin

STYLE 212

Maple, Dark Cherry Finish, mahogany finished neck, ebonized finger-board and bridge, pearl posi-
celluloid guard plate, sound hole fancily inlaid and bevelled, top edge fancily inlaid and bound with
oid, a fancily inlaid stripe down back, American patent heads, finely hand polished.

Price, $8.13.

Regal Manufacturing Co., Indianapolis, catalogue, 1901, "The 20th Century Guitar-Mandolin Style 212." Photograph by Jim Bollman, courtesy Stu Cohen.

THE 20TH CENTURY GUITAR-MANDOLIN

STYLE 214

Beautiful Curly Sycamore Body, Rosewood Finish, mahogany finished neck, ebonized finger-board and bridge, pearl positions, celluloid guard plate, sound hole fancily inlaid and bevelled, both edges, top and back, bound with celluloid and fancily inlaid, a fancily inlaid stripe down back, American patent heads, finely hand polished.

Price, $11.25.

Regal Manufacturing Co., Indianapolis, catalogue, 1901, "The 20th Century Guitar-Mandolin Style 214." Photograph by Jim Bollman, courtesy Stu Cohen.

The late nineteenth and early twentieth centuries produced its share of musical oddities, including the aptly named guitar-mandolin. Described by one wholesaler as "a mandolin with a guitar shaped body, it has a fingerboard the same as on a mandolin and is played in the same manner," Regal was making this instrument by the time of their 1901 catalogue. Two models of "20th Century"-brand guitar-mandolins were featured, and are reproduced here. Their solid, slightly curved top "tulip" shaped headstock carries through to 1932, as well as the oval soundhole, floating bridge, "clamshell" one-piece tailpiece and four-on-a-plate tuners. In the style of the times, these early models featured faux finishes on both the bodies and necks, and a modified "batwing" pickguard under the strings. A surviving early version labeled "Royal" features a natural finished spruce top, mahogany or rosewood back and sides, top and back bound in white celluloid, marquetry and fine lines around the soundhole and top as well as down the backstripe. Regal sold these instruments through Montgomery Ward (their 1915-16 catalogue), and wholesalers H. C. Schultz and the Tonk Bros.

Two late examples of guitar-mandolins have surfaced that utilize Regal's tenor guitar body. They have similar decorative features as used on low-cost Regal mandolins and guitars of the period. Besides the standard tenor guitar body size and shape described in Chapter Six of this book, these guitar-mandos came with a black body finish, rose "decalcomania" on the bass side of the top, white (probably painted) binding, Bell brand tailpiece, ten frets to the body with eighteen frets total and a slightly curved end of the fingerboard.

Chapter Four
Harp Guitars

"An instrument that is destined to win no uncertain place in the esteem of lovers of stringed instruments is the Orchestral guitar, manufactured by the Wulschner Music Co., of Indianapolis. The instrument is unique, inasmuch as it is the nearest approach yet known to the Italian harp. Owing to the use of twelve strings a compass an octave greater than the standard instrument is possible. The tonal qualities of the instrument are superb and captivate all who hear it played. For ordinary solo work, the first six strings and finger board, which are just like the Regal guitar, can be used, so that there is nothing new to learn. Meanwhile the artist can get effects with the Orchestral guitar impossible in others with limited compass."—The Music Trade Review, September 1, 1900.

Harp Guitar

Summary

Instrument: Harp guitar.

Model: "Orchestral guitar," "Auditorium Bass Guitar," harp guitar.

Years Made: 1899-1937.

Brand(s): Regal.

Quality: High.

Special Features: A regular guitar neck of six strings plus a "contra-bass" neck of five or six strings.

Woods: Spruce over birch, mahogany or rosewood, mahogany neck.

Measurements: For earliest known, width lower bout 19 1/8", upper bout 15" and depth, 4 ¼".

Logos Used: "Regal" in pearl script, paper sound hole label and wooden medallion, green "Regal" decal on headstock.

Known Original Wholesale List Price: $60.00-90.00.

Harp guitars were a musical phenomena of the late nineteenth and early twentieth century (Gibson first built them around 1902), another oddity from the same time period that produced the guitar-mandolin described in the previous chapter. Consisting of a regular guitar neck with a second, unfretted one containing bass strings, harp guitars usually featured an enlarged body to support the extra tension of the added lower and heavier (and, therefore, exerting more pull on the neck and body) bass strings.

Regal of Indianapolis began making harp guitars in 1899. Photos of two examples are included here. While structurally similar, they have slightly different decoration. The three harp guitars I've seen share an oversized guitar body, two rectangular pin bridges each holding six strings, slotted headstocks, twelve frets to the body, eighteen frets total, spruce tops, two piece rosewood back and rosewood sides, white bound tops and headstocks, white bound neck extensions (none have a second full neck) and what appear to be mahogany necks. Based on the sound hole labels for the three guitars, all appear to have been made around 1900, while the Indianapolis factory was still owned by the Wulschner family.

Harp guitar, with paper soundhole label and "Wulschner and Son" soundhole medallion, circa 1900. Full front view. Photograph/courtesy Frank Ford/Gryphon Stringed Instruments.

Harp guitar, with paper soundhole label and "Wulschner & Son" soundhole medallion, circa 1900. Full back view. Photograph/courtesy Frank Ford/Gryphon Stringed Instruments.

Harp guitar, serial number 9994, with paper soundhole label and "Wulschner and Son" soundhole medallion, circa 1900. Full front view. Photograph/courtesy Intermountain Guitar and Banjo.

Harp guitar, serial number 9994, with paper soundhole label and "Wulschner and Son" soundhole medallion, circa 1900. Full back view. Photograph/courtesy Intermountain Guitar and Banjo.

Harp guitar, serial number 9994, with paper soundhole label and "Wulschner and Son" soundhole medallion, circa 1900. Photograph/courtesy Intermountain Guitar and Banjo.

NO. R 615-C GUITAR

SPECIFICATIONS: Concert size; spruce top; birch back and sides; colored inlay around sound hole and top edge; both edges bound with white celluloid; nickel plated tail piece; ebonized bridge; 12 string; mahogany colored back and sides in gloss lacquer finish.

NO. R 90 HARP GUITAR

SPECIFICATIONS: Fine double neck Harp Guitar with six contra bass strings; carved spruce top; mahogany back and sides; beautifully finished in hand rubbed natural mahogany and spruce; mahogany necks; full toned with deep basses; edges of body bound with white celluloid; hand fitted bridges; best grade of strings.

NO. R 615-12 GUITAR

SPECIFICATIONS: Jumbo size; spruce top; birch back and sides; sound hole and top edge inlaid with colored wood inlay; both edges bound with white celluloid; nickel plated tail piece; wide neck and finger board; 12 strings; ebonized bridge; dull satin finish.

TRADE MARK Regal

16

"No. R 90 Harp Guitar," Tonk Bros. catalogue, 1937, courtesy Tony Marcus, Regal Musical Instrument catalogue, 1937, courtesy The National Music Museum.

There are no further documented examples of Regal-made harp guitars until 1928, when a Regal "Auditorium Bass Guitar" with two necks and twelve total strings shows up in the H. C. Schultz catalogue. Unfortunately, a photograph was not included with the description, which features "birchwood in imitation rosewood finish." The price was $60.00 wholesale.

Finally, in our story of Regal harp guitars, the company sold a harp guitar model from 1934 to 1937 (see catalogue illustration). Unlike the harp guitars from turn-of-the-century Regal, these featured two full mahogany necks and a carved spruce top with floating bridges and tailpieces. The guitar neck had a slotted peghead with fourteen frets clear of the body and twenty frets total. In other words, Regal took their roundhole archtop guitar and reengineered it to produce this model of harp guitar. This version is pictured in both a natural and shaded top. The guitar wholesaled for $90.00.

Dressed to the nines, this unknown group of uptown entertainers featured a Regal harp guitar (standing, second from right). Circa 1900. Courtesy of Ron Middlebrook.

Chapter Five

Banjos

Regal was never a major player in the banjo market. In fact, there were periods when Regal didn't make, advertise, or assemble from parts made by others any banjos at all. With the exception of one design patented by the company in 1928, their instruments were unexceptional, and made little impression on banjo buyers. It should be an indication of their quality that Regal banjos are not highly sought after nor coveted by today's banjo players or collectors.

Wulschner

Summary

Instrument: Five String Banjo.

Model: Five String Banjo, Ladies Banjo, Piccolo Banjo and Banjorine.

Years Made: 1896-1897.

Brand(s): The Regal.

Quality: Low to mid grade.

Special Features: None.

Woods: Maple shell, mahogany neck (on higher grade models).

Measurements: 8″ rim (Piccolo), 10″ rim (Ladies), 11″ rim (regular Five String) and 12″ (Banjorine).

Logos Used: None shown.

Known Original Retail List Price: $22.50-57.50.

The first banjos to bear "The Regal" designation were marketed by Emil Wulschner & Son. Their 1896/1897 catalogue, reproduced here, shows six models of five string banjos, plus a "Piccolo," a "Ladies Banjo" and a "Banjorine." Jim Bollman, an expert on Victorian banjos, concluded from examining this Wulschner catalogue that, as best could be told from the pictures and descriptions contained therein, these Regal branded instruments were in part or whole made by Lyon & Healy of Chicago or Cole of Boston and supplied to Wulschner by Lyon & Healy. The Regal Style C very closely resembles the Washburn (Lyon & Healy's brand) Style 1130, and the Style A the Washburn Style 1120. Some of the peghead shapes (Styles D and E) and inlay patterns (Style E, Ladies Banjo/Style H and Banjorine/Style I) appear to have been made by Cole.

BANJOS—"THE REGAL."

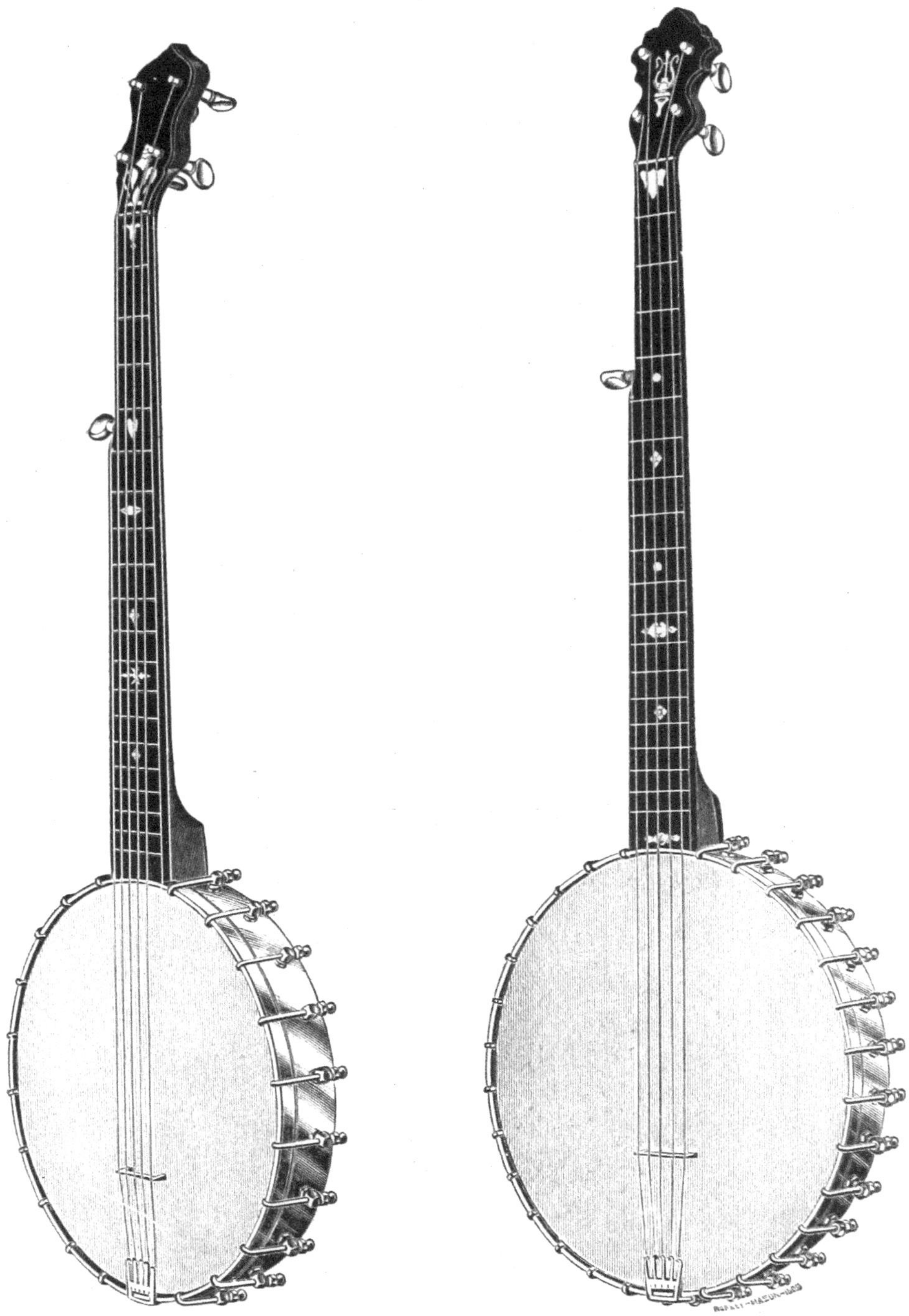

Style A Style B

Style A. 11-inch Nickel Plated Shell, Both Edges Wired, Finely Polished Maple Shell Inside, a Beautifully Proportioned Neck, Ebony Fingerboard with Pearl Position Ornaments, Ebony Veneered and Pearl Inlaid Headpiece, 21 Nickel Plated Hexagon Brackets, White Celluloid Pegs...Each, $22.50

Style B. 11-inch Nickel Plated Shell, Both Edges Wired, Heavy Maple Shell Inside, Stained and Polished, 29 Nickel Plated Hexagon Brackets, Extra Heavy Ebony Fingerboard with Pearl Position Dots and Ornaments, Elaborate Pearl Design in Headpiece, a Beautifully Proportioned and French Polished Neck, White Celluloid Pegs. 26.13

Emil Wulschner & Son, Indianapolis, IND., The "Regal" Banjos, 1896-1897 catalogue, p229-233. Photographs by Jim Bollman, courtesy Stu Cohen.

BANJOS—"THE REGAL."

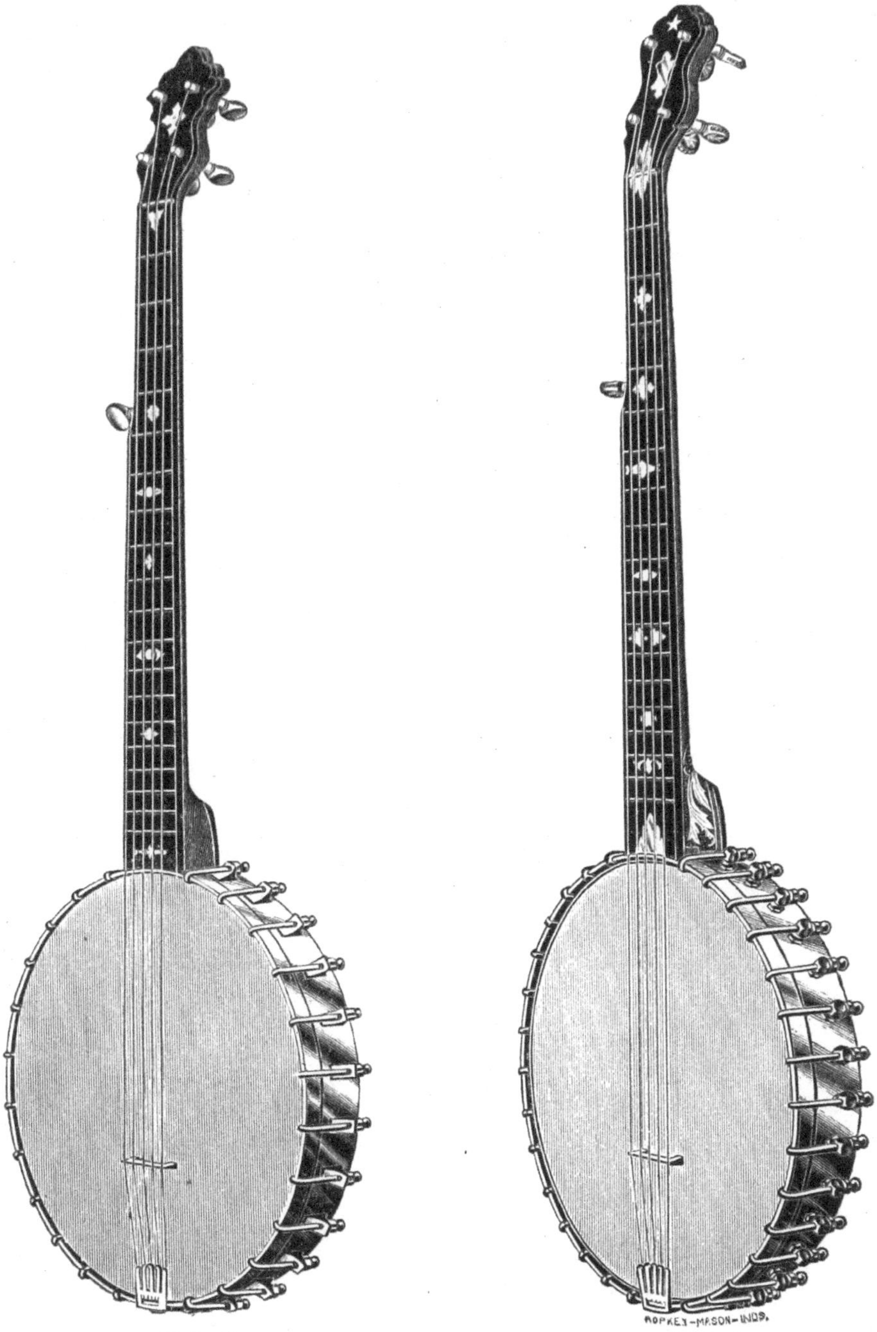

Style C   Style D

Style C. 11-inch Nickel Plated Shell, Both Edges Wired, Heavy Maple Shell Inside, Stained and Polished, 25 Nickel Plated Standard Brackets, Beautifully Proportioned and French Polished Neck, Extra Heavy Ebony Fingerboard with Beautiful Pearl Position Dots and Ornaments, Pearl Inlay in Headpiece, Nickel Plated Staypiece, White Celluloid Pegs. .... Each, $30.00

Style D. 11-inch Nickel Plated Shell, Both Edges Wired, Heavy Maple Shell Inside Stained and Polished, 31 Nickel Plated Hexagon Brackets, Extra Heavy Rabbeted Strainer Hoop, Beautifully Proportioned and Hand Carved Mahogany Neck, Extra Heavy Ebony Fingerboard, Elaborate Pearl Inlaid Fingerboard and Headpiece. Nickel Plated Staypiece, Fancy Celluloid Pegs. .... " 40.63

Emil Wulschner & Son, Indianapolis, IND., The "Regal" Banjos, 1896-1897 catalogue, p229-233. Photographs by Jim Bollman, courtesy Stu Cohen.

BANJOS "THE REGAL."

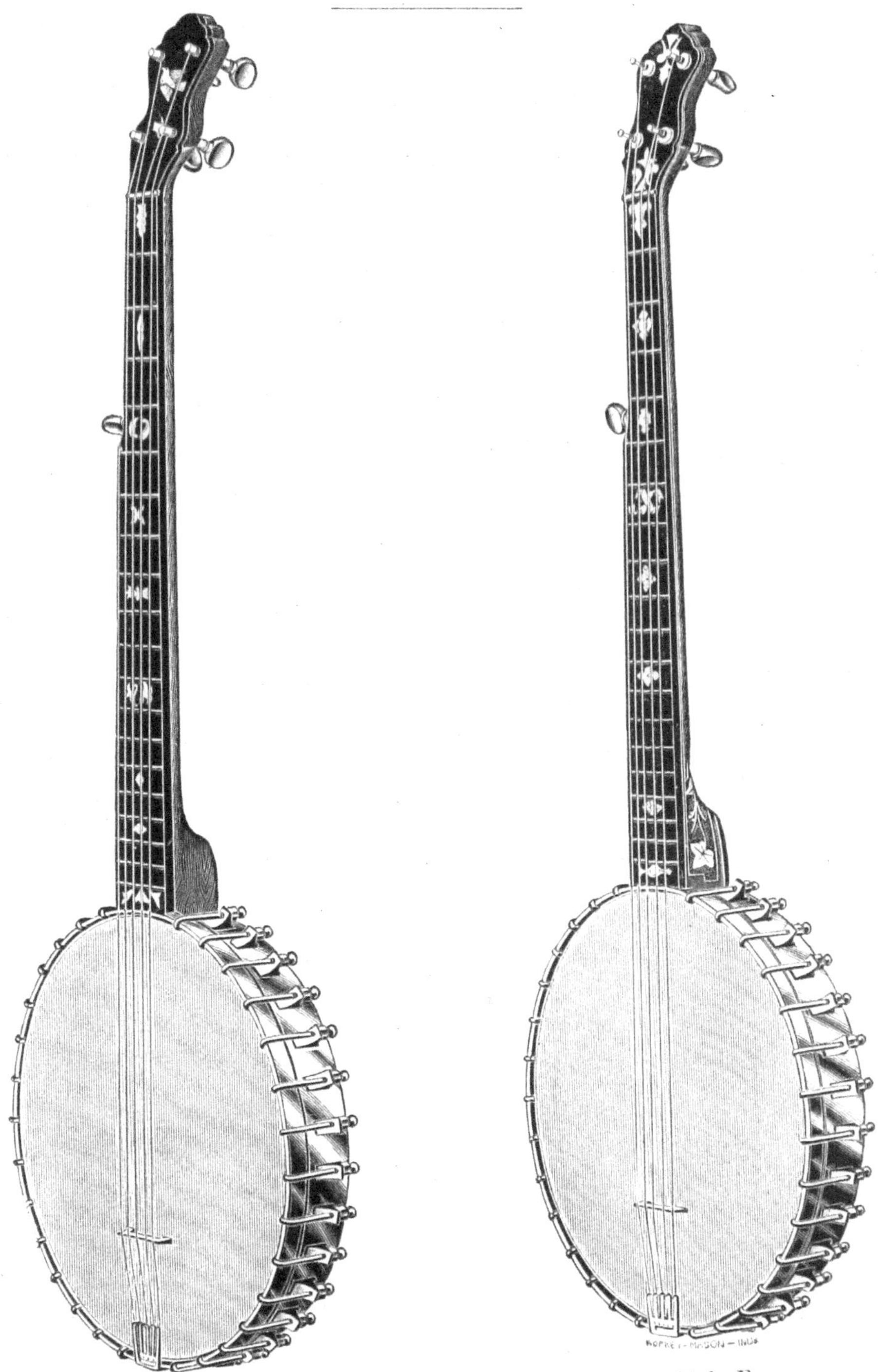

Style E Style F

Style E. 11-inch Nickel Plated Shell, Both Edges Wired, Extra Heavy Rabbeted Strainer Hoop, Heavy Maple Shell Inside Stained and Polished, Extra Heavy Ebony Fingerboard with Elaborate Inlayings of Pearl, Beautifully Proportioned and Polished Mahogany Neck, 31 Standard Nickel Plated Brackets and Hexagon Head Bracket Screws, Elaborate Inlaying of Pearl in Headpiece, Nickel Plated Staypiece, White Celluloid Pegs .... Each, $48.50

Style F. 11-inch Nickel Plated Shell, Both Edges Wired, Extra Heavy Maple Shell Inside Stained and Polished, 31 Nickel Plated Standard Brackets and Hexagon Head Bracket Screws, Extra Heavy Rabbeted Strainer Hoop, Nickle Plated Staypiece, Extra Heavy Ebony Fingerboard with Very Elaborate Inlayings of Pearl, Elegantly Hand Carved and Polished Neck, Elaborate Pearl Inlaid Headpiece, Champion Safety Keys with White Celluloid Buttons .... " 57.50

Emil Wulschner & Son, Indianapolis, IND., The "Regal" Banjos, 1896-1897 catalogue, p229-233. Photographs by Jim Bollman, courtesy Stu Cohen.

PICCOLO BANJO—"THE REGAL."

Style G.

Style G. 8-inch Nickel Plated Shell, Both Edges Wired, Extra Heavy Maple Shell Inside Stained and Polished, Extra Heavy Rabbeted Strainer Hoop, 12 Nickel Plated Standard Brackets and Hexagon Head Bracket Screws, Beautifully Proportioned and Polished Neck, Heavy Ebony Fingerboard with Beautiful Pearl Inlay, Pearl Inlaid Headpiece, Nickel Plated Staypiece, White Celluloid Pegs .. Each, $27.50

LADIES' BANJO—"THE REGAL."

Style H. 10-inch Nickel Plated Rim, Extra Heavy Maple Shell Inside, Stained and Polished, Extra Heavy Rabbeted Strainer Hoop, 17 Nickle Plated Standard Brackets, Beautifully Proportioned and French Polished Neck, Extra Heavy Ebony Fingerboard with Elaborate Pearl Inlayings, Heavy Veneered Headpiece with Elaborate Pearl Design, Nickel Plated Staypiece ....Each, $30 00

Style H

Emil Wulschner & Son, Indianapolis, IND., The "Regal" Piccolo and Ladies' Banjos, 1896-1897 catalogue, p232. Photographs by Jim Bollman, courtesy Stu Cohen.

BANJORINES "THE REGAL."

Style I

Style I. 12-inch Nickel Plated Shell, Extra Heavy Maple Shell Inside, Stained and Polished, Extra Heavy Rabbeted Strainer Hoop, 31 Nickel Plated Standard Brackets and Hexagon Head Bracket Screws, Nickel Plated Staypiece, Elegantly Proportioned and Polished Mahogany Neck, Extra Heavy Ebony Fingerboard Elaborately Pearl Inlaid, Elaborate Inlayings of Pearl in Headpiece, White Celluloid Pegs..........Each, $43.75

Emil Wulschner & Son, Indianapolis, IND., The "Regal" Banjorines, 1896-1897 catalogue, p233. Photographs by Jim Bollman, courtesy Stu Cohen.

20TH CENTURY BANJOS

STYLES 80, 81, 82

STYLE 82

Nickel Shells, wood-lined, cherry finished necks, calfskin heads, ebonized finger-boards, **pearl positions,** German silver frets.

Style 80—Seven nickel plated brackets	**Price,**	**$6.00**
" **81**—Thirteen nickel plated brackets	"	**6.75**
" **82**—Seventeen nickel plated brackets	"	7.25

Regal Manufacturing Co., Indianapolis, catalogue, 1901, "The 20th Century Banjos Styles 80, 81, 82." Photograph by Jim Bollman, courtesy Stu Cohen.

20TH CENTURY BANJOS

STYLES 83, 84, 85, 86

STYLE 86

Nickel Shells, wood-lined, cherry finished necks, ebonized finger-boards, pearl positions, German silver frets, wired edge, calfskin heads.

Style 83—Twenty-one nickel plated brackets	Price,	$ 8.13
" 84—Twenty-five nickel plated brackets	"	8.63
" 85—Thirty-one nickel plated brackets	"	9.38
" 86—Thirty-nine nickel plated brackets	"	10.00

Regal Manufacturing Co., Indianapolis, catalogue, 1901, "The 20th Century Banjos Styles 83, 84, 85, 86." Photograph by Jim Bollman, courtesy Stu Cohen.

The University Banjos

Have the same attention given to all details of material and workmanship as are found in University Mandolins and Guitars. They will satisfy the most critical player, and are fully warranted.

THE UNIVERSITY BANJO

STYLE 90

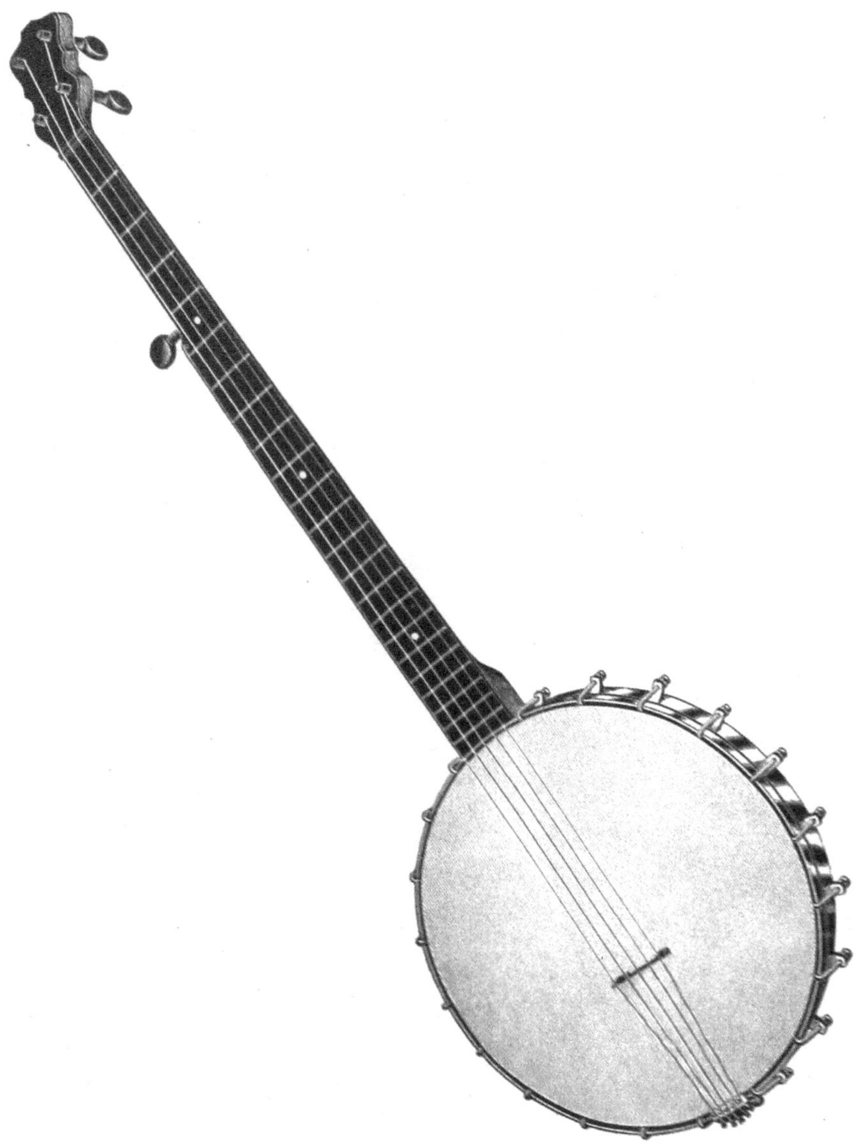

Eleven-inch Nickel Plated Shell, wood-lined, cherry neck, veneered head-piece, double **wired edges, nickel** plated stay piece, ebony finger-board, three octaves, pearl positions, twenty-one nickel plated **brackets, Elite tail-piece**, fine calf head.

Price, $10.00.

Regal Manufacturing Co., Indianapolis, catalogue, 1901, "The University Banjo Style 90." Photograph by Jim Bollman, courtesy Stu Cohen.

The University Banjo

STYLE 91

Eleven-inch Nickel Plated Shell, wood-lined, cherry neck, veneered head-piece, pearl inlaid, double wired edges, nickel plated stay piece, ebony finger-board, three octaves, pearl positions, twenty-three nickel plated brackets, Elite tail-piece, fine calf head.

Price, $11.88.

Regal Manufacturing Co., Indianapolis, catalogue, 1901, "The University Banjo Style 91." Photograph by Jim Bollman, courtesy Stu Cohen."

THE UNIVERSITY BANJO

STYLE 92

Eleven-inch Nickel Plated Shell, wood-lined, cherry neck, veneered head-piece fancily pearl **inlaid, double** wired edges, nickel plated stay piece, ebony finger-board, three octaves, with positions fancily pearl **inlaid, twenty-**five nickel plated brackets, Elite tail piece, fine calf head.

Price, $18.75.

Regal Manufacturing Co., Indianapolis, catalogue, 1901, "The University Banjo Style 92." Photograph by Jim Bollman, courtesy Stu Cohen.

The University Banjo

STYLE 93

Eleven-inch Nickel-Plated Shell, wood-lined, cherry neck, veneered head-piece, inlaid with a fancy pearl design, double wired edges, nickel plated stay piece, three octaves, ebony finger-board fancily inlaid in positions with pearl ornaments, twenty-seven nickel plated brackets, Elite tail piece, fine calf head.

Price, $21.25.

Regal Manufacturing Co., Indianapolis, catalogue, 1901, "The University Banjo Style 93." Photograph by Jim Bollman, courtesy Stu Cohen."

THE UNIVERSITY BANJO

STYLE 94

Eleven-inch Nickel Plated Shell, wood-lined, Spanish cedar neck, veneered head-piece **elaborately pearl inlaid,** three octaves, ebony finger-board very fancily inlaid with pearl ornaments, double wired **edges, nickel plated stay piece,** twenty-nine nickel plated brackets, Elite tail-piece, fine calf head.

Price, $25.00.

Regal Manufacturing Co., Indianapolis, catalogue, 1901, "The University Banjo Style 94." Photograph by Jim Bollman, courtesy Stu Cohen."

Regal Manufacturing Company

Summary

Instrument: Five String Banjo.

Model: Five String Banjo

Years Made: 1901.

Brand(s): 20th Century, University.

Quality: Low.

Special Features: None.

Woods: Unknown rim wood, cherry or Spanish cedar neck.

Measurements: 11″ rim.

Logos Used: None shown.

Known Original Retail List Price: $6.00-$25.00.

The only other surviving indication of Regal's Indianapolis banjos is contained in a 1901 catalogue. As is discussed elsewhere in this book, this catalogue only contains Regal's lower priced "University" and "20th Century" lines. Again, Jim Bollman indicates that these five strings are all low-grade banjos made or supplied by Lyon & Healy.

The catalogue indicates the Wulschner family's last attempts at banjo marketing before the firm was taken over by a group of Indianapolis business men. By the fall of 1901, Regal had either redesigned their banjo line to be made in the Indianapolis factory, their supplier had changed the designs, or Regal had moved to a new firm for banjos.

Hunter Patent

Summary

Instrument: Banjo.

Model: Tenor, Five String, Banjo-Mandolin, Banjo-Guitar and Plectrum.

Years Made: 1928-1939.

Brand(s): Regal.

Quality: Low to medium grade.

Special Features: Regal/Hunter patented shoe flange, resonator.

Woods: Birch rim and resonator with "hardwood" neck, mahogany rim and resonator with mahogany neck.

Measurements: 11″ rim, 13 ½″ resonator, 23″ tenor scale, 27″ plectrum scale.

Logos Used: Regal metal "badge" on resonator by heel, Regal green headstock decal (1937-1939).

Known Original Wholesale List Price: $16.50-45.00.

April 22, 1930. A. E. HUNTER Des. 81,007

BANJO OR SIMILAR ARTICLE

Filed Sept. 14, 1928 2 Sheets-Sheet 1

Fig. 1

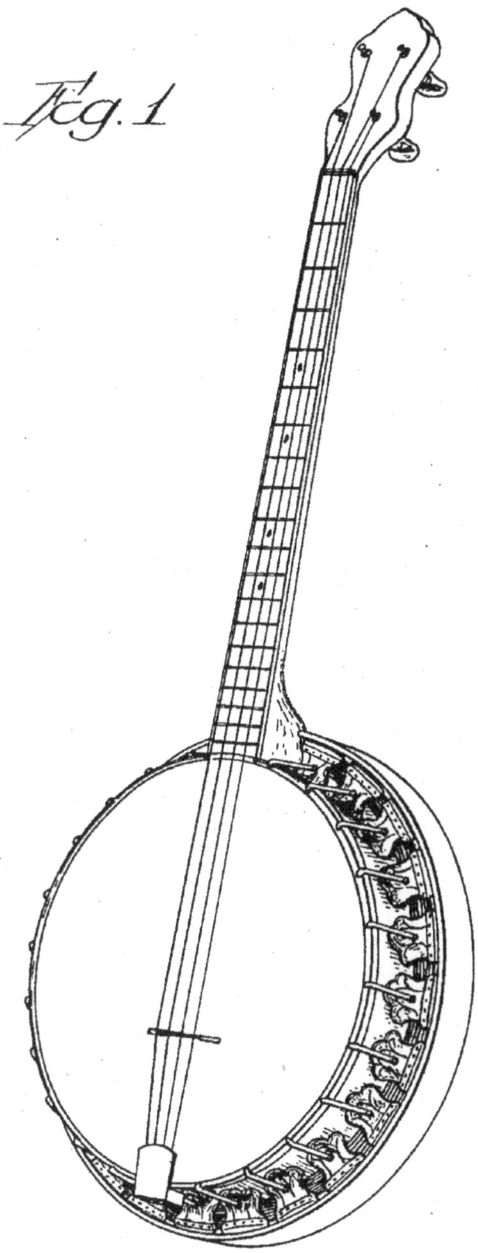

Inventor:
Albert E. Hunter
John C. Carpenter
Atty:

Patent drawing, "A. E. Hunter, Banjo or Similar Article. Filed Sept. 14, 1928."

March 15, 1932. A. E. HUNTER **1,849,091**

BANJO

Filed Sept. 14, 1928

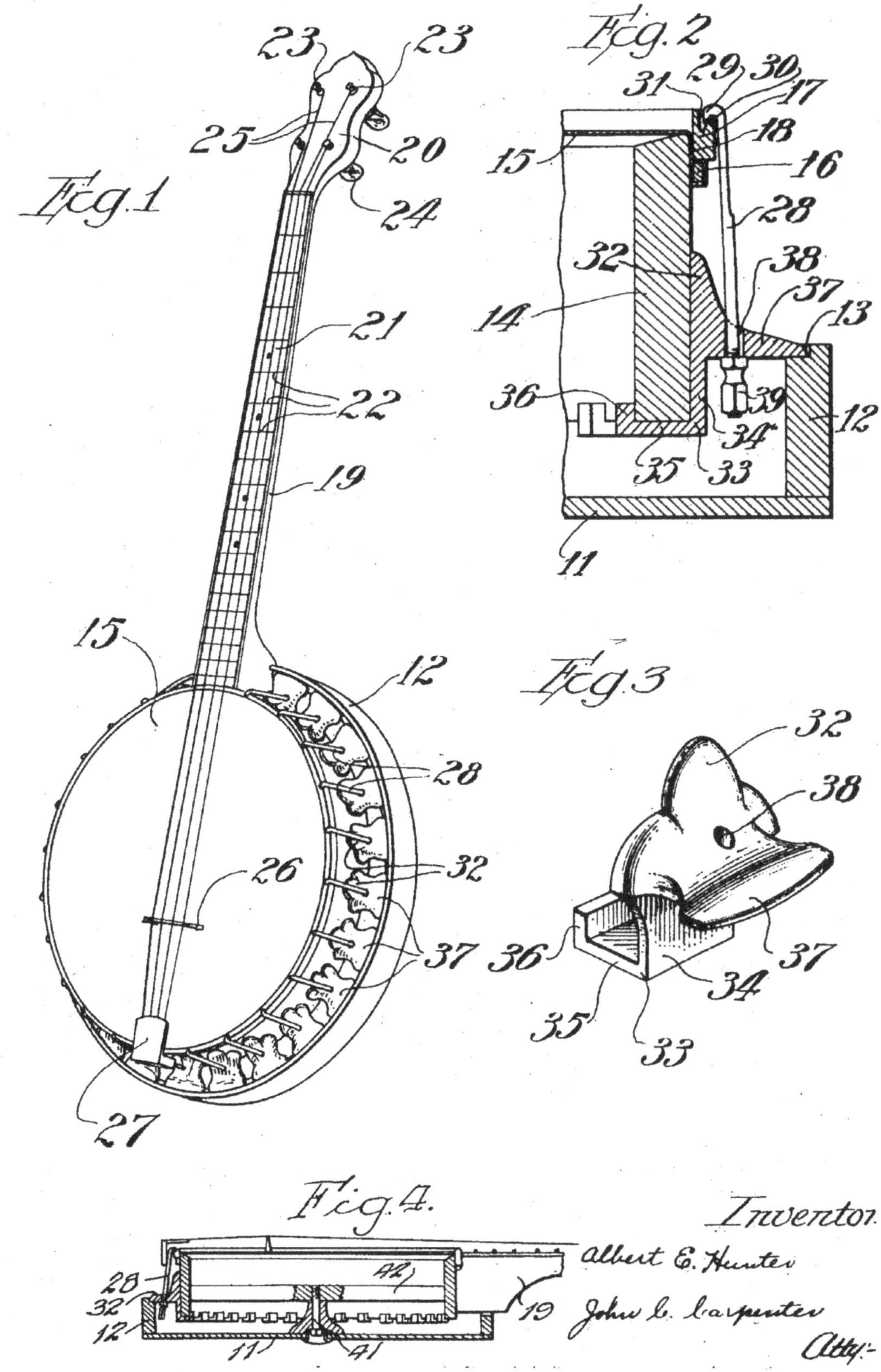

Patent drawing, "A. E. Hunter, Banjo. Filed Sept. 14, 1928."

April 22, 1930. A. E. HUNTER Des. 81,007

BANJO OR SIMILAR ARTICLE

Filed Sept. 14, 1928 2 Sheets–Sheet 2

Fig. 2

Inventor:
Albert E. Hunter

John E. Carpenter
Atty.

Patent drawing, "A. E. Hunter, Banjo or Similar Article. Filed Sept. 14, 1928."

Once Regal was acquired by Lyon & Healy, moved to Chicago and spun-off into its own entity, there are no indications of what banjo models they were selling or even if they were in the banjo business at all. For twenty years, I found no record of banjos that could be tied to Regal.

That all changed in 1928, when Regal executive Albert Hunter applied for two patents toward a new banjo design. Besides the physical attributes of the instrument, the main structural innovation was a head tightening system that integrated the banjo's shoe (the part which the head-tightening bracket passes through) with the "flange" or (closed back) resonator top. In his patents, Hunter claimed that this provided an improved and faster method for tightening the head by attaching the shoes to the bottom rather then through the walls of the rim and also improved the tone of the instrument.

The three Hunter-designed models Regal offered were a birch rim and resonator with a "hardwood" neck, mahogany with a mahogany neck and "figured African" mahogany with a three piece mahogany neck. All came with an eleven inch rim, thirteen and a half inch resonator and patented shoe flange, and were available at various times with tenor, five string, banjo-mandolin, banjo-guitar and plectrum necks.

According to catalogue descriptions, the all birch Regal banjo featured a "rim of heavy seven-ply construction. Resonator is made of . . . five-ply construction with swelled back, beautifully inlaid with colored wood inlaying and bound with white celluloid. Finished in two tone shaded walnut. . . Hardwood neck of three-ply construction [two piece neck w/center stripe] with veneered headpiece. Fine ebonized [white bound] fingerboard. Metal tone ring. Top hoop of heavy nickeled brass. Covered pattern tailpiece. Good friction pegs. Heavy nickel plated arm rest." The all-mahogany banjo was of similar construction and parts. The Regal high-end mahogany instrument featured upgraded pearl headstock and fingerboard inlays, and geared tuning pegs.

One odd-ball model has surfaced, which I believe to be made of birch. It's hard to tell, because the wooden resonator is covered in purple marbleized "MOTS" material and the fingerboard is made of white "MOTS."

Chapter Six

"Four Strings, No Waiting": The "Original" Tenor Guitar

Tenor Guitar

Summary

Instrument: Tenor Guitar.

Model: ¾ size guitar body with "tulip/rabbit ears" headstock and tenor banjo neck.

Years Made: 1925-1936.

Brand(s): Regal, S. S. Stewart, KlearTone.

Quality: Low to high grade.

Special Features: ¾ size guitar body, 19 fret tenor banjo-style neck.

Woods: All birch, spruce over birch, spruce over mahogany, spruce over figured mahogany, spruce over rosewood, poplar or mahogany neck.

Measurements: 21" scale, 7 3/8"-7 ½" upper bout, 10 3/8"-10 ½" lower bout, 1 and 1/8"-1 and ¼" nut width, 3 ¼" deep at the end pin.

Logos Used: Regal oval paper soundhole label some with "Tenor Guitar" added, Regal headstock medallion decal (low-grade) or pearl (high-grade) (1925-1936), green Regal headstock decal (one known example), rectangular white plate with black printing attached with two tacks to headstock "KlearTone" in script and above it "Reg US Patent Office," "S. S. Stewart" headstock decal.

Known Original Wholesale List Price: $6.50-$120.00.

After Regal's success with President Frank Kordick's radical mandolin design, the next masterstroke by the company was the introduction of their tenor guitar. As early as 1924, instrument makers had been experimenting with melding the fingerboard (and therefore the fingering) of a tenor banjo to the more "soothing" tones of the guitar. The tenor guitar was designed to give the banjoist the ability to achieve a guitar "sound" without having to relearn left hand chords and scales. The tenor guitar was also marketed to ukulele players. Regal introduced their version, a nineteen fret tenor neck with a twenty-one inch scale mounted on a three-quarter-sized guitar body, in October of 1925 at the Illinois Products Expo and in advertisements in the Music Trade Review. By contrast, Gibson and Martin would not include tenor guitar models in their catalogues until 1927.

In 1926, Regal claimed that:

"The resonance and sweetness of the Tenor Guitar, combined with its grace of construction and comparative ease of playing make it a favorite among those who wish to play their own accompaniments.

"The Tenor Guitar is extremely popular with Radio fans, as it blends beautifully with other string instruments and the piano, and is rich in possibilities, whether it is used in orchestra work, solo playing or accompanying the human voice.

"It has often been called the 'Most Versatile of all String Instruments.'

"In a Mandolin orchestra use the Tenor Guitar for chord work and for Mandola parts.

PROGRESSIVE MUSICAL INSTRUMENT CORPORATION

The Tenor Guitar is the latest addition to the "REGAL" family of plectrum instruments. It has a three-quarter size Guitar body with a twenty-one inch standard Tenor Banjo neck and scale. It can be strung, tuned and played as a Tenor Banjo or Ukulele and, used either way, produces a wonderfully pleasing tone.

"REGAL" Tenor Guitar No. 80—Top, back and sides of selected figured birch; hardwood neck; fine ebonized fingerboard; genuine ebony bridge; best grade steel strings; patent tuning keys. Finished in a dull satin mahogany color.

Style Number 80 *Price $10.00*

"REGAL" Tenor Guitar No. 81—Back and sides of selected figured birch; top of clear spruce; hardwood neck; fine ebonized fingerboard; genuine ebony bridge; best grade steel strings; patent tuning keys. Finished in a dull satin walnut color.

Style Number 81 *Price $15.75*

Mail Your Orders to 319 Sixth Avenue, New York, N. Y.

"Tenor Guitar No. 80," and "Number 81," Progressive Musical Instrument Corporation (PMI) catalogue, circa 1928. Courtesy the National Music Museum.

"In addition to the above, although the Tenor Guitar is most popular player with the Tenor Banjo tuning, it may be strung up as a Ukulele and is a most welcome guest at picnics, glee clubs and boating parties.

"A Tenor Guitar doubles the joys of your vacation."

In the same year, Regal began claiming to be the "Originators of the Tenor Guitar." The fact that these tenor guitars were mainly advertised as Regal made and not under the disguise of the various distributor house brands leads one to believe that Regal saw this as a proprietary money maker that they wanted to keep under their own control.

Initially, Regal offered four styles utilizing the three-quarter size body, standard tenor banjo neck that joined the body at the twelfth fret and "tulip/rabbit ears" headstock shape. All had natural finish "ladder-braced" spruce tops, a floating bridge and tailpiece, with the difference being the back and sides varied from either birch, mahogany, figured mahogany or rosewood.

The entry-level walnut or cherry-color stained birch one piece back and sides model was offered from 1925 through 1932. It came with black celluloid binding around the top, back and soundhole; wood marquetry rosette; Bell brand tailpiece; ebonized fingerboard, headstock overlay and heel cap; "hardwood" (probably poplar, basswood or birch) neck; friction tuning pegs and fingerboard dots at frets five, seven and ten.

The next level tenor guitar replaced birch with mahogany for the back and sides of the instrument. Other appointments were the same. It was also offered through 1932.

The "De Luxe" tenor guitar utilized "figured" or "flamed" mahogany for the two-piece back, sides and neck bound in ebony, with added marquetry around the top and for the center backstripe. The ebony fingerboard was inlayed with a dot at fret three, diamond fret five, two dots and a cross at fret seven, two crosses fret ten, diamond fret twelve, and two dots at fret fifteen. The ebony headstock veneer featured the Regal medallion logo rendered in pearl. The tailpiece was an adjustable Waverly banjo-style and the tuning pegs geared Grover pancake tuners.

By 1928, Regal saw fit to expand their tenor guitar line by introducing two new models using the original design. On the high end was a rosewood guitar with a spruce top; on the low-end, an all-birch guitar.

The "Professional" rosewood model, like the others that preceded it, would be available from Regal until 1932. To rosewood back and sides was added pearl binding around the top and soundhole, black/white celluloid fingerboard binding, fancier inlays and gold-plated hardware.

The all birch tenor, which stayed in the Regal catalogue until the demise of the three-quarter size body nineteen fret guitar in 1936, came with a mahogany or cherry stained birch top (some in a natural finish) and body, painted binding and was a downgraded version of the spruce over birch guitar. From 1932-1934, the all birch tenor was also available in a "Crystalline" finish (see Chapter Nine fmi). And, an unusual variation of the three-quarter size tenor has shown up recently online. This spruce over birch all natural finish instrument is decorated with a black silkscreen pattern on the lower bout both front and back, along with the vinyl fingerboard (called "pyralin") used on other Regal products from 1930 through 1935. Marked as a "factory second," this guitar may have been thrown together from parts (the soundhole rosette and bridge were not typical to this model) and/or made late in the life of this instrument.

After the demise of the original Regal tenor guitar, the company went on to build other tenor models. Unfortunately, these were just four string versions of their six string's, full sized guitar bodies with eighteen or twenty fret necks altered to accept fewer strings (for more about these Tenor Guitars, see Chapters Seven and Eight).

DETROIT H.C. SCHULTZ, INC WHOLESALE EXCLUSIVELY CLEVELAND

Regal Tenor Guitars

Style Number 2052

No. 2052. Back and sides of fine figured mahogany; best grade spruce top; fine mahogany hand-shaped neck; fingerboard inlaid with genuine pearl position figures; pearl "REGAL" ornament in head; geared tuning pegs; heavy banjo-pattern tailpiece. Hand-rubbed to a high piano polish.
Price, each...**$40.00**

Regal Tenor Guitars, "No. 2052," H. C. Schultz catalogue, 1928. Courtesy Elderly Instruments.

Chapter Seven

Flattop Guitars

Wulschner

Summary

Instrument: Flattop guitar.

Model: Wulschner.

Years Made: 1896-1900.

Brand(s): Regal.

Quality: Medium to high grade.

Special Features: Ladder-braced top.

Woods: Natural finish spruce top, rosewood back and sides, cedar neck.

Known Measurements: 13″-14″ lower bout, 8 ½″-9 13/16″ upper bout, body depth at endpin 3 5/8″-3 15/16″, nut width 1 ¾″-2″, 25″ scale.

Logos Used: Regal square paper soundhole label, wooden soundhole medallion "Wulschner & Son, Trade Mark, Regal, Indianapolis, IND," pearl crown headstock logo, "Regal" pearl script in peghead.

Known Original Wholesale List Price: $22.50-$97.50.

The Indianapolis music retailer Emil Wulschner supposedly began selling guitars under the Regal name in 1895. His 1896-1897 catalogue gives us the best idea of the flattop guitars represented by his Regal line. There are five different styles of guitar, the 102/103, the 104, 106, 108 and 110. The higher the number, the fancier the trimmings (decoration) of the instrument. Like the guitar maker Ashborn fifty years before, Wulschner effectively made the same instrument over and over, just changing inlay and binding to increase the price (and profits!).

All Regal guitars from this catalogue (reproduced here) came with twelve fret to the body "Spanish" cedar necks, eighteen fret ebony fingerboard, a slotted headstock, rosewood back and sides, three-on-a-plate top-geared tuners, modified pyramid bridges and a natural finished spruce top. All were available in "Standard" and "Grand Concert" size. Some models came with a "Three-quarter" or "Auditorium" body. The 102/103 also came in a mahogany body. A twenty-five inch scale seems standard for all models.

The small sample of Regal Guitars that have survived from this period, while none are absolutely identical to any model shown, agree with the illustrations and general descriptions in the 1896-1897 catalogue. Two of the instruments have the "crown" logo on the headstock in engraved pearl, four have leaf-like pearl inlays in the headstock resembling fingerboard inlays, two have stars and one has "Regal" in pearl script. Fingerboard inlays vary from simple dots, stars, diamonds or shamrocks at the third, fifth, seventh, tenth and twelfth frets to a variety of free-standing inlays on one of the "crown" logo guitars. Serial numbers, incised into the top of the headstock and on the neck block inside the instrument, are known for three instruments. Four have paper labels that read (emphasis theirs):

206 EMIL WULSCHNER & SON, INDIANAPOLIS, IND.

"REGAL" GUITARS.

FRANKFORT, IND.

Wulschner & Son, Indianapolis:

GENTLEMEN—The "Regal" Guitar I purchased of you some time ago is undoubtedly the finest instrument I ever played on, and I have played on all the leading makes. Its tone is sweet, clear, and has that great volume so long sought by leading soloists. It is truly "perfection, musically and mechanically," and **I shall use no other.**

Yours most truly, LOUIS C. GLENDOLYN.

Styles 102¾-103 GC

Rosewood, Neatly Inlaid and Celluloid Edges, beautiful colored wood Inlay around Soundhole, Spanish Cedar Neck, Oval Ebony Fingerboard, Pearl Position Dots, inlaid strip down the Back, Elegantly Polished.

Style 102¾	Three-quarter Size	Each,	$22.50
" 102 S.	Standard Size	"	23.75
" 103 S.	" " Mahogany	"	30.00
" 102 GC.	Grand Concert Size	"	21.88
" 103 GC.	" " " Mahogany	"	28.00

Emil Wulschner & Son, Indianapolis, IND., "'Regal' Guitars," 1896-1897 catalogue, p206. Photographs by Jim Bollman, courtesy Stu Cohen.

EMIL WULSCHNER & SON, INDIANAPOLIS, IND. 207

"REGAL" GUITARS.

METROPOLITAN SCHOOL OF MUSIC, INDIANAPOLIS.

Emil Wulschner & Son:

GENTLEMEN—Having given your "Regal" Guitars and Mandolins a thorough test, I pronounce them perfect as to tone, quality, correctness of scale and general excellency, and can heartily recommend them to those desirous of a really first class mandolin or guitar.

Yours truly, F. M. PLANQUE,

Teacher of Mandolin, Guitar and Banjo, Metropolitan School of Music, Indianapolis.

Styles 104 S-104 A

Rosewood, Spanish Cedar Neck, Oval Ebony Fingerboard, Pearl Position Dots, beautiful colored wood Inlayings around Soundhole, beautiful Inlaid strip down the back, Edges and Soundhole Celluloid Bound, Elaborate colored wood Inlayings around Edges, Elegantly Finished.

Style 104 S.	Standard Size	Each,	$29.00
" 104 GC.	Grand Concert Size	"	35.25
" 104 A.	Auditorium Size	"	44.00

Emil Wulschner & Son, Indianapolis, IND., "'Regal' Guitars," 1896-1897 catalogue, p207. Photographs by Jim Bollman, courtesy Stu Cohen.

"REGAL" GUITARS.

INDIANAPOLIS.

Wulschner & Son:

GENTLEMEN—The "Regal" Mandolin and Guitar I have examined very carefully and pronounce them far superior to anything on the market. The instruments having a perfect model, perfect scale and sweet and powerful correct tone.

FRANK Z. MAFFEY,
Teacher of Mandolin, Guitar and Banjo

Styles 106 S-106 GC

Rosewood, with richly Inlaid and Celluloid Bound Edges, Spanish Cedar Neck, Oval Ebony Fingerboard, **Pearl Position Ornaments**, handsome colored wood Inlayings around Soundhole, beautiful Inlaid strip down **the back**, **White Front**, Extra Fine Head, Elegantly Finished.

Style 106 S.	Standard Size	Each,	$35.00
" **106 GC.**	Grand Concert Size	"	42.50

Emil Wulschner & Son, Indianapolis, IND., "'Regal' Guitars," 1896-1897 catalogue, p208. Photographs by Jim Bollman, courtesy Stu Cohen.

Wulschner & Son Regal, probably Style 106 guitar, serial number 3799. Full front view, photograph/courtesy Tom Benson.

Wulschner & Son Regal, probably Style 106 guitar, serial number 3799. Close-up of top, photograph/courtesy Tom Benson.

Wulschner & Son Regal, probably Style 106 guitar, serial number 3799. Close-up of rosewood back, photograph/courtesy Tom Benson.

Wulschner & Son Regal, probably Style 106 guitar, serial number 3799. Back of headstock, photograph/ courtesy Tom Benson.

"Notice. All 'REGAL' Guitars are made by hand, and the very finest material obtainable is used in their construction.

"The careful and experienced workmanship on each part of the instrument, together with our peculiar method of tone balancing, gives to the 'REGAL' Guitars that richness of tone and vibratory quality for which they are noted and which is unobtainable in the machine-made instruments.

"The scale is absolutely correct and each instrument is fully warranted.

Wulschner & Son Regal, probably Style 106 guitar, serial number 3799. Top of headstock with serial number, photograph/courtesy Tom Benson.

"None genuine unless branded with our registered trade-mark 'REGAL.'"

Below the paper label was a wooden medallion incised with the words "Wulschner & Son, Trade Mark, Regal, Indianapolis, IND."

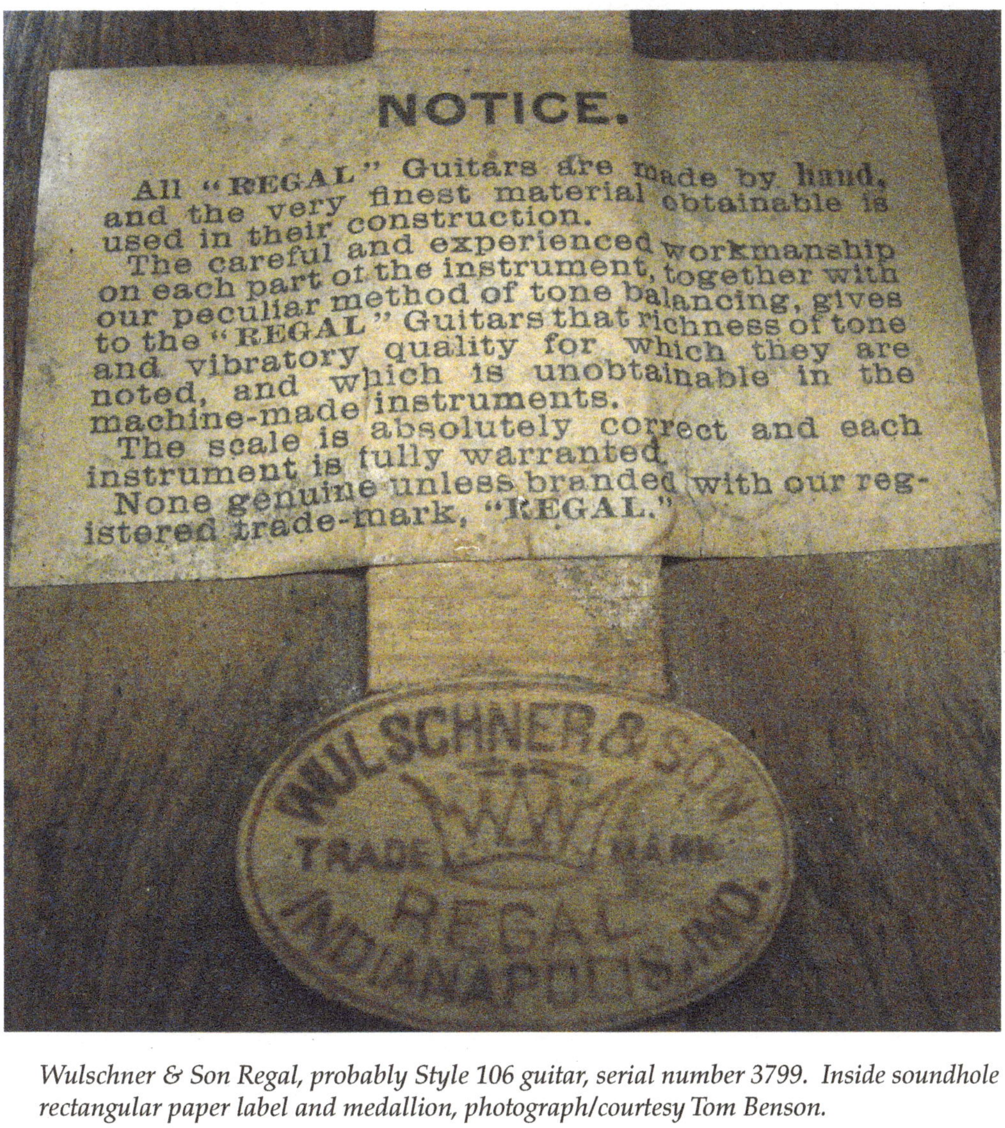

Wulschner & Son Regal, probably Style 106 guitar, serial number 3799. Inside soundhole rectangular paper label and medallion, photograph/courtesy Tom Benson.

Every guitar differs in some manner from the others (for example, nut widths vary from 1 ¾" to 2"), so, this small sample makes it difficult to reach any definitive conclusions about Regal-made instruments from this period. It is possible to conclude from the variations in features that Wulschner was probably making some of their instruments, especially after moving into their factory in 1898, and outsourcing others. Some writers have suggested the Larson Brothers as the makers of Wulschner/Regal guitars. But, it is just as likely that Lyon & Healy, who were providing Wulschner with Regal-brand banjos, could have made the guitars of this period as well.

"REGAL" GUITARS.

Emil Wulschner & Son:

DEAR SIRS—I use and can cheerfully recommend the "Regal" Mandolins and Guitars. In my estimation they excel all other makes. For depth and sonority of the Bass Strings and ringing brilliancy of the upper register, and with their absolutely true scale, places them far in the lead of all other makes and anything I have ever seen.

I wish you success with them, which you undoubtedly will have as they need only to be seen to be appreciated.

Yours truly, PROF. CHAS. W. HUME,
Teacher of Mandolin and Guitar.

Styles 108S-108 GC

Rosewood, Spanish Cedar Neck, Oval Ebony Fingerboard with Pearl Position Ornaments, Elaborate Inlayings of Colored Wood Around Sound Hole, Edges Elaborately Inlaid with Beautiful Colored Woods, Fingerboard and Headpiece Celluloid Bound, Handsome Stripe in Back, Pearl Ornaments Inlaid in Headpiece, Extra Fine Patent Head, Elegantly Finished. A superb instrument in every respect and especially designed for the use of Artists and Teachers.

Style 108 S.	Standard Size..	Each	$52 50
" 108 GC.	Grand Concert Size	"	60 50

Emil Wulschner & Son, Indianapolis, IND., "'Regal' Guitars," 1896-1897 catalogue, p209. Photographs by Jim Bollman, courtesy Stu Cohen.

210 EMIL WULSCHNER & SON, INDIANAPOLIS, IND.

"REGAL" GUITARS.

Emil Wulschner & Son, Indianapolis, Ind.

GENTTLEMEN—The "Regal" mandolins and guitars are surely wonderful instruments, and I cannot refrain from expressing my admiration of the "Regal" guitar and mandolin purchased of you recently. Their tone is full, rich and pure, combined with a perfect fingerboard. I take pleasure in adding my recommendation to those you have received from so many others. Yours truly,

E. E. NOEL,

Teacher of Mandolin and Guitar.

Styles 110S-110A

Rosewood, Very Elaborate Inlayings Around Soundhole, Spanish Cedar Neck, Oval Ebony Fingerboard with Fancy Pearl Position Ornaments and Celluloid Bound Edges, Top Very Elaborately Inlaid Around the Edges and Celluloid Bound, Handsome Inlaid Stripes Around the Back and Through the Centre, Headpiece Elaborately Inlaid and Celluloid Bound Both Front and Back, Elegantly French Polished. A very handsome instrument in every respect.

Style 110 S.	Standard Size	Each.	$75.00
" 110 G. C.	Grand Concert Size	"	85.00
" 110 A.	Auditorium Size	"	97.50

Emil Wulschner & Son, Indianapolis, IND., "'Regal' Guitars," 1896-1897 catalogue, p210. Photographs by Jim Bollman, courtesy Stu Cohen.

Regal Manufacturing Company

Summary

Instrument: Flattop guitar.

Model: Regal, "20th Century," "University."

Years Made: May, 1900-1904.

Brand(s): Regal, "20th Century," "University."

Quality: Low to high grade.

Special Features: Ladder-braced top.

Woods: Natural finish spruce top; rosewood, maple, oak, sycamore or mahogany back and sides; cedar neck.

Known Measurements: 24"-24 1/4" scale, 1 ¾" nut, 12 ¾"-14 5/8" lower bout, 9"-10 5/8" upper bout, 3 3/8"-4 1/16" deep at the end pin.

Logos Used: Paper soundhole label "The University Guitar Strictly High Grade," wooden soundhole medallion "University, R.M.Co., Mandolins & Guitars," wooden soundhole medallion, pearl script in peghead.

Known Original Wholesale List Price: $4.38-$62.50.

The Regal Manufacturing Company was formed by the Wulschner family in May, 1900 and sold to a group of local investors by August of 1901. By the beginning of 1904, Regal of Indianapolis was out of business.

From 1900 to 1904, Regal Manufacturing sold three "lines" of varying quality. The "20th Century" brand was used for factory-made, low-priced guitars; "University" for quality, although somewhat factory-made, instruments; and "Regal" for top-of-the-line, handmade guitars. The surviving catalogue from 1901 only shows "20th Century" and "University" brand guitars and is reproduced here.

As one can see, the Style 300/301, 250-260, 262 and 264 are all low-grade instruments. Many feature tailpieces and all have some type of faux finish on the body and/or neck to give the impression of a higher priced guitar. Quality begins with the "University" series. Rosewood back and sides coupled with a "Spanish" cedar neck, ebony fingerboard and bridge, pearl inlays, celluloid and marquetry binding are all standard for these models, from the plain Style 420 on up to the heavily inlaid 430. An extant Style 426 features a short 24 ¼" scale, a nut width of 1 ¾", upper bout of 10 5/8" and lower bout of 14 5/8", with a depth of 4 1/16" at the end pin. This may be what the company called their "Auditorium" size guitar. Another "University," recently sold by Vintage Instruments in Philadelphia, was a top-of-the-line Style 430. It is probably a regular-sized model, with a 12 ¾" lower bout, 9" upper bout, 3 3/8" depth at endpin, 24" scale, and 1 and 13/16" wide nut.

Although no catalogue has yet to surface for Regal-branded guitars of this period, one beautiful example of a Regal guitar was published in the book Vintage Guitars (String Letter Publishing, 2001). This very fancy model reminds one of a Lyon & Healy Washburn and of later high end guitars made by Regal. As best can be seen in the published photograph, the guitar features a two piece natural finish white bound spruce top; fingerboard and soundhole with a black ring rosette; abalone top and soundhole trim; Washburn style modified rectangular bridge with flared inlaid ends, straight saddle and white pins with abalone insets; heavily column inlaid fingerboard and headstock; probably rosewood back and sides; twelve frets to the body; slotted headstock; eighteen fret neck; top geared tuners with white buttons; "Regal" in pearl script in the headstock; and an oval soundhole wooden medallion inscribed with "Regal Manufacturing Co., Trade Mark, Regal, Indianapolis, IN, USA."

20TH CENTURY GUITARS

STYLES 300–301

Style 300—Maple, Red Shaded, cherry finished neck, walnut finger board and **bridge**, inlaid sound hold, varnish finish, American patent heads...**Price, $4.38**

" 301—Same, with patent tail piece.. " **$4.38**

Regal Manufacturing Co., Indianapolis, catalogue, 1901, "The 20th Century Guitars Styles 300-301." Photograph by Jim Bollman, courtesy Stu Cohen.

20TH CENTURY GUITARS

STYLES 250—251

Style 250—Maple, Mahogany Finish, hand polished, cherry finished neck, ebonized finger-board and bridge, pearl positions, inlaid sound hole, edges and sound hole bevelled, American patent heads..**Price, $5.00**

" 251—Same, with patent tail piece.. " **5.00**

Regal Manufacturing Co., Indianapolis, catalogue, 1901, "The 20th Century Guitars Styles 250-251." Photograph by Jim Bollman, courtesy Stu Cohen.

20TH CENTURY GUITARS

STYLES 252 - 253

Style 252 —**Maple, Rosewood Finish,** hand polished, cherry finished neck, ebonized fingerboard and bridge, pearl positions, inlaid sound hole, sound hole and edges bevelled, American patent heads	**Price,**	**$6.25**
" 253 —Same, with patent tail piece	"	**6.25**
" 252¾—Same as 252, ¾ size	"	**6.25**
" 253¾—Same as 253, ¾ size	"	**6.25**

Regal Manufacturing Co., Indianapolis, catalogue, 1901, "The 20th Century Guitars Styles 252-253." Photograph by Jim Bollman, courtesy Stu Cohen.

20TH CENTURY GUITARS

STYLES 254—255

Style 254—Quarter sawed oak, hand polished, cherry finished neck, ebonized finger-board **and** bridge, pearl positions, sound hole inlaid and bevelled, top edge inlaid and celluloid bound, fancily inlaid stripe down back, American patent heads........................**Price, $7.50**

" 255—Same, with patent tail piece.......................... .... " **7.50**

Regal Manufacturing Co., Indianapolis, catalogue, 1901, "The 20th Century Guitars Styles 254-255." Photograph by Jim Bollman, courtesy Stu Cohen.

20TH CENTURY GUITARS

STYLES 250–257

Style 256—Maple, Dark Cherry Finish, hand polished, cherry finished neck, ebonized fingerboard and bridge, pearl positions, sound hole fancily inlaid and bevelled, top edge fancily inlaid and celluloid bound, fancily inlaid stripe down back, American patent heads........ **Price, $8.13**

" **257**—Same, with patent tail piece........ " **8.13**

" **256 G C**—Same as 256, grand concert size........ " **9.38**

" **257 G C**—Same as 257, grand concert size........ " **9.38**

Regal Manufacturing Co., Indianapolis, catalogue, 1901, "The 20th Century Guitars Styles 256-257." Photograph by Jim Bollman, courtesy Stu Cohen.

20TH CENTURY GUITARS

STYLES 258–259

Style 258—Maple, Fancily Grained in Imitation of Rosewood, hand polished, cherry finished neck, ebonized finger-board and bridge, pearl positions, sound hole fancily inlaid and bevelled, top edge fancily inlaid and rosewood bound, a fancily inlaid stripe down back, American patent heads...Price, $ 9.00

"	259—Same, with patent tail piece..	"	9.00
"	258 G C—Same as 258, grand concert size......................................	"	10.25
"	259 G C—Same as 259, grand concert size......................................	"	10.25
"	258 A—Same as 258, auditorium size..	"	11.25
"	259 A—Same as 259, auditorium size..	"	11.25

Regal Manufacturing Co., Indianapolis, catalogue, 1901, "The 20th Century Guitars Styles 258-259." Photograph by Jim Bollman, courtesy Stu Cohen.

20TH CENTURY GUITARS

STYLE 260

Style 260—Quarter Sawed Sycamore, Highly Flamed Finish, hand polished, cherry finished neck, ebonized finger-board and bridge, pearl positions, veneered **head-piece, sound** hole and top edge fancily inlaid, both edges, front and back celluloid **bound, a fancily** inlaid stripe down back, American patent heads.. **Price, $11.25**

Regal Manufacturing Co., Indianapolis, catalogue, 1901, "The 20th Century Guitars Style 260." Photograph by Jim Bollman, courtesy Stu Cohen.

20TH CENTURY GUITAR

STYLE 262

Style 262 – **Solid Mahogany,** hand polished, cherry finished neck, ebonized finger-board and bridge, pearl positions, veneered head-piece, edges and sound hole fancily inlaid, edges celluloid bound, both front and back, a fancily inlaid stripe down back, American patent heads.. **Price, $12.50**

" **262 G C**—Grand concert size.. " **13.75**

Regal Manufacturing Co., Indianapolis, catalogue, 1901, "The 20th Century Guitars Style 262." Photograph by Jim Bollman, courtesy Stu Cohen.

20TH CENTURY GUITAR

STYLE 204

Birds Eye Maple, Highly Flamed, hand polished, cherry finished neck, **ebonized finger-board and bridge, pearl positions,** veneered head-piece, sound hole and edges both back and **front elaborately** inlaid **and celluloid bound, an elaborately** inlaid colored wood star in top back of bridge, an elaborately **inlaid** stripe **down back, American patent heads.**

Price, $15.00.

Regal Manufacturing Co., Indianapolis, catalogue, 1901, "The 20th Century Guitars Style 264." Photograph by Jim Bollman, courtesy Stu Cohen.

University Guitars

Like the University Mandolins, are fully warranted in every respect. For a strictly high-grade Guitar the market affords no equal instrument for the prices asked. Every part is so perfectly made as to yield a thorough satisfaction to all musicians.

THE UNIVERSITY GUITAR

STYLE 420

Style 420—**Rosewood,** Spanish cedar neck, ebony finger-board and bridge, pearl positions, veneered head-piece, sound hole and top edge inlaid and celluloid bound, inlaid stripe down back, nickel plated patent heads, French polished............................**Price, $16.25**

" 420¾—¾ size.. " 16.25

" 420 G C—Grand concert size.. " 18.75

Regal Manufacturing Co., Indianapolis, catalogue, 1901, "The University Guitar Style 420." Photograph by Jim Bollman, courtesy Stu Cohen.

The University Guitar

STYLE 422

Rosewood, Spanish cedar neck, ebony finger-board and bridge, positions ornamented with pearl, veneered head-piece, sound hole and both edges, front and back, inlaid and celluloid bound, inlaid stripe down back, nickel plated patent head, French polished.

Price, $20.00.

Regal Manufacturing Co., Indianapolis, catalogue, 1901, "The University Guitar Style 422." Photograph by Jim Bollman, courtesy Stu Cohen.

THE UNIVERSITY GUITAR

STYLE 424

Style 424—**Rosewood,** Spanish cedar neck, ebony finger-board and bridge, positions fancily inlaid with pearl, finger-board bound with celluloid, veneered head-piece, pearl inlaid sound hole and edges, front and back, fancily inlaid and celluloid bound, inlaid stripe down back, nickel plated patent heads, French polished ....**Price, $26.25**
" 424 G C—Grand concert size.. " **28.75**

Regal Manufacturing Co., Indianapolis, catalogue, 1901, "The University Guitar Style 424." Photograph by Jim Bollman, courtesy Stu Cohen.

THE UNIVERSITY GUITAR

STYLE 426

Style 426—Rosewood, Spanish cedar neck, ebony finger-board and bridge, positions very fancily pearl inlaid, finger-board bound with celluloid, veneered head-piece, ornamented with pearl, sound hole and edges, front and back, celluloid bound and very fancily inlaid, a fancily inlaid stripe down back, nickel plated patent heads, French polished.......**Price, $31.88**

" **426 A**—Auditorium size.. " **37.50**

Regal Manufacturing Co., Indianapolis, catalogue, 1901, "The University Guitar Style 426." Photograph by Jim Bollman, courtesy Stu Cohen.

University-Brand guitar Style 426, Regal Manufacturing Company, Indianapolis, full front view. Photograph/courtesy Tony Klassen/New Era Guitars.

University-Brand guitar Style 426, Regal Manufacturing Company, Indianapolis, close-up of top binding and soundhole rosette. Photograph/courtesy Tony Klassen/New Era Guitars.

University-Brand guitar Style 426, back of headstock.

University-Brand guitar Style 426, soundhole medallion label

University-Brand guitar Style 426, Regal Manufacturing Company, Indianapolis, full back view. Photograph/courtesy Tony Klassen/New Era Guitars.

THE UNIVERSITY GUITAR

STYLE 428

Style 428—**Rosewood,** Spanish cedar neck, ebony finger-board and bridge, positions elaborately pearl inlaid, finger-board celluloid bound, veneered head-piece fancily pearl inlaid, sound hole and edges, front and back, celluloid bound and elaborately inlaid, a very fancily inlaid stripe down back, nickel plated patent heads, French polished......... **Price, $41.25**

" 428 G C—Grand concert size.. " **45.00**

Regal Manufacturing Co., Indianapolis, catalogue, 1901, "The University Guitar Style 428." Photograph by Jim Bollman, courtesy Stu Cohen.

THE UNIVERSITY GUITAR

STYLE 430

Style 430—Rosewood, Spanish cedar neck, ebony finger-board and bridge, finger-board bound with celluloid and elaborately inlaid with a fancy pearl flower design, veneered head-piece, pearl inlaid, sound hole and edges, front and back, celluloid bound and elaborately inlaid, an elaborately inlaid stripe down back, gold plated patent heads, French polished .... Price, $58.75

" 430 G C—Grand concert size .... " 62.50

Regal Manufacturing Co., Indianapolis, catalogue, 1901, "The University Guitar Style 430." Photograph by Jim Bollman, courtesy Stu Cohen.

Chicago Parlor

Summary

Instrument: Flattop guitar.

Model: 12 fret slot head "Parlor."

Years Made: 1914-1932.

Brand(s): Regal, Concertone.

Quality: Low to medium grade.

Special Features: None.

Woods: Birch; spruce over birch, oak or mahogany; "hardwood" or mahogany neck.

Measurements: N/A.

Logos Used: Paper soundhole label.

Known Original List Price: $15.00-33.75 wholesale, $1.95-25.98 retail.

After the move to Chicago, Regal continued to produce guitars in the same styles as those made or sold out of the Indianapolis factory. These were ladder-braced, slot-headed, twelve frets to the body with an eighteen fret fingerboard instrument designed for gut or very light steel strings, which came in a variety of styles and quality.

The lowest grade guitars had birch bodies or spruce over birch shaded to simulate mahogany or rosewood. The best of the lot was eventually incorporated into the "Regal Superior" line. Its spruce top and soundhole were bound in black celluloid with veneered fine lines, birch back and headstock bound in celluloid only and an ebonized fingerboard topped off a "hardwood" neck. A slightly higher grade guitar was available with oak back and sides.

The best of the affordable instruments was also a "Superior." It came with mahogany back and sides, a spruce top, mahogany neck with rosewood headstock overlay, ebonized fingerboard, and rectangular ebony bridge.

Variations on many of these low to medium-grade six strings were sold beginning in 1914 through the Montgomery Ward mail-order catalogue. The Regal spruce over mahogany guitar had colored wood marquetry around the soundhole, top, back and down the back stripe; along with an "ebonized" headstock overlay and fingerboard bound in white celluloid. From 1928-1931, one of the best quality Montgomery Ward guitars by Regal was the Serenader/Professional, another spruce over mahogany guitar.

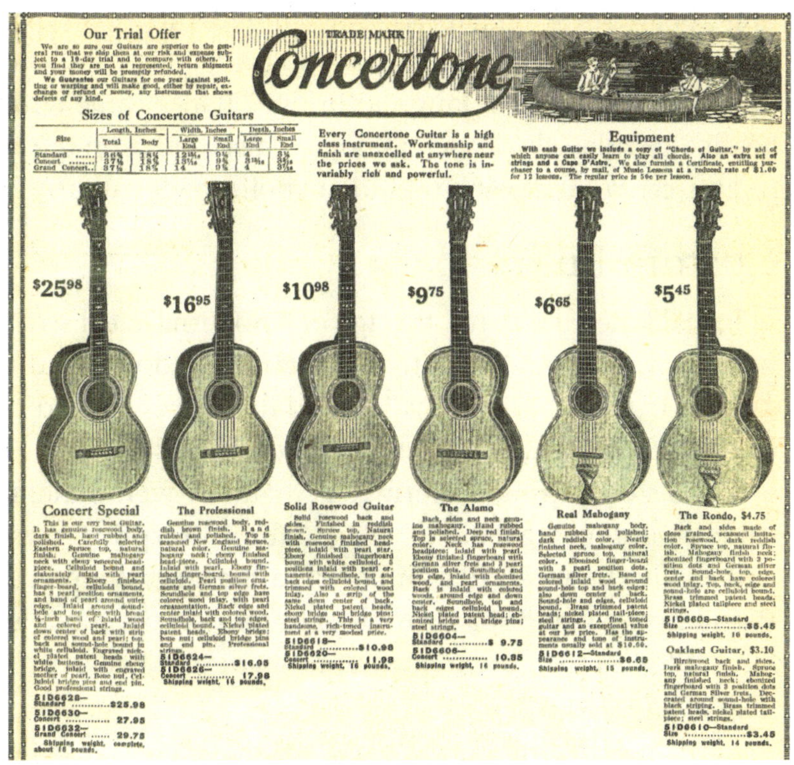

"Concertone" guitars, probably Regal-made, Montgomery Ward catalogue, 1917, courtesy the Chicago History Museum.

Superior

Summary

Instrument: "Superior" flattop guitar.

Model: 12 fret slot head.

Years Made: 1914-1932

Brand(s): Regal "Superior," Montgomery Ward Concertone "Professional," "Artists'."

Quality: High.

Special Features: Pearl binding and inlay.

Woods: Natural spruce top, rosewood back and sides, mahogany neck.

Measurements: 24 ½" scale, upper bout 9 7/8"-10", lower bout 13 ½"-14", nut width 1 ¾" on some models.

Logos Used: Regal pearl headstock medallion, paper soundhole label.

Known Original List Price: $13.75-31.75 retail, $30.00-55.00 wholesale.

The "flagship" models of Regal guitars eventually became known as the top of the "Superior" line. Comparable to the fancier Washburns of the same period (which Regal very well might have made along with their own labeled instruments), their spruce over rosewood bodies were generously appointed in pearl. Montgomery Ward bragged that "there is no better Guitar made or sold under any name or at any price than the instrument shown above."

The Montgomery Ward "Professional" made by Regal and offered in two sizes came with mother-of-pearl and colored wood marquetry-bound top and soundhole, white celluloid bound spruce top, rosewood back bound in wood marquetry and marquetry back stripe, mahogany neck, ebony fingerboard, pearl Regal-esq crown inlaid into the rosewood headstock veneer and an ebony rectangular bridge. The "Artists'" three sizes upgraded the headstock veneer to ebony and added pearl inlays to each wing of the rectangular bridge. It also came with a ten day trial. Interestingly the "seagull" headstock inlay shown in catalogues also found on the mahogany/spruce "Superior" model is reminiscent of that used on Indianapolis made guitars.

Custom Built

In 1928, Regal entered the age of "modern," steel strung guitars with their "Custom Built" line (there were also "Custom Built" tenor guitars, mandolins and ukuleles, see below and under the chapters on each instrument). These "X" braced flattops eschewed the fancy decoration of the Victorian period, and placed a premium on stability, sound and volume. The "Custom Built" series differed from most of Regal's other guitar offerings in that they were serial numbered and, with two exceptions, were only sold under the Regal name. One of those exceptions were the Washburn guitars, made first for Lyon and Healy. Between 1930 and 1937, after L&H stopped selling stringed instruments, Regal provided Washburns to the Tonk Bros. distributors. Those models were essentially the same as the "Custom Built" line, but with a different headstock shape and heavier construction (see page 93-97 of Washburn Prewar Instrument Styles fmi).

In describing their new models, Regal copywriters told their distributors that:

"'Regal Custom Built' Guitars are the finest money can buy. Strictly hand made by expert workmen who have used a great deal of skill and care in producing these instruments. Their craftsmanship shows in

Regal Guitars

Style Number 2019

No. 2019. Standard Size. Birch back and sides, mahogany finish; spruce top; colored block inlaying around soundhole and top edge; fancy decalcomania strip down center of back; both edges and soundhole bound with white celluloid; rubbed and polished. **Price, each**.......... **$11.70**

No. 2012. Same as No. 2019 excepting top and back edges are plain. **Price, each**.......... **$9.80**

No. 2073. Same description as No. 2019 excepting it is ¾ or Ladies' Size. **Price, each**.......... **$11.70**

"Regal Guitars" "No. 2019, 2012 and 2073," H. C. Schultz catalogue, 1928. Courtesy Elderly Instruments.

DETROIT **H.C. SCHULTZ, INC** WHOLESALE EXCLUSIVELY CLEVELAND

Regal Guitars

Style Number 2023

No. 2023. Standard Size. Birch back and sides, finished in imitation rosewood; selected spruce top; double row of black and white wood block inlaying around soundhole, both edges and down center of back; fine shaped neck with white celluloid bound head; fingerboard bound with white celluloid together with inlaid fancy pearl position figures; highly finished in grained imitation rosewood; rubbed and polished. **Price, each**..***$19.20***

No. 2021. Same as No. 2023, excepting back edge is only bound with white celluloid and has a metal tailpiece in place of pin bridge. **Price, each**..***$15.00***

No. 2060. Same as No. 2021. Concert Size, Mexican Style. 12 strings. **Price, each**..............................***$20.50***

No. 2075. Same as No. 2023, but in Jumbo Size. Three pearl position marks. Plain head. **Price, each**..............***$30.00***

No. 2070. Auditorium Bass Guitar. Double neck. 12 strings. Birchwood in imitation rosewood finish. **Price, each**....***$60.00***

"Regal Guitars" "No. 2023, 2021, 2060, 2075 and 2070," H. C. Schultz catalogue, 1928. Courtesy Elderly Instruments.

DETROIT **H.C. SCHULTZ, INC** WHOLESALE EXCLUSIVELY CLEVELAND

Regal Guitars

Style Number 2014

No. 2014. A popular standard size guitar made of selected figured birch, shaded in a rich mahogany color as pictured above. Front and back edges and soundhole bound with white celluloid. Hand-rubbed and polished.
Price, each **$10.50**

No. 2055. Same as No. 2014 but in Grand Concert Size.
Price, each **$12.00**

No. 2061. Same as No. 2014 but in Jumbo Size, top and back edges plain.
Price, each **$16.80**

"Regal Guitars" "No. 2014, 2055 and 2061," H. C. Schultz catalogue, 1928. Courtesy Elderly Instruments.

DETROIT **H. C. SCHULTZ, INC** WHOLESALE EXCLUSIVELY CLEVELAND

Regal Guitars

Style Number 2018

No. 2018. Standard Size. Back and sides made of birch, top of spruce, shaded a deep mahogany; soundhole and both edges bound with colored inlaying and white celluloid; fingerboard bound with white celluloid; **hand-rubbed and polished.**

Price, each **$15.00**

No. 2017. Same as No. 2018 without inlaying on back edge and the instrument is not rubbed.

Price, each **$12.00**

"Regal Guitars" "No. 2018 and 2017," H. C. Schultz catalogue, 1928. Courtesy Elderly Instruments.

DETROIT **H.C. SCHULTZ, INC** WHOLESALE EXCLUSIVELY CLEVELAND

Regal Guitars

Style Number 2027

No. 2027. Standard Size. Back and sides of genuine quarter-sawed oak, highly figured; fine spruce top; both edges, soundhole and center of back **heavily** inlaid with bright colored wood block inlaying; white celluloid binding around both edges, soundhole, fingerboard and headpiece; fancy pearl positions inlaid in fingerboard; finished in attractive golden cak; well rubbed and polished.
Price, each **$19.40**

No. 2026. Same as No. 2027 with the exception of the fingerboard which has three pearl position dots and no binding on edge or head. **Price, each** **$17.10**

"Regal Guitars" "No. 2027 and 2026," H. C. Schultz catalogue, 1928. Courtesy Elderly Instruments.

Regal Guitars

Style Number 2028

No. 2028. Standard Size. Genuine mahogany back and sides; high grade spruce top; double row of colored wood inlaying around soundhole, both edges and down center of back; ebonized headpiece with white celluloid binding; fingerboard bound with white celluloid; fancy pearl position figures inlaid in fingerboard; hand-rubbed and highly polished.
Price, each...**$20.30**

No. 2065. Mexican Style. 11 strings. Standard Size. Same as No. 2028 excepting that the fingerboard and head are plain and fancy pearl figures in fingerboard replaced with three pearl dots.
Price, each...**$21.00**

"Regal Guitars" "No. 2028 and 2965," H. C. Schultz catalogue, 1928. Courtesy Elderly Instruments.

Regal Guitars

Style Number 2029

No. 2029. Standard Size. Genuine rosewood back and sides; well-seasoned close-grain eastern spruce top; genuine mahogany neck and fine ebonized fingerboard; rosewood headpiece; handsomely inlaid around soundhole, both edges and down center of back; highly rubbed and polished.
Price, each... **$26.00**

No. 2032. Same as No. 2029 with the addition of fancy inlaid fingerboard bound with white celluloid and white celluloid bound head.
Price, each... **$30.00**

No. 2030. Same as No. 2029 except back edge is bound with celluloid only.
Price, each... **$25.00**

"Regal Guitars" "No. 2029, 2032 and 2030," H. C. Schultz catalogue, 1928. Courtesy Elderly Instruments.

"REGAL SUPERIOR" Guitar No. 73 as pictured above; back and sides of genuine mahogany with best grade of spruce top obtainable. Sound hole, both edges and center of back neatly inlaid with black and white veneer lines; genuine mahogany neck with rosewood veneered head piece; ebonized oval finger board with five pearl position figures; pearl ornament in head; genuine ebony bridge; fine trimmings; hand rubbed to a dull satin-like finish; carefully adjusted and inspected.

Style Number 73 *Price $22.00*

"REGAL SUPERIOR" Guitar No. 71 has back and sides made of the best grade of figured birch; close-grained spruce top; sound hole inlaid with a rosette of five black and white veneer lines; top edge bound with black celluloid and inlaid with two veneer lines; back edge bound with black celluloid only; fine hardwood neck with black veneered head; ebonized finger board with three pearl position dots; best grade of trimmings; dull satin polished finish; carefully adjusted and inspected.

Style Number 71 *Price $15.00*

Mail Your Orders to 319 Sixth Avenue, New York, N. Y.

"Guitar No. 71" and "Guitar No. 73," PMI catalogue, circa 1928. Courtesy the National Music Museum.

PROGRESSIVE MUSICAL INSTRUMENT CORPORATION

"REGAL SUPERIOR" Guitar No. 76 as pictured above. Truly a handsome instrument for those wanting beauty as well as tone; sound hole and top edge heavily inlaid with wide band of genuine iridescent pearl backed up with small black and white block inlaying; row of black and white block inlaying around sides at top and back edges; back and sides of rosewood with fine eastern spruce top. Genuine mahogany neck with "REGAL" nameplate in headpiece; fancy celluloid bound fingerboard. Highly polished.

Style Number 76 *Price $50.00*

"REGAL SUPERIOR" Guitar No. 75 pictured above. An exceptionally fine instrument with selected rosewood back and sides and the finest spruce top obtainable; neatly inlaid around sound hole, front and back edges and down through center of back with fine black and white wood lines; oval ebonized finger board bound with black and white celluloid; genuine mahogany neck and rosewood veneered head; pearl ornament in head, genuine ebony bridge with white bridge pins. Highly rubbed and polished.

Style Number 75 *Price $30.00*

Mail Your Orders to 319 Sixth Avenue, New York, N. Y.

"Guitar No. 75" and "Guitar No. 76," PMI catalogue, circa 1928. Courtesy the National Music Museum.

the small details such as rounded corners and edges, proper adjustment of neck and strings, hand ovaled fingerboards and hand tapered bridges.

"Each 'Regal Custom Built' Guitar is carefully inspected and adjusted before leaving the factory and then stamped with a serial number and guaranteed for one year against defects in workmanship or materials. They are made in five styles selling at unusually low prices for this type of instrument.

"These guitars are built entirely for musical quality and a welcome relief from the vulgar and gaudy ornate."

As the Regal "Custom-Built" guitar line seems obviously to be a direct challenge to C.F. Martin's guitar line of the late 1920s, it is serendipitous that the Grossman Music Company's catalogue of 1928 features the two company's offerings on opposing pages. This presents an opportunity to compare Regal's "imitations" of the twelve fret slot-headed acoustics that Martin produced during 1928.

Regal No. 1 and 2 are versions of C.F. Martin's "Concert Size" 0-18. Both companies use a natural finished spruce top over sides and back of mahogany. Although Regal claims to have used an ebony fingerboard as did Martin during this period, some versions of the Regal guitar utilized dyed maple or other woods for the fretboard and rectangular bridge. The Regal No. 1 would run a dealer $20.00 (all prices are wholesale) and the No. 2 $25.00, as opposed to $40.00 for the Martin. Regal's No. 3 "Custom," approximately the size of Martin's "Grand Concert" 00-18, cost $28.00; the Martin would run you $45.00. Martin and Regal also made these models with rosewood back and sides. Martin's were a bit fancier then Regal's, but, the basic guitar by both companies came with the same features. Regal's "Concert Size" No. 4 ran $45.00, with Martin charging $55.00 for their 0-21, and Regal's "Grand Concert" No. 5 cost $50.00, compared to the Martin 00-21 at $60.00.

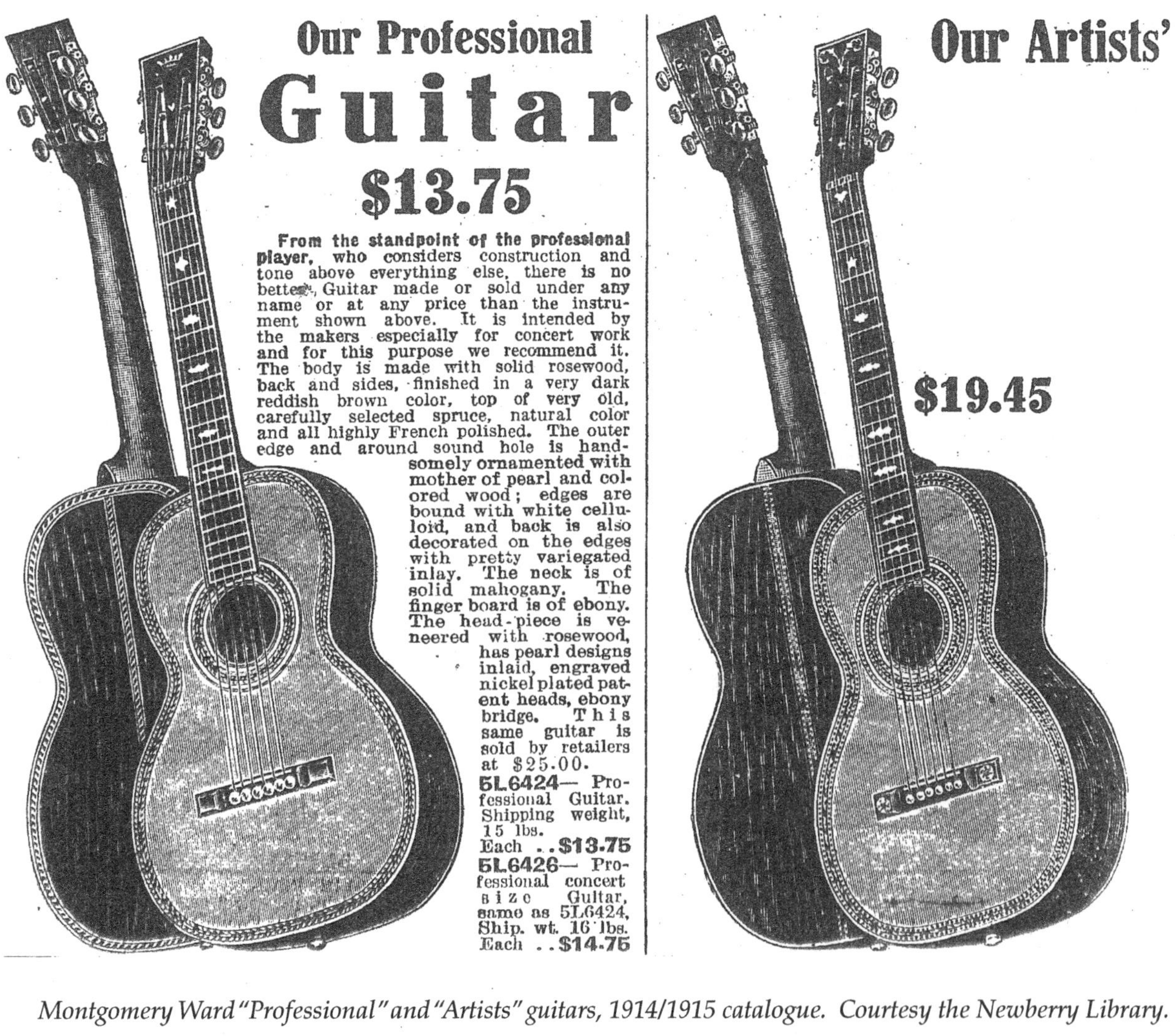

Montgomery Ward "Professional" and "Artists" guitars, 1914/1915 catalogue. Courtesy the Newberry Library.

This high-end Regal guitar, shown here next to a suspiciously similar-looking Washburn from the same period, is the equivalent of the Montgomery Ward "Artist" model. Photograph/courtesy Gary Selufsky.

This soundhole close-up with oval label of a high-end Regal guitar is the equivalent of the Montgomery Ward "Artist" model. Photograph/ courtesy Gary Selufsky.

This top close-up of a high-end Regal guitar is the equivalent of the Montgomery Ward "Artist" model. Photograph/courtesy Gary Selufsky.

This back close-up of a high-end Regal guitar is the equivalent of the Montgomery Ward "Artist" model. Photograph/courtesy Gary Selufsky.

This back view of a high-end Regal guitar is the equivalent of the Montgomery Ward "Artist" model. Photograph/courtesy Gary Selufsky.

REG. U.S. PAT. OFFICE KLEARTONE GROSSMAN MUSIC COMPANY, CLEVELAND, OHIO

C. F. Martin Guitars

The high standards of tone and workmanship established since 1833 by C. F. Martin, Sr., rigidly observed by his descendants of three generations, have made Martin Guitars, and kindred instruments world famous. A Martin instrument, when it leaves the factory, is in perfect playing condition and is guaranteed to remain so, with reasonable care, indefinitely.

Style 17

Style 18

Style 21

Style 28

Mahogany body, top and neck; rosewood bridge, fingerboard and head veneer. Body bound with rosewood; top bordered with black and white wood. Small white position marks and side dots. Lacquer finish, natural color.

No. 2-17—Amateur Size $32.50

Mahogany body and neck, spruce top, ebony bridge and fingerboard. Body bound with rosewood, top bordered with black and white wood. Pearl position dots, white side dots. Lacquer finish, natural color.

No. 0-18—Concert Size $40.00
No. 00-18—Grand Concert Size 45.00
No. 000-18—Auditorium Size 50.00

Style 42

Style 21

Rosewood body, spruce top, mahogany neck, ebony fingerboard and bridge. Body bound with rosewood, bordered front and back with black and white wood. Marqueterie inlay around soundhole and back center strip. Pearl position marks, white side dots.

No. 0-21—Concert Size $55.00
No. 00-21—Grand Concert Size 60.00

Style 28

Rosewood body, spruce top, mahogany neck, ebony fingerboard and bridge. Body and top bound and inlaid with ivory-celluloid and black and white marqueterie. Pearl position marks, white side dots.

No. 0-28—Concert Size $75.00
No. 00-28—Grand Concert Size 80.00
No. 000-28—Auditorium Size 85.00

Style 42

Rosewood body, spruce top, mahogany neck, ebony fingerboard and bridge. Body and fingerboard bound with ivory-celluloid top bordered and inlaid with pearl, elaborate pearl position marks, small side dots.

No. 0-42—Concert Size $110.00
No. 00-42—Grand Concert Size 115.00

Style 45

Rosewood body, spruce top, mahogany neck, ebony fingerboard and bridge. Body, fingerboard and head bound with ivory-celluloid. Top, back and sides richly bordered with pearl; rosewood head veneer inlaid with pearl; elaborate pearl position marks, small side dots. Very handsomely ornamented.

No. 0-45—Concert Size $155.00
No. 00-45—Grand Concert Size 160.00
No. 000-45—Auditorium Size 170.00

Style 45

[66] ***We Carry a Complete Stock of "Martin" Instruments at All Times***

Two pages from the circa 1928 catalogue of the Grossman Music Company, Cleveland, Ohio, showing guitars from the C. F. Martin Company on one side and, facing, the Regal "Custom-Built" series on the other. As an added bonus, the top bracing pattern is shown for the Regals.

Regal "Custom-Built" Guitars

Nos. 1-2

No. 3

Regal "Custom-Built" Guitars are strictly hand made, designed for the Artist and excel in musical tone qualities. They are neat in appearance, beautiful in simplicity and are marked by skilled workmanship in every detail. Each guitar is adjusted and tested before leaving the factory, is stamped with a serial number, and is guaranteed to the purchaser against defects in workmanship and materials for one year from date of purchase.

No. 1—"Custom-Built" Guitar

Concert Size. Genuine mahogany back and sides and clear white spruce top. Genuine mahogany neck finished to match the body. Genuine ebony fingerboard with a scientifically correct scale. Black and white wood lines inlaid around soundhole and black fiberloid binding on top edge **$20.00**

No. 2—"Custom-Built" Guitar

Concert Size. Selected genuine mahogany back and sides and selected clear white spruce top. Genuine mahogany neck finished to match body. Top edge and soundhole inlaid with neat, black and white veneer lines in addition to black fiberloid binding on top and back edges **$25.00**

No. 3—"Custom-Built" Guitar

Grand Concert Size. A specially built, large size guitar constructed of the very finest materials obtainable. Top is of selected, clear white spruce; back and sides of finest grade mahogany. Inlaying and binding same as on Concert Size No. 2. Exceptional tone qualities **$28.00**

No. 4—"Custom-Built" Guitar

Concert Size. Genuine rosewood back and sides and finest eastern spruce top. Genuine mahogany neck, carefully hand shaped and finished to match body. Genuine ebony fingerboard with a scientifically correct scale and smooth, hand finished frets to insure easy fingering. Hand rubbed and polished, showing the beautifully figured grain of the rosewood **$45.00**

No. 5—"Custom-Built" Guitar

Grand Concert Size. A most beautiful, artistically designed guitar worthy of the finished Artist. Back and sides are of the finest rosewood and top of the very finest eastern spruce obtainable. Inlaying and binding are the same as on No. 4. Carefully adjusted and tested and guaranteed to the purchaser against defects in workmanship and materials for one year from date of purchase **$50.00**

No. 4

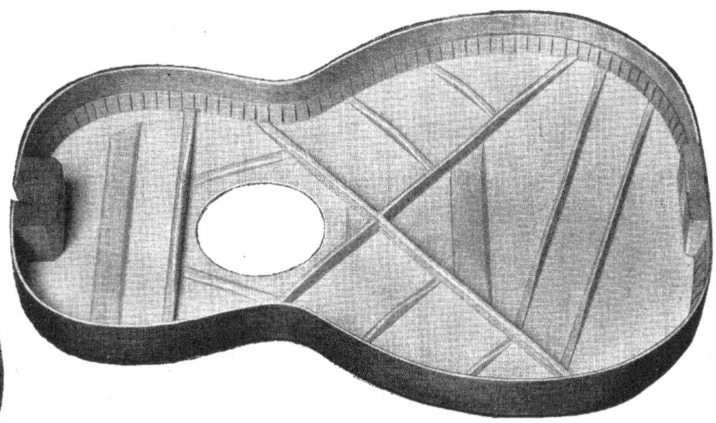

Actual photograph, showing inside construction of the top or sounding board of Regal "Custom-Built" Guitars. The position of each rib has a distinct acoustical significance upon the tone and resonance of the instrument.

No. 5

Regal "Custom-Built" Guitars are Guaranteed to the Purchaser [67]

Custom Built: Six String

Summary

Instrument: Flattop guitar.

Model: "Custom Built."

Years Made: 1928-1949 (some models).

Brand(s): Regal, Washburn, Marveltone.

Quality: High grade.

Special Features: "X" braced, 12 fret slotted peghead, serial number stamped onto paper soundhole label.

Woods: Natural finished spruce over mahogany, spruce over rosewood, mahogany neck.

Measurements: 24 ¼-24 ½" scale, 9 ¾-10 1/4" upper bout, 13 ¼-13 ½" lower bout, 3 7/8-4" endpin depth, nut width 1 7/8" ("Concert Size"); 24 1/2-24 5/8" scale, 9 7/8-10" upper bout, 14-14 1/8" lower bout, 4-4 1/16" endpin depth, nut width is 1 7/8" ("Grand Concert Size").

Logos Used: Regal paper soundhole label with "Custom Built" added, Regal oval metal back of headstock badge (1931), pearl script headstock, medallion pearl headstock (pre-1935), green Regal headstock decal (1935-onward), "Marveltone" in pearl on headstock (1935).

Known Original Wholesale List Price: $20.00, $25.00, $28.00, $45.00 and $50.00.

The entry level "Custom Built" Regals were natural spruce over mahogany with twelve frets to the body and eighteen frets total (later ones with twenty frets) slotted headstock mahogany neck, available in "Concert" (two models) and "Grand Concert" sizes. The guitars came with an ebony (changed in 1935 to "ebonized") fingerboard, bridge and headstock overlay (later ones rosewood), and three-on-a-plate tuners (earlier ones with top gears, later ones with bottom gears). Later Models 1 and 2 came with a floating pickguard that contoured to the soundhole (see photographs). The No. 1 had a soundhole rosette of black and white wood lines and a top edge bound with black fiberoid and fine lines, and fingerboard dots at fifth, seventh and ninth (later ones twelfth) frets. The No. 2 and 3 added a black bound back edge, a five line rosette, and a two piece back with an inlaid back stripe. And, in the 1939 catalogue, Regal offered the "Grand Concert" size guitar with a rosewood fingerboard and bridge and flush teardrop pickguard, along with a "square neck for Hawaiian playing." .

Some of the No. 3 and No. 5 (see below) "Grand Concert" guitars were labeled "Marveltone" and sold by Targ & Dinner of Chicago, who had been using the "Marveltone" trade name since at least 1926. Strangely enough, Montgomery Ward had shown several models of Regal-looking Marveltone guitars, along with a top bracing diagram identical to that shown for the "Custom Built" Regals during the same time period, in their 1929 catalogue. Were these made for Targ & Dinner, and then sold through Montgomery Ward? Did Regal have extra stock T&D didn't take and off-loaded them to Wards?

The top end of Regal's "Custom Built" series were natural spruce topped, rosewood back and sides and mahogany necked guitars that came in "Concert" and "Grand Concert" sizes. Appointments followed those of the mahogany No. 2 "Custom Built" guitars, although some guitars had fancier pearl fingerboard markings.

Regal Custom-built No. 2 model guitar, "Concert Size," serial number 5834. Various detail shots show-off the floating contoured pickguard, strap button, top binding and soundhole rosette, bridge, tuners and "Custom Built" soundhole label.

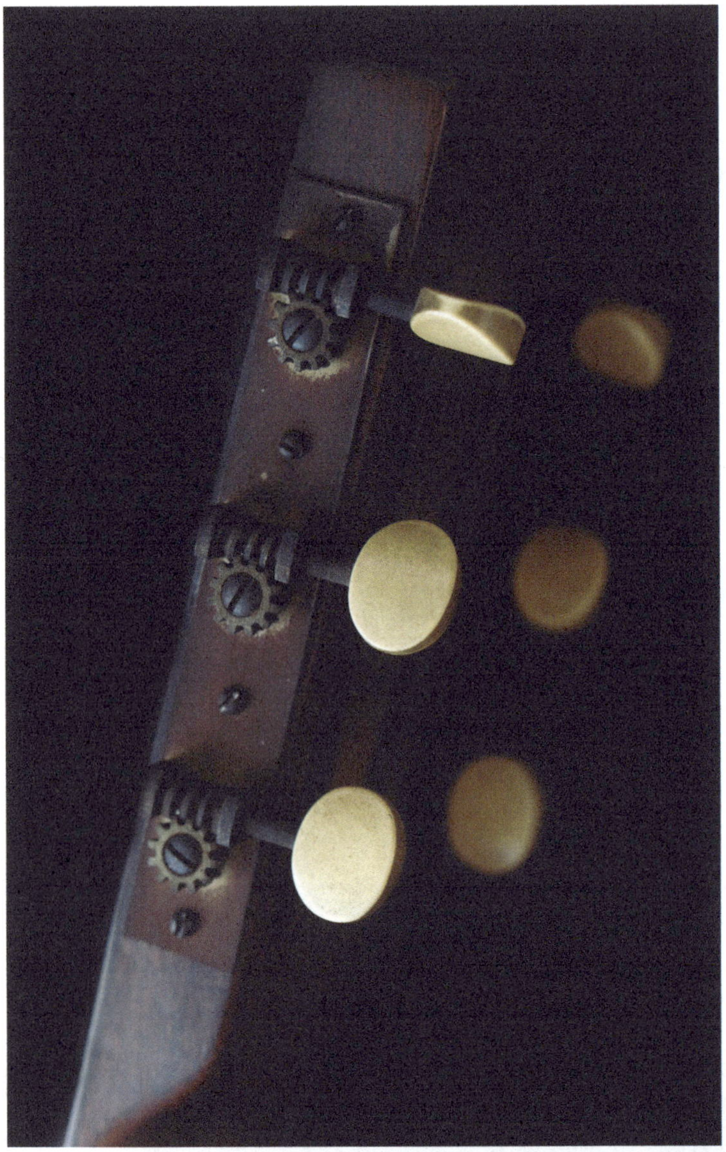

Regal Custom-built No. 2 model guitar, "Concert Size," serial number 5834. Various detail shots show-off the floating contoured pickguard, strap button, top binding and soundhole rosette, bridge, tuners and "Custom Built" soundhole label.

Rich Full-Toned Guitars

Best Guitars on EASY PAYMENTS

"Tone Quality of Marveltone Guitar Is Unsurpassed"!
Write Langdon Bros. of Langdon Bros.' Hawaiian Studios
Famous Concert and Radio Artists

"We have used your Marveltone Grand Concert Guitars professionally, and consider them among the finest instruments made. Their rare tone quality—first consideration of the professional—is fittingly matched by the beauty of construction."
LANGDON BROS.

$29.85 Cash Price

Features of the Fine Hand Construction
Master craftsmen, skilled in the making of fine musical instruments, have created our Marveltone Guitar. Guaranteed for one year from date of purchase against any defects in workmanship or materials. Over 25,000 feet of selected, genuine Mahogany are gone over before enough can be found to make only 100 of these guitars. Spruce top; ebonized fingerboard, smoothly fretted with nickeled silver. Balanced, hand-shaped neck. Instrument is finished with a thin, transparent coat of varnish. Ship. wt. 11 lbs.

$5 DOWN FOUR DOLLARS A MONTH

For Easy Payments Use Order Blank on Page 456

551 D 753—Grand Concert size.
Cash Price.......................... **$29.85**
Easy Payment Price.......................... **33.75**

551 D 1086—Three-ply veneer Guitar Case covered with good grade imitation leather; side opening. For above guitar. Ship. wt. 1 lb. **$12.95**

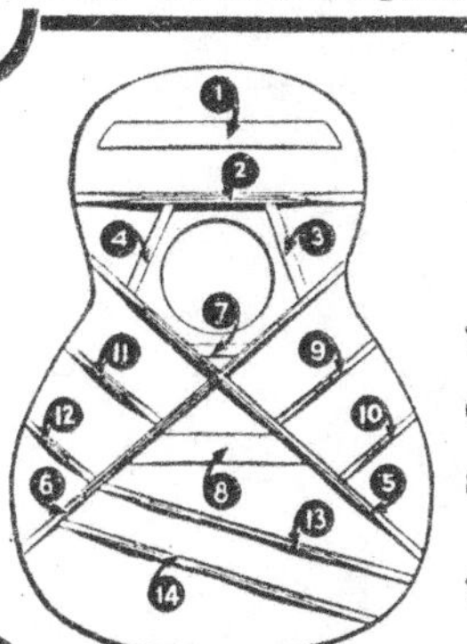

Superiority of Sound Board
1. Reinforcing bar; relieves neck strain.
2. Supporting arch.
3 and 4. Remove lateral strain.
5 and 6. Give tensile strength to top without binding against vibrations.
7. Prevents temperature changes from checking wood at soundhole.
8. Bridge rib—permits top greatest sensitivity to vibration.
9, 10, 11 and 12. Reinforcing bars.
13 and 14. Lower end braces; prevent top from "pulling in back of bridge."

The "Serenader" Concert Size Guitar

The tone of this beautiful instrument has been acclaimed by artists. Back, sides and neck of selected genuine mahogany. The Ebony fingerboard is decorated with floral designs of inlaid pearl. All edges bound with white ivorette. Inlaid around top edge and sound hole is a wide band of hand-cut iridescent mother-of-pearl. Ship. weight 11 pounds. For easy payments use Order Blank on Page 456.

$5 DOWN THREE DOLLARS A MONTH

551 D 817—Cash Price.......................... **$24.95**
Easy Payment Price.......................... **27.95**

551 D 1070—Imitation leather side-opening Guitar Case for above. Flannel lined. Ship. wt. 11 lbs.................. **$5.25**

Genuine Mahogany

$24.95 Cash Price 551 D 817

1929 Montgomery Ward catalogue listing for "Marveltone" guitars sold by B&D wholesalers out of New York City and probably made by Regal (for example, the bracing diagram is the same as that used by Regal in their listings for the "Custom Built" models). Courtesy the Chicago History Museum.

"Marveltone" brand Regal in the "Grand Concert" size, the equivalent of the "Custom-Built No. 3," full front view.

"Marveltone" brand Regal in the "Grand Concert" size, the equivalent of the "Custom-Built No. 3," close-ups of headstock inlay and top with replaced bridge.

Regal "No. 5 Custom-Built" guitar with rosewood back and sides. Full front view, with close-ups of inlaid headstock medallion and paper "Custom-Built" soundhole label. Photographs/courtesy Spruce Tree Music.

Regal "No. 5 Custom-Built" guitar with rosewood back and sides. Full back view, with close-up of metal plate on the reverse of the headstock. Photographs/courtesy Spruce Tree Music.

Custom Built: Tenor Guitar

Summary

Instrument: Tenor guitar.

Model: "Custom Built."

Years Made: 1931-1949.

Brand(s): Regal.

Quality: Medium grade.

Special Features: Full size guitar body, banjo style neck and headstock.

Woods: All mahogany, spruce over mahogany.

Measurements: 23" scale, 13 3/4" lower bout, 1 and ¼" nut width ("Grand Concert Size").

Logos Used: Regal "Tenor Guitar" paper soundhole label, medallion headstock, green decal headstock.

Known Original Wholesale List Price: $9.50-$28.00.

Along with the regular guitar line, Regal offered the first of their full size guitar-bodied pin-bridged tenor guitars with fourteen frets to the body and a total of twenty frets. Regal told their wholesalers these guitars with four string necks were "Built to meet the growing demand for a large-bodied tenor with fine tone quality and great volume, these instruments have become very popular within just a short time." The No. 1 "Custom Built" tenor came with an all mahogany body and the No. 3, a natural spruce top with a three-ring soundhole rosette over mahogany back and sides and ebony fingerboard.

Some transitional guitars (or ones assembled later from left-over parts) with three quarter sized "original" tenor bodies and floating bridge/tailpiece configuration, but with the "Custom Built" twenty fret necks, have survived. Versions of these guitars continued to be offered until 1949.

"Birch: The Forgotten Tone Wood"

There are a number of ways that instrument manufacturers save time and money. One is to make a line of instruments with the same dimensions using a variety of woods and decoration. This way, one set of jigs and machinery can be used to produce a number of models. Another way to economize production is to use some parts, like a neck or body, on a variety of instrument types. A final way to increase profits is to use "non-traditional" instrument materials. Many low-end guitars, mandolins, tenor guitars and stringed instruments in the ukulele family made in the 1920s-1960s utilize birch for bodies and sometimes necks. Most commonly

Montgomery Ward 1930/1931 catalogue listing for the "Diamond Head" guitar (on right). Courtesy Gerry Clarke.

used these days for plywood, birch is an American wood that, while not as attractive as mahogany or rosewood, was plentiful and cheap. As we show within these pages, Regal (and other manufacturers such as Oscar Schmidt, Harmony and Kay, to name a few) utilized all these methods to produce a large number of low-cost stringed instruments.

This sub-section deals with some of the "birch beauties" (my label) that Regal produced in great numbers over the course of its entire history. There's nothing scientific in my choice of these models over others. They just seemed to "rise to the surface" above all the other thousands of stringed instruments produced in Regal's Chicago factory. And, in case you hunger for more, scroll on over to the Ukulele chapter where there's a whole raft of painted birch-bodied gems.

So, sit back and enjoy a troll through (as my friend Lynn Michael would say) "birch, the forgotten tone wood."

Vinyl Fingerboard

Summary

Instrument: Flattop guitar.

Model: "The Diamond Head."

Years Made: 1930-1934.

Brand(s): Regal.

Quality: Low grade (but who cares?).

Special Features: Vinyl "pyroxylin" fingerboard, two color silkscreen of Diamond Head on top.

Woods: Spruce over mahogany, spruce over birch (1934), "hardwood" neck.

Measurements: Scale length 24 7/8", nut width 1 and 13/16", upper bout 10", lower bout 14 1/8", end pin depth 4".

Logos Used: Medallion Regal headstock decal.

Known Original List Price: $4.50-22.50 retail, $16.00 wholesale.

I'm cheating a little bit by starting off this section of "birch beauties" with a spruce over walnut-shaded birch guitar more commonly made with a mahogany back and sides. Called alternately "The Diamond Head" or the "Volcano," Regal made this "Two-in-one Guitar" (i.e.: it could be set up either for regular "Spanish" or, with a nut riser, "Hawaiian" lap playing) for sale through the Montgomery Ward catalogue. It even came with two different books so you could learn whichever style that suited you. If something about this guitar happens to look familiar, yes, the top silkscreen is just a rearranged version of the one used by Gibson for some of their Kel Kroydon instruments. Before you start concocting some sort of conspiracy theory about Regal and Gibson working together, it is a more likely scenario that both Regal and Gibson outsourced the silkscreening, which was applied after the body was finished, to the same shop. This ladder-braced guitar also came with Regal's two-piece vinyl "pyroxylin" twenty fret fingerboard. Just apply a light pearl-colored piece of vinyl to the fingerboard, cover certain frets with dark colored vinyl with cut-out patterns, and, "viola," instant inlay. Some even had palm trees "inlayed" into their headstocks utilizing the same method (just the cost-saving measure needed to weather the Depression). To finish off this twelve fret to the body slot-headed guitar, the soundhole, top and back were bound with black fibre. As the Depression worsened, mahogany turned to birch with a basswood neck, the binding became white paint, the fingerboard ebonized, and the number of frets was reduced to eighteen.

Luckily for us, Regal utilized their vinyl fingerboard treatment for other instruments as well (and these are all true "birch beauties"). There was the "Regal Silver Spray" flattop mandolin, which, along with a vinyl (some used a celluloid plastic called "pyralin") fingerboard, featured a rose decalcomania on its black and yellow sunburst top, and red painted top and soundhole binding. And guitar models too numerous to mention also got the vinyl treatment both during the Great Depression and afterwards.

One worth discussing is the "Pagoda" guitar. Oriental motifs can be found in almost every decorative item (lamps and furniture, to mention two) from the 1920s up through the 1950s. This craze slopped over to musical instruments, and Regal (and their competitors) made several different models with oriental-themed decoration. The all birch "Pagoda" had twelve fret to its small six string or three quarter-size tenor black lacquered body (it came both ways), with the "scene" in silver or multiple colors and painted white or red binding. Mostly, these came with a white "pearlette" (i.e.: plastic) "MOTS" fingerboard, but there are surviving examples with the vinyl board from the "Volcano" guitar. Another is the related "Gondolier," with its vinyl fingerboard and all birch body covered with, as the catalogues put it, "artistically stenciled decoration portraying a realistic scene of a Gondolier rowing through the streets of Venice." Italy, here we come!

Le Domino

Summary

Instrument: Flattop guitar.

Model: "Le Domino."

Years Made: 1930-1934.

Brand(s): Regal.

Quality: Poor.

Special Features: Decalcomania dominos.

Woods: Birch or spruce over birch, birch or maple neck.

Measurements: 13 ½" wide lower bout, scale 24 5/8", nut width 1 ¾.

Logos Used: Paper soundhole label, "Le Domino" headstock decal.

Known Original Wholesale List Price: $12.75-$15.00.

Regal acquired the "Le Domino" brand from the defunct J. R. Stewart Company, a Chicago-based manufacturer that didn't survive the first year of the Depression. Stewart began making their line of "Le Domino" brand instruments in 1926. They all had birch bodies finished in black. The "Le Domino" model guitars, mandolins, banjos and ukuleles all were decorated with decalcomania, that is, outsourced domino decals applied as fingerboard markers, body binding, rosettes and headstock logos. When Regal took over the "Le Domino" trademark, they kept making ukuleles (see Chapter Nine for a photograph of one), banjo ukuleles, mandolins (at least until 1936), tiples, and four string tenor and six string flattop guitars (or selling off Stewart's stock of them complete with the J. R. Stewart logo!). The flattop and tenor, which Regal discontinued when they began making the "Big Boy" (see Chapter Eight) in 1934, was a twelve fret to the body slot head with an eighteen fret ebonized fingerboard, three-on-a-plate tuners, and a pin bridge on a ladder-braced top.

Buck Jones and Other Cowboy Guitars

Summary

Instrument: Flattop guitar.

Model: "Buck Jones," "Jerry Smith"/"Hop Along Cassidy" and others.

Years Made: 1937-1950+ (all models), 1940-1943 (Buck Jones).

Brand(s): Regal, Montgomery Ward.

Quality: Low grade (but collectible!).

Special Features: Stenciled/silkscreened Western scenes on front of body.

Woods: Birch.

Measurements: "Buck Jones": 37" by 13" and ¾ size 36" by 12" ("Concert Size"); "Smith"/"Cassidy": 25 1/4" scale, 15 3/16"-15 ½" lower bout, 11 5/16" upper bout, 4 1/16" deep at end, nut =1 and 13/16" ("Auditorium Size").

Logos Used: Regal green and blue w/multiple colors headstock decals, stenciled "Regal" in white on headstock.

Known Original List Price: $4.88-$7.95 retail ("Buck Jones"), $13.50-$22.00 wholesale ("Smith"/"Cassidy")

From the 1930s through the 1950s, the image of the cowboy was a dominant one in American culture. Every Saturday, little buckaroos would crowd the movie theatres across the country for the latest installment of their heroes' adventures. These cinematic idols and their ilk made the effortless jump to television when it took over America's entertainment needs in the 1950s.

And, many of these cowboy stars were also musical stars. Those like Gene Autry and Roy Rodgers always carried their guitars and were likely to break into song when there was a break in the action. So, it was only natural that partnerships between those cowboy performers and the companies that made their guitars became prevalent. The performers themselves favored real, high end models aimed to boast sales among their adult audiences. However, there were also low-cost models made for their young followers. These were made of birch and featured western scenes and/or pictures of their heroes silkscreened or painted on the front.

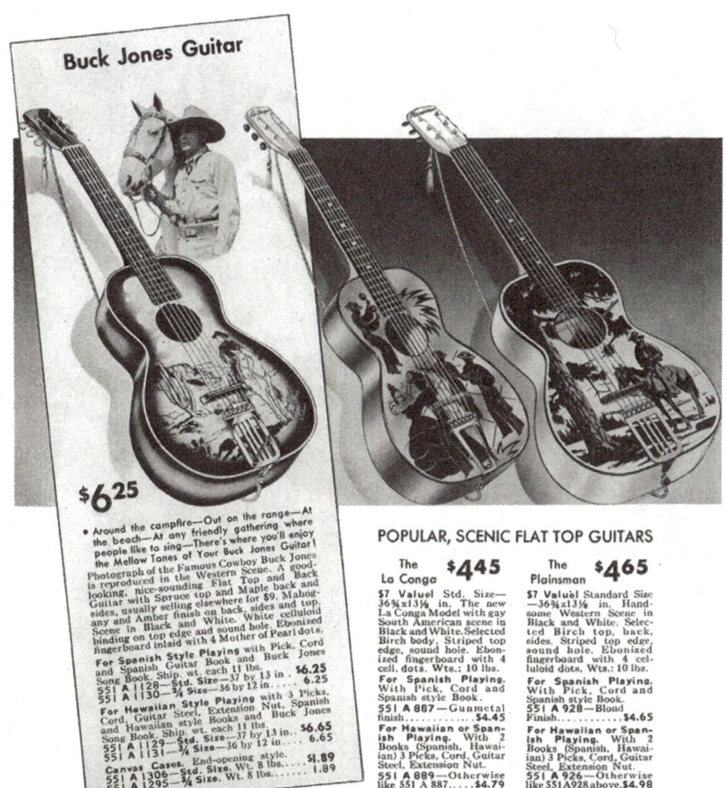

Montgomery Ward Fall/Winter 1941 catalogue listing for the "Buck Jones" and other models of "cowboy" guitars. Courtesy Gerry Clarke.

The king of these "cowboy" guitars was the Harmony Company of Chicago, who made countless models sold through another Chicago concern, Sears. Regal, which ran far behind Harmony, still made a number of popular models. Michael Wright, in his chapter on "Cowboy Guitars" in the Vintage Guitars book, lists eight different possible Regal-made "cowboy" guitars,

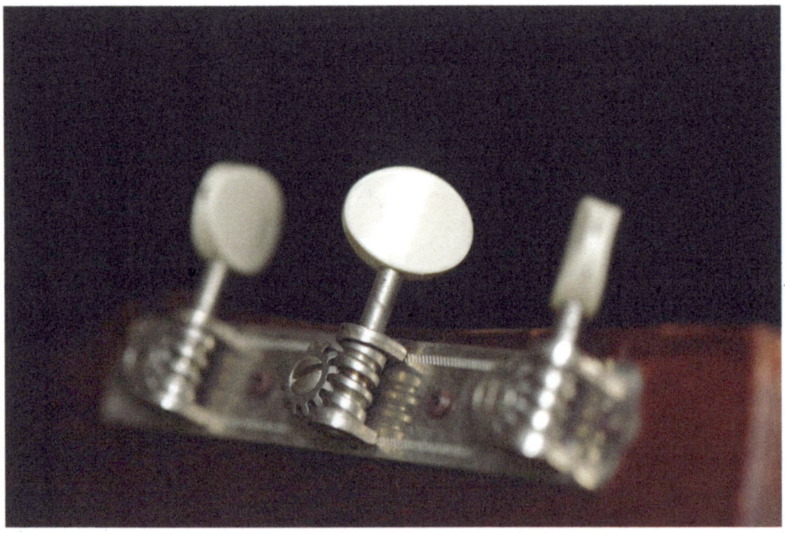

Unusually large-size "cowboy" guitar, the "Jerry Smith/ Hop Along Cassidy" model. Close-ups of body illustration, headstock and tuners.

four of which sold through Montgomery Ward under its house brand. Two of the best known were the Montgomery Ward "Buck Jones" and the Regal "Smith"/"Cassidy."

Charles "Buck" Jones (1891-1942), was a cowboy movie star. He started in silent movies as a stuntman, eventually working his way up to starring roles in the 1920s. Jones made the transition to sound westerns, and his career was only cut short by his untimely death at the end of 1942. The Montgomery Ward guitar featured Buck on his horse riding through a desert scene rendered in two colors. Little cowboys could fire their Daisy "Buck Jones" model air rifle and then strum their Montgomery Ward "Buck Jones" guitar "around the campfire, out on the range, at the beach, [or] at any friendly gathering where people like to sing" as the 1941 Ward's catalogue advertised (see illustration).

The original 1940 "Buck Jones" guitar came in both "standard" and "3/4" sizes, had a maple top and soundhole with celluloid binding, an ebonized fingerboard and the nickel or chrome plated tuner "valve" covers used on all Regal models made for Ward during the War years. The guitar had twelve frets to the body, a solid headstock and eighteen frets total. By the last model in the spring/summer of 1943, the top had become spruce and the bridge had changed from a floating bridge/tailpiece arrangement to a pin bridge held down by two screws.

The other notable Regal cowboy guitar has been sometimes called the "Jerry Smith, the Yodeling Cowboy" or "Hop Along Cassidy" guitar. Featuring a cowboy on a raised steed, cactus and a Cassidy-style cowboy hat, this guitar was offered by Regal from sometime (probably late) in the 1940s through the 1950s. It came in two sizes, "Standard" and "Auditorium," with various finishes and single top color stencil/silkscreen on its birch body, three-on-a-plate tuners, and one of three different headstock logos.

Faux Wood Grained

Summary

Instrument: Flattop guitar.

Model: Faux wood grained.

Years Made: 1939.

Brand(s): Regal, South Sea Islands Studios, Ball McIntire, Griffin.

Quality: Low grade.

Special Features: Painted faux wood graining on body.

Woods: Probably birch.

Measurements: "Concert Guitar" 13 1/8" lower bout, 3 5/8" deep at endpin; "Auditorium Guitar" 15 ½" by 19 ½."

Logos Used: Paper soundhole label, green headstock decal.

Known Original Wholesale List Price: $7.50-$9.50.

Everything in the world of guitars is not as it seems. These gorgeously-grained twelve fret to the body slot or solid headed guitars are imposters of the lowest sort. They all feature "pattern inlaid wood tops" of painted faux woodgraining, ebonized fingerboard, "stenciled panel," eighteen total frets, rectangular ebonized bridge attached to the top with two screws, painted white binding around top and soundhole, painted white fingerboard markers and three-on-a-plate tuners. The guitar was available in both round and square neck models, with the square necks having painted fret numbers on the treble side of the fingerboard.

And, 'beware' as other makers used similar patterns on their own guitars.

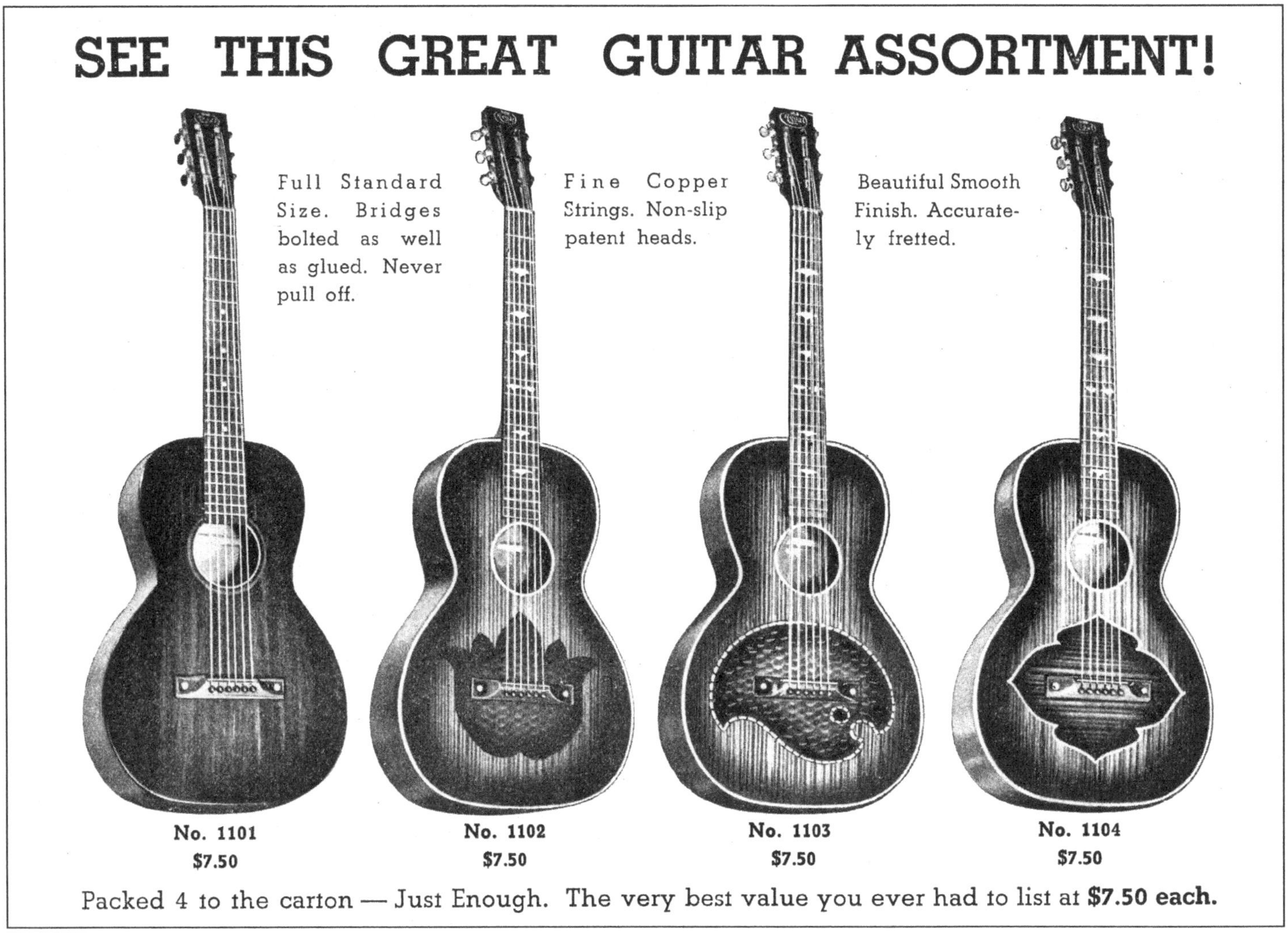

A page of additional faux wood-grained guitars from Regal's 1939 catalogue.

Is It A Kay or Is It A Regal?

One of the hardest conundrums to unravel is the connection between Kay, Regal and the Oahu Publishing Company of Cleveland, Ohio. Oahu utilized, through a very clever pyramid scheme, its network of teachers to sell instruments, sheet music and accessories, as well as recruit students that became other teachers that sold instruments, sheet music and accessories. Oahu hid the outsourcing of their manufacturing, and then featured a photograph in their catalogues of the Kay factory with "Oahu" pasted over the Kay sign to complicate the ruse. It is well-known that Kay made the majority of Oahu's guitar offerings of the 1930s, a fact that Michael Wright has written about in his book Guitar Stories Volume Two (Vintage Guitar Books, 2000). However, a number of Oahu guitars that appear to have been made during that decade have turned up with Regal labels. Did Regal share some of its models with Oahu because Kay couldn't keep up with Oahu's demands? Did Kay and Regal's sharing of parts and resources lead to these Oahu models? Or, did Kay make these guitars for both Regal and Oahu (which seems unlikely)? Let's review the evidence and try to unravel the mystery below.

This young lady seems pleased to be holding a Regal faux wood-grained guitar in this snapshot from 1948.

Oahu Faux Painted

Summary

Instrument: Flattop guitar.

Model: "MOTS," faux painted rosewood pattern.

Years Made: 1930-1934.

Brand(s): Regal, Oahu.

Quality: Low grade.

Special Features: "Mother-of-toilet-seat" ("MOTS") plastic fingerboard and headstock with matching pickguard, faux painted birch back and sides to resemble rosewood, large neck with Hawaiian setup on some models.

Woods: Spruce over birch, poplar/basswood neck.

Measurements: 13" lower bout, 9 ¼" upper bout, 1 and 13/16" nut width, 24 1/4" scale length, 3 ¾" deep.

Logos Used: Regal or Oahu paper soundhole label, Regal or Oahu metal headstock badge.

Known Original Wholesale List Price: $13.50-$15.00.

One "over-the-top" guitar that comes labeled either "Oahu" or "Regal" serves up a lot of flash but ultimately not much substance. This small bodied guitar came with a ladder-braced spruce top; faux rosewood-grained birch back and sides; matching grey marbled pickguard and headstock overlay; white "pearlette" ("MOTS") fingerboard; green, white and black vines with flowers decalcomania that covers part of the pickguard; colored marquetry and white celluloid around the soundhole and top; ebonized rectangular bridge; decalcomania backstripe; white heelcap; three-on-a-plate tuners; and twelve frets to the body fingerboard with eighteen frets total. The slotted headstock is reminiscent of the classic "Stromberg-Voisinet" shape used by Kay in reverse (some have a regular-shaped slotted peghead) and the metal oval headstock nameplate reads either "The Mark of Better Instruments, Regal, Made by Regal Musical Instrument Co., Chicago" or "Honolulu Conservatory, Oahu, Of Music."

This 1935 group of holiday merry-makers includes a faux-finished Regal ala Oahu. Too bad Jim seems to only know banjo technique!

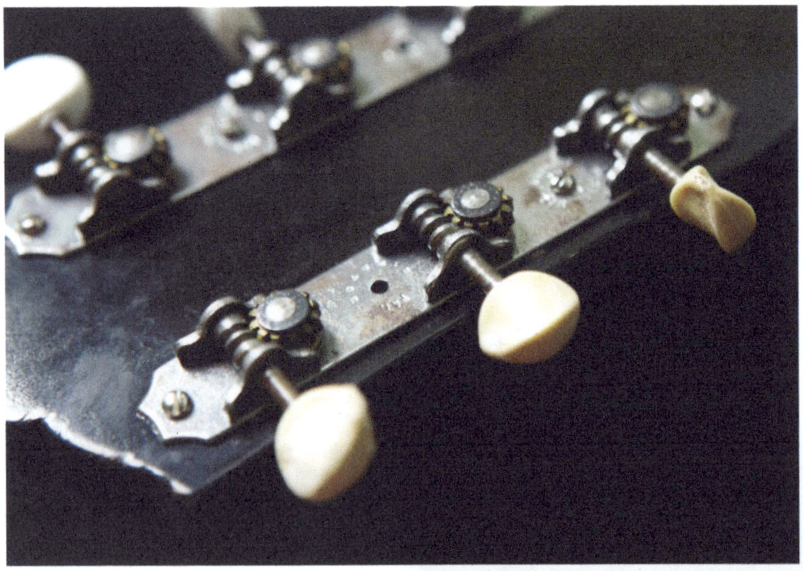

Oahu-style Regal, full front body view with close-ups of the Kluson tuners and headstock decal. Note the pickguard ala Washburn and "Jumbo" Recording King guitars made by Regal and the Oahu-style two-color vine silkscreen. The riveted tuner gears suggest that this guitar was made during World War II.

"Regahu" Models

Summary

Instrument: Flattop guitar.

Model: Regal Oahu.

Years Made: 1935-1939.

Brand(s): Regal, Kahlua, Associated Teachers.

Quality: Low to medium grade.

Special Features: Rounded, peaked trade mark Oahu headstock shape.

Woods: Various.

Measurements: Various.

Logos Used: "Kahlua" on white plastic headstock overlay, green headstock decal, paper soundhole label, blue with multiple colors headstock decal, "Associated Teachers" headstock stencil.

Known Original Wholesale List Price: $11.50 and $17.50 for two different models.

There are a number of different guitar models with either Regal or assorted other designations that sport a common variation of the "classic" Oahu headstock design. All look as if someone had taken an Oahu made by Kay and badly traced the headstock curves, eliminating all subtlety and beauty from the design.

The ones labeled "Regal" include an all mahogany twelve fret to the body "Standard Size" guitar in the 1939 Regal catalogue, a late 1940s/1950s natural spruce topped, mahogany back and sides square neck with Waverly three-on-a-plate tuners and a Regal pickguard that measures 15 ¼ inches at the lower bout and 4 ¼ inches deep at the end pin, as well as three late 1930s-1940s large square necked Hawaiians with Oahu gold and black silkscreened vines and flowers on the lower bout of the body (one with a Regal pickguard) of either spruce over mahogany or all mahogany construction. The one shown has a shaded two-piece ladder-braced spruce top, mahogany back and sides, rectangular screwed bridge, maple square neck with a ebonized fingerboard and the Oahu body vine silkscreen. It measures 1 and 13/16" at the nut, 11 and 1/8" upper bout, 15 ¼" lower bout, 3 13/16" deep at the endpin and has a 25 ½" scale.

Gibson Shapes, Regal-made

When Regal began shifting its guitars over from the older, ladder-braced Victorian parlor-style to the modern, "X" braced steel string instruments, they first created versions of Martin's 0 and 00 styles. Regal's next step was toward larger and different body shapes and a fourteen fret to the body, twenty fret fingerboard. And their guitars started to look a lot like Gibson's.

Both manufacturers had been providing Montgomery Ward with instruments for its retail catalogue throughout the 1930s. Later in the 1930s, after Regal Musical Instrument had begun referencing Gibson in their guitar making, Regal and Gibson were both involved making the Tonk Bros. Washburn line. So, they had a related history outside of these referential guitars.

Groton GUITARS

GROTON NO. 1

Fortunate indeed is the beginning guitarist who starts his studies on a Groton Model B & D Guitar. Only a few dollars more than the cheapest commercial grade instrument in cost the Groton No. 1 has the tone action and feel of a fine instrument—one which will speed the student's progress materially. Auditorium size, back and sides of selected mahogany, top of close-grained spruce, neck of three-ply construction to prevent warping, large, easy action frets, fine hand-rubbed satin finish.

Price $15.00
Challenge, keratol case 5.50

GROTON NO. 2

A Super Auditorium size guitar suitable for high grade amateur and even professional plectrum style playing, an unusually fine value at its modest price. Back and top are both arched, the back and sides being of selected mahogany, the top carved and hand shaped to a beautiful arch from selected spruce, seasoned and treated for sounding board purposes. Body bound top and bottom with white celluloid, the neck is of three-ply laminated wood, with fine rosewood fingerboard jointing body at 14th fret. Hand rubbed satin finish over blended shading of natural mahogany and shaded top; bracket type guardplate of heavy tortoise celluloid. Beautifully decorated, clean and sturdy workmanship throughout.

Price $25.00
Archcraft keratol case 9.50

Groton No. 1 KG-11 body shaped guitar, with Groton No. 2 archtop (see Chapter Eight). CMI catalogue, 1937, courtesy The National Music Museum.

KG-11 Shape

Summary

Instrument: Flattop guitar.

Model: Gibson Kalamazoo KG-11 body shape.

Years Made: 1935-1955.

Brand(s): Regal, American Conservatory, Serenader, Washburn, Rannigan & Cummer Music Center, Recording King, Groton.

Quality: Medium grade.

Special Features: Ladder top bracing, electronic pickups in some models.

Woods: Spruce over mahogany, maple or birch, poplar neck or maple neck.

Measurements: 24 1/4″ scale, 1 and 13/16″ nut width, 15″-15 3/16″ lower bout, 3 3/4″-4″ deep.

Logos Used: "American Conservatory" in white silkscreen on headstock, B&J paper soundhole label, Serenader headstock decal, white "Groton" script on headstock, paper soundhole label, green headstock decal, white silkscreened "Rannigan & Cummer Music Center" on headstock, "Recording King" silkscreened in white on headstock, blue with multiple colors headstock decal, "Regal" stenciled on the headstock in white, "Regal" embossed on red marbled plastic headstock overlay.

Known Original List Price: $13.50-27.50 wholesale, $10.95-22.25 retail.

Regal began utilizing the "big bottomed" Gibson KG-11 body shape for their "full size" tenor guitars in 1931. Labeling the body shape "Grand Concert Size," Regal used it for their "Custom Built" line and its variants. However, Regal waited until 1935 to introduce its first "modern" six string guitar using the KG-11 shape and style.

The Regal "Junior" or "Junior Jumbo" started life looking very much like its Gibson counterpart, although the Regal's utilized a bigger body. The "Junior" came with a brown sunburst top; mahogany back and sides; white celluloid bound top, back and soundhole; fourteen fret to the body rosewood fingerboard; twenty total frets; rectangular rosewood bridge with two screws (late 1930s onward); and three-on-a-plate tuners. The tortoise pickguard on the "Junior Jumbo" resembles those used by Regal for "Washburn" and "American Conservatory" brands, a teardrop on the Regal and Recording Kings or, on the Groton, a "lobster claw" shape as used on the other Regal-made Bacon guitars. Possibly due to cost-cutting measures or the disruption in the supply of mahogany during World War II, Regal switched to maple back and sides with a poplar neck and ebonized fingerboard, headstock overlay and rectangular bridge by 1943. Wartime guitars also featured (as did those of other makers) tops made up of small multiple pieces of wood. After the War, the mahogany back and sides had returned for some models, along with a rosewood fingerboard and bridge. Three-on-a-plate tuners were supplied by Kluson and Regal also added a black finish to the back of their headstocks in a triangular pattern with a natural finish neck and black heel. Starting in 1939, the "standard" Regal headstock shape was a "paddle" with a subtle curve at the top ending in a slight rounded point, used most notably on guitars branded "Playtime Deluxe." Square neck Hawaiian models were added, which were only twelve frets to the body and eighteen frets total. And fingerboards became bound in white celluloid.

The last of the "Junior Jumbos" came with a natural finish top and many or all of them may have been "parts guitars" assembled by Harmony after buying Regal's assets in the mid-1950s. A number have the

Branded 'Rannigan & Cummer Music Center," this KG-11-shaped guitar was made by Regal, and comes complete with pickup. Photograph/courtesy Goldtone Instruments Inc.

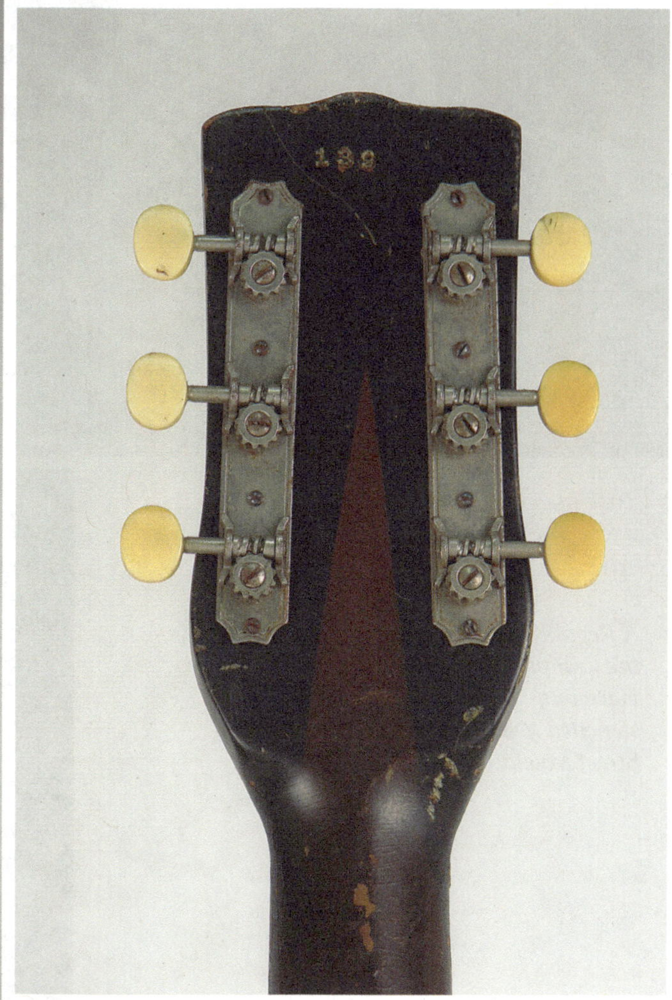

Branded 'Rannigan & Cummer Music Center," this KG-11-shaped guitar was made by Regal, and comes complete with pickup. Photograph/courtesy Goldtone Instruments Inc.

A Regal KG-11-style guitar made late in the Company's history and finished by Harmony. Note the Harmony bridge and stenciled headstock logo. Courtesy Lark Street Music.

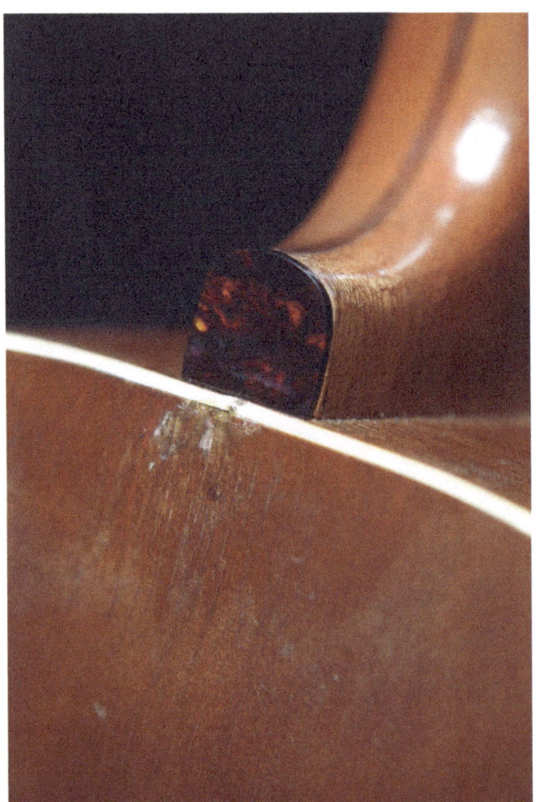

Harmony "bat winged" bridge and headstock shape (see photos), and some have necks that look as if they were made for an archtop guitar.

Over the twenty years that Regal used this body shape, the same basic guitar was sold under a myriad of labels through a number of different companies. Tonk Bros. distributors of Chicago first listed the "American Conservatory" brand (a trade name purchased by Regal from Lyon & Healy through Tonk) version of this guitar in 1935 and Regal also made the Tonk Bros. Washburn variety (another former Lyon & Healy brand), the Style 5240 (aka: the "Junior"), in 1937 and 1938. The Bacon Banjo Company offered their "Groton No. 1" guitar between 1936 and 1937, B&J in New York City sold a model utilizing the "Serenader" trade name and the "Regal Junior Jumbo" appeared in the Montgomery Ward catalogue in 1943 and 1945, as well as in Regal's own starting in 1939.

KG-11 Shape: "Rhumba," "Gipsy," "Bolero"

Summary

Instrument: Flattop guitar.

Model: "Rhumba," "Gipsy," "Bolero."

Years Made: 1937.

Brand(s): Regal.

Quality: Low grade.

Special Features: Plastic headstock overlay with multi-colored Caribbean-influenced graphics.

Woods: Poplar neck, birch back.

Measurements: As above.

Logos Used: "Regal" painted on plastic headstock overlay.

Known Original Wholesale List Price: $11.00-$15.00.

Variations on the Regal "Junior Jumbo" were three models with a Caribbean influence. The "Gipsy" and "Rhumba" (spelled "Rumba" on the instrument's headstock and "Rhumba" in the catalogue listing) came with birch back and sides, "hardwood" neck, and floating bridge/tailpiece combination. The top on the "Gipsy" was probably also birch, although the "Rhumba" and "Bolero" came with spruce tops; soundhole, top and back bound with white celluloid; and a rosewood fingerboard. The "Bolero" added a bound fingerboard, rectangular rosewood pin bridge and a pickguard with a tropical scene. All came with a white plastic headstock overlay painted with the company name, guitar model and a dancer portraying the various model names. The two "Rhumba" guitars I've seen have a woman dancing on a sombrero in red, green, pink and black, "Regal" and "Rhumba" in black script on the peghead, a black painted back of the headstock, along with a white painted neck and sides.

Let's "Rumba!" Well, even if Regal's headstock overlay outsourcers couldn't spell, the guitar is still super cool. Besides the colorful overlay, dig the white painted sides and neck. Photographs/ courtesy Atomic Guitars.

KG-11 Shape: Radio-Tone Amplifying Guitar

Summary

Instrument: Flattop guitar.

Model: Radio-Tone Amplifying guitar.

Years Made: 1949.

Brand(s): Regal.

Quality: Low grade.

Special Features: Built-in metal amplifying device, radio wave decoration.

Woods: Spruce over "hardwood" or birch, all birch.

Measurements: Width 14", depth 3 3/4", scale length 25 1/4", nut width 1 3/4".

Logos Used: "Radio Tone" stenciled in white on headstock and etched into tailpiece.

Known Original Wholesale List Price: $22.00 and $37.50.

A third variant on the "Junior Jumbo" is the "Radio-tone Amplifying Guitar." These guitars look great but unfortunately are on the low end of the quality scale. Neither electric nor a true resophonic, these introductory-level Radio-Tones came in two models. Essentially the same instrument with or without the amplifying attachment, the only different appears to be that the "normal" guitar had a rectangular pin bridge and the "amplifying" guitar had the bridge built into its metal amplifier.

The body decoration features twin radio towers rising up from the tail end of the top with "lightening bolt" radio waves coming out above the single "Cyclops" soundhole screen, with this theme echoed on the headstock with more waves/bolts surrounding the stenciled logo. There is a metal plate/bridge assembly replacing (or mounted in) the soundhole, with a tailpiece holding down the strings. The fingerboard is made of rosewood, the top binding painted on as is the headstock overlay. The fourteen fret to the body round neck was joined at some point by a twelve fret square neck Hawaiian with eighteen total frets. All of the ones I've seen come in a natural finish except one birch sunburst example that closer to the "Rhumba" et al shown above.

REGAL STUDIO AND LESSON PLAN GUITARS

No. 510

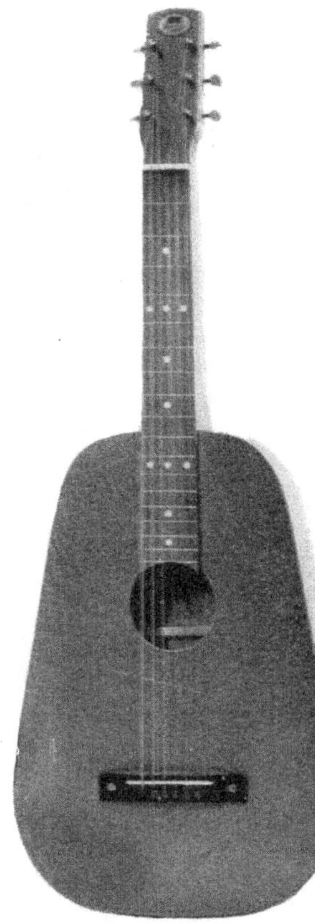

No. 511

No. 513

***Regal* Model No. 510 Guitar.** Conventional shape, standard size with a square or flat shaped neck for easy positioning upon the lap. Stenciled numbered frets to quickly guide the beginner. Two tone walnut color in a very durable lacquer finish. Sound hole and top edge decorated with white stripe. The pin type bridge is bolted to the top as well as being glued. It will not pull off. A sturdy instrument of selected hardwoods to withstand repeat usage. — **$13.50** each

Side opening, soft shell case...each **$6.00**

End opening, covert cloth bag, button fasteners...each **4.90**

***Regal* Model No. 511 Hawaiian type Guitar.** A grand new shape for studio use where something distinctly different is needed. Ideal for youngsters. Easy to hold. Good tone. Good looking. Glossy, metallic-like lacquer finish. A big value at our low price. — **$14.50** each

Challenge, side opening case to fit...each **$7.50**

***Regal* Model No. 513 Radio-tone Amplifying Guitar.** It's NEW! It's DYNAMIC! Loud tone without electrification. Built-in metallic amplifying device, beautifully engineered and heavily nickel plated. Adjustable bridge. Large orchestra size body. Attractively decorated with radio antenna design. Flashy tailpiece with built-in receptacle for owner's identifying name card. This instrument is just the thing for schools and studios. Fine side opening case included with each Guitar. — **$37.50** each

"It's NEW! It's DYNAMIC!" It's the Regal Model No. 513 Radio-tone Amplifying Guitar. From the Regal 1949 catalogue, courtesy Dennis Buchholz/Leaning Dog Guitars.

LG Style

Summary

Instrument: Flattop guitar.

Model: LG Gibson style.

Years Made: 1940s.

Brand(s): Regal, McKinney.

Quality: Medium grade.

Special Features: Ladder-braced.

Woods: Spruce over mahogany or birch, mahogany? or maple? neck.

Measurements: 4″ deep at the end pin, 24 3/8″ scale square neck, 25 ½″ scale round neck, 14″ lower bout, 1 7/8″ nut width on square neck, and 1 and 11/16″ nut width on round neck.

Logos Used: Paper soundhole label, green headstock decal, "McKinney" stenciled in white on headstock.

Known Original Wholesale List Price: N/A.

By the 1940s, Regal had followed Gibson into making an "LG" shaped guitar. The majority of the ones I've seen are twelve fret to the body/eighteen fret total Hawaiian square necks, but I've also owned a twenty fret, fourteen fret to the body round neck.

Both Hawaiian and "Spanish" versions feature a natural spruce top over mahogany back and sides (birch on one example), teardrop pickguard, rosewood fingerboard (ebonized on the birch guitar) and screwed on rectangular bridge, white bound soundhole and top, "Playtime" headstock shape, painted black headstock back with triangular pattern described above and soundhole rosette of black fine lines (see photos).

"B&D"

Since the birth of the "vintage" guitar market in the 1960s, there has always been a great deal of mystery surrounding the "B&D" flattop guitars marketed by the Bacon Banjo Company. Their mystique comes from a combination of rarity, quality of construction, as well as over-the-top appointments such as heavily engraved and colored "MOTS" ("mother of toilet seat," i.e.: plastic) headstocks and fingerboard inlays. Not the least of their fame comes from one of their most notable adapters, "Cosmic American Guitarist" John Fahey. At the height of his popularity, the late Fahey utilized a "B&D Senorita" for both recordings and performances. The iconic image of John Fahey holding the "Senorita" (shown here), strangely reversed by his record company, was known to a generation of guitar nerds, and still holds sway today.

In 1924, Martin made a few of their 0-18 model in a dark finish with the Bacon name in the peghead for sale through the Connecticut manufacturer. Bacon, primarily known for its banjos, did not offer guitars again until the introduction of their "S" series of banjos (so known because all model names began with an "S"), when they borrowed the "Senorita" name for their new line of flattop, Hawaiian and tenor guitars. From period catalogues and viewing surviving examples from the early 1930s, I do not believe these "Senorita" slot-headed twelve fret to the body flattop guitars, fifteen fret tenor guitars, or fourteen fret round and "F" holed archtop "Troubadours" were made by Regal. These instruments do not resemble concurrent Regal guitars nor the later Regal-made Bacons in construction details or in serial numbering.

Close-up details of a pair of Regal guitars with the Gibson "LG" body style.

A pair of Regal guitars, a twelve fret Hawaiian (right) and a fourteen fret to-the-body "regular" guitar (left), with the Gibson "LG" body style.

Senorita

Summary

Instrument: Flattop Guitar.

Model: "Senorita."

Years Made: 1935-1939.

Brand(s): "B&D."

Quality: High grade.

Special Features: Engraved "MOTS" headstock overlays, engraved "MOTS" fingerboard inlays, "lobster claw" pickguard shape.

Woods: Spruce over mahogany, spruce over rosewood.

Measurements: Scale length 25 3/8", lower bout 15 5/8", upper bout 11 5/16", depth at endpin 4 5/8", 1 and 13/16" nut width ("Super Auditorium"); 25 3/8" scale, 1 3/4" nut width, 4 1/2" deep, 15 1/4" lower bout, 11 and 1/2" upper bout ("Auditorium").

Logos Used: Blue paper "Bacon Banjo Co." soundhole label, "B&D" and "Bacon" on headstock.

Known Original Wholesale List Price: $50.00-$80.00.

The guitar (and guitarist) that started the Bacon "mystique," John Fahey, as he appeared in 1967, on the cover of his Vanguard LP, Requia (complete with backwards photograph). Photograph by Marvin Lyons, design by Murray Klein, courtesy Vanguard Records.

After hearing and seeing photographs of Fahey's Bacon, Tony Klassen of New Era Guitars acquired this "S-6," serial number 1019. Inspired by the Bacon, Tony is now building his own version of the "B&D Senorita S-6." Photographs/courtesy Tony Klassen/New Era Guitars.

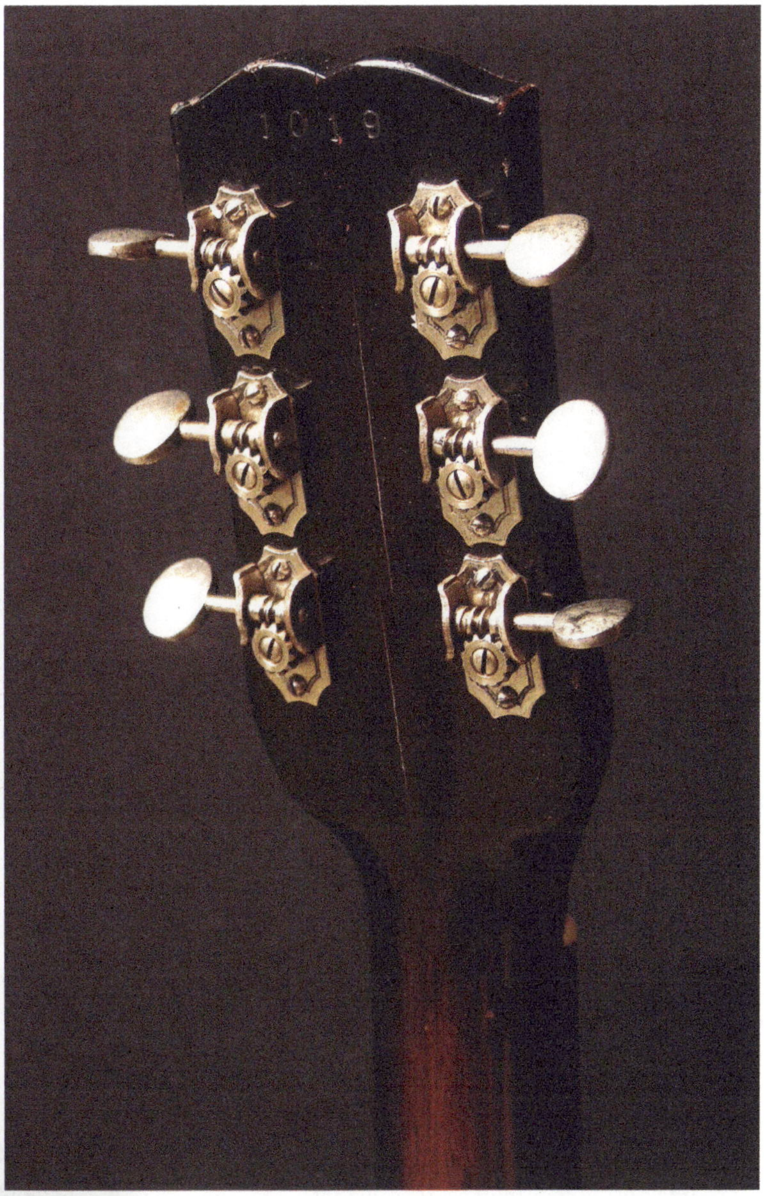
1019

BACON BANJO Co. Inc.
GROTON-CONN.
MFRS.
BANJOS, GUITARS and STRINGS

John Fahey's "B&D Senorita" guitar as it appears today. The pickguard, bridge and tuners are unoriginal. Photography by Sabsphotography.co.uk, courtesy Gary Melnyk.

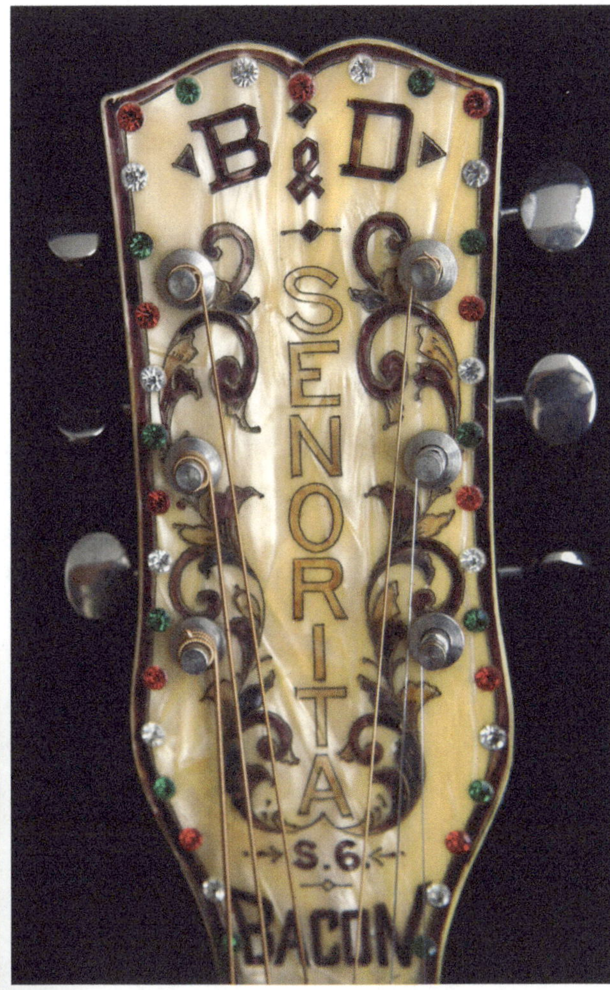

A "B&D S-6" (serial number 1147) built with the body shape of an S-1. Courtesy Lark Street Music.

Two models of the later Regal-made "B&D Senorita" guitars with the black plastic headstock overlay, an "S-1" (on top) and "S-6" (bottom), as shown in the CMI catalogue for 1937. Courtesy the National Music Museum.

"'Duke' and his 'Swingbillies,' WLAW, Lawrence, Mass."

By 1936, Bacon was advertising that "Bacon & Day Guitars introduce many exclusive, new features, improving greatly the accepted standards of tone quality, carrying power and durability of construction. The necks are of laminated woods, reinforced by full length steel bars, permitting warp-proof construction. Being much thinner than customary, they greatly facilitate execution."

Bacon offered four models of Regal-made flattop guitars. Besides the "Groton" "Junior Model," already discussed in the previous section, the "Senorita" came in three versions. The "S-1" was an "Auditorium" size guitar (on top in the catalogue photograph here), with back and sides made of mahogany. The "S-2" also featured mahogany back and sides, but was "Super

Roy Bookbinder with his later "B&D Senorita S-6." Photographer and date unknown, courtesy Roy Bookbinder.

Auditorium" sized, as was the "S-6," with rosewood back and sides (on the bottom in the catalogue photograph here). The "Auditorium" body shape is reminiscent of some other high-end Regal-made guitars featured in the next section, and the "Super Auditorium" body shape is similar if not the same as the Washburn Style 5244 produced for the Tonk Bros. by Regal. The 5244 even came with the "lobster-claw" pickguard found on the "Senorita" model Bacons.

The three transitional Regal-made "Senorita S-6" guitars shown here date from the mid-1930s. They all feature the out-sourced engraved "MOTS" with rhinestones headstock overlays ala Bacon's high-end banjos and block engraved fingerboard inlays found on "B&D" guitars from the first half of the 1930s, but substitute the Regal "heart-shaped" headstock, "lobster-claw" pickguard (one has an unoriginal guard), two piece back with backstripe, "X" braced top and the four digit serial numbers incised in the back of the headstock utilized by Regal. They all would have originally come with a rectangular rosewood bridge with compensated saddle; white top, soundhole and back celluloid binding; white celluloid heelcap; fourteen frets to the body; and twenty frets total. Since these all appear to have been made individually or at least in small batches, there are some minor differences between these three "S-6s." Most notably, the "Fahey" guitar does not say "S-6" on the headstock, and serial number 1147 is an "Auditorium" rather then a "Super Auditorium" sized guitar.

By 1936, Bacon had dropped the rhinestones and fancy "MOTS" for a simpler layered black with white letters headstock overlay and dot fingerboard inlays. The "S-2" also came as a twelve fret to the body, nineteen frets total Hawaiian with ladder bracing. These models were at least advertised through the collapse of the Bacon Banjo Company in 1939/1940, although it is difficult to tell how many were made. (Note: See the section below on the Regal "Jumbo" model for information about other late model "B&D" guitars.)

The Washburn Body Used On Other Regal Models

Summary

Instrument: Flattop guitar.

Model: Washburn Solo 5257 style body.

Years Made: 1937.

Brand(s): Regal, Radio Tone.

Quality: High grade.

Special Features: "MOTS" headstock overlay, pearl fingerboard bar inlays, deco headstock with disc overlay.

Woods: Spruce over rosewood.

Measurements: 15 1/4" lower bout, 11 and 1/2" upper bout, 4 1/2" deep, =25 3/4" scale, 1 7/8" nut width.

Logos Used: Regal script on headstock, "Radio Tone" in pearl on headstock, Radio Tone paper soundhole label.

Known Original Wholesale List Price: $100.00.

Along with the "B&D" and Washburn guitars, Regal made a handful of other high grade guitars in the late 1930s. These included a number of instruments that appear to use recycled parts from the Tonk's Washburn models.

One guitar combines the Washburn 5257 with a Montgomery Ward Recording King "Jumbo." The body comes from the 5257, complete with a Washburn-style pickguard, white celluloid bound soundhole, natural spruce top and two-piece rosewood back with black fine lines on top and around the soundhole, and back centerstripe of three gold lines. The fourteen fret to the body, twenty frets total rosewood fingerboard has a dot at five, seven, nine and twelve; the neck a white celluloid heelcap; the Recording King headstock shape is topped with a white "MOTS" headstock overlay with "Regal" and the Regal crown logo in black; and the back of the probably poplar or basswood neck is finished in black. As on the earlier Recording King "Jumbo," the tuners are Kluson three-on-a-plate with gears held on by slot-headed screws and amber opaque tuner buttons. The Regal/Recording King mahogany rectangular bridge is held on by a screw on each end covered with a white dot. Altogether, a very unusual and odd guitar.

The unknown musician with the Oklahoma Night Riders at the far right holds what appears to be a Regal-made Washburn 'Solo' Model 5257/5246. This body was utilized by Regal for a number of other high-end guitars branded with various names

Another high-end late-30's Regal utilizing a Washburn body is the "Custom Built" "Radio Tone" guitar. The Radio Tone brand was initially used for low-quality instruments sold by the Hawaiian Teachers Limited of Hollywood, California. Regal made these originally mail-order guitars, but it is unclear if the Hawaiian Teachers was actually a separate company or just a Regal-created phantom. By 1937, Radio Tone instruments were being listed in the Regal catalogue, including the high-end version shown here, and the Radio Tone name continued to be used by Regal for an "amplifying" guitar into the late 1940s (see above). The sunburst "X" braced spruce top of the "Radio Tone" is bound in white celluloid as is the soundhole and two-piece rosewood back. Black and gold fine lines accent the top, soundhole and backstripe. The fingerboard is ebony with groups of three vertical rectangular bars of pearl at frets three, five, seven, nine, twelve and fifteen, and bound in white. With fourteen frets to the body and twenty frets total, an ebony rectangular bridge, seven piece mahogany neck, ebony heel cap and individual tuners with metal buttons, this instrument is essentially a Washburn. Topping off this guitar is a pearl inlayed logo in the rosewood headstock overlay with "lightening bolt" radio waves emanating from the "Radio Tone" name.

Finally, there are the two guitars built for the musicians of WLS radio. Both Regal and WLS were located in Chicago and there was probably some type of relationship between the two firms.

One of the country stars of WLS in the 1930s was Myrtle "Lulu Belle" Cooper. Born December 24, 1913 in Boone, North Carolina, Lulu Belle began working with the singer "Red" Foley on the WLS National Barn Dance in 1932. In 1934, she married her new performing partner, "Skyland" Scotty Wiseman.

It is unclear when Lulu Belle began using Regal guitars. She is pictured in various WLS publications of the 1930s and 1940s with two different Washburn/Radio Tone-like instruments. The first is similar to the sunburst "Radio Tone" shown and described above. Both her first partner, "Red" Foley and Lulu are

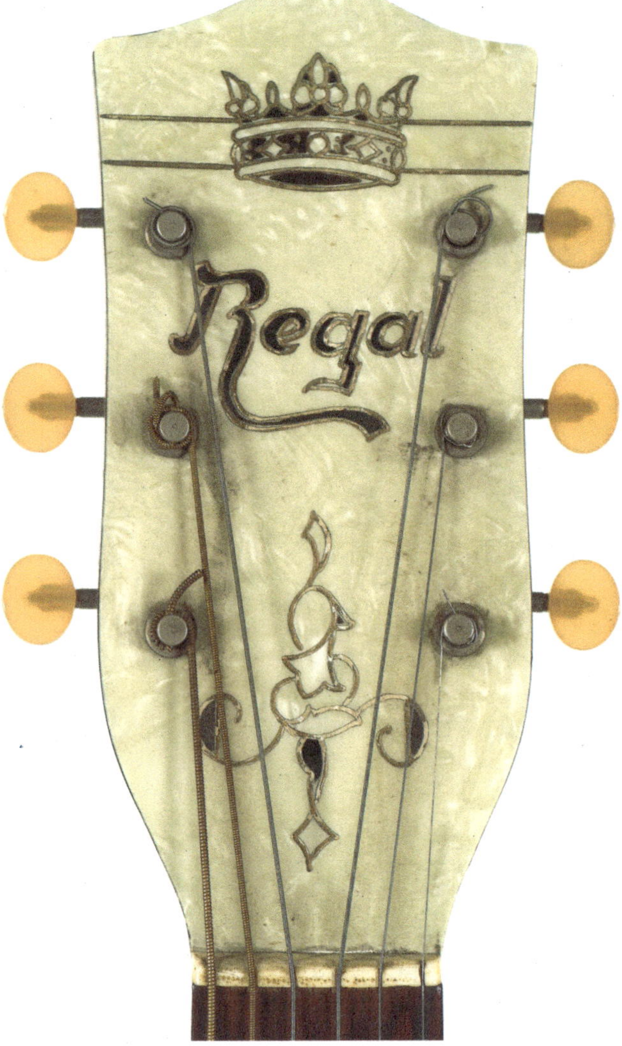

Here is just one example of a Washburn body, marked with the model number 5257, joined to a Regal-brand neck. Spruce top, rosewood back and sides ala Washburn join a neck of probably poplar, maple or basswood. Although the body (serial number 700) dates from circa 1935/1936, the tuners are typical of the first half of the 1940s, as is the plastic headstock overlay. Photography by Dave Matchette/Elderly Instruments, courtesy Stan Werbin.

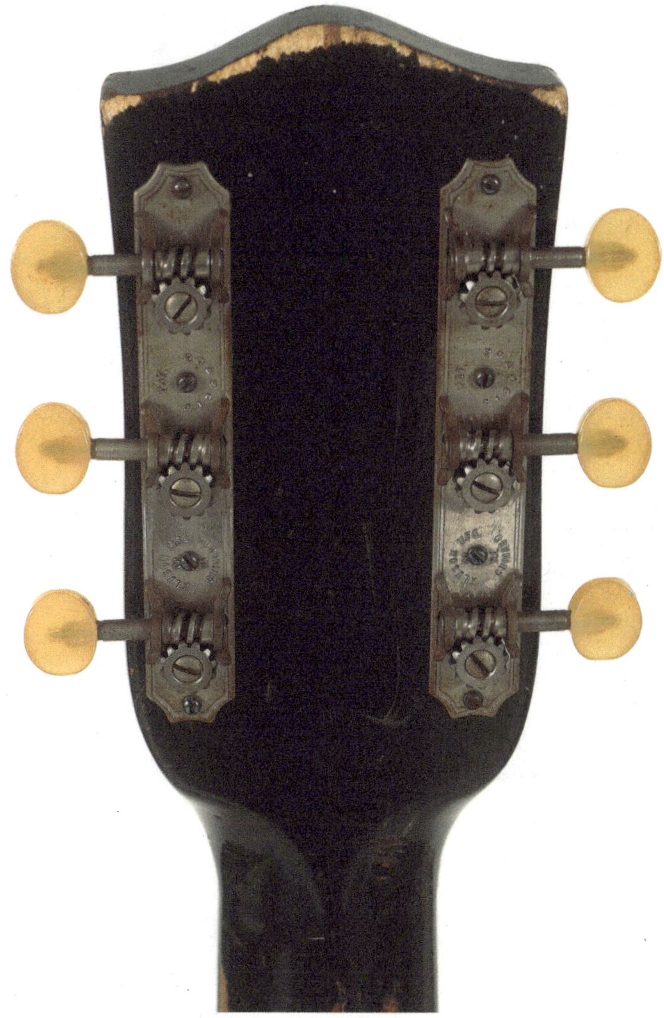

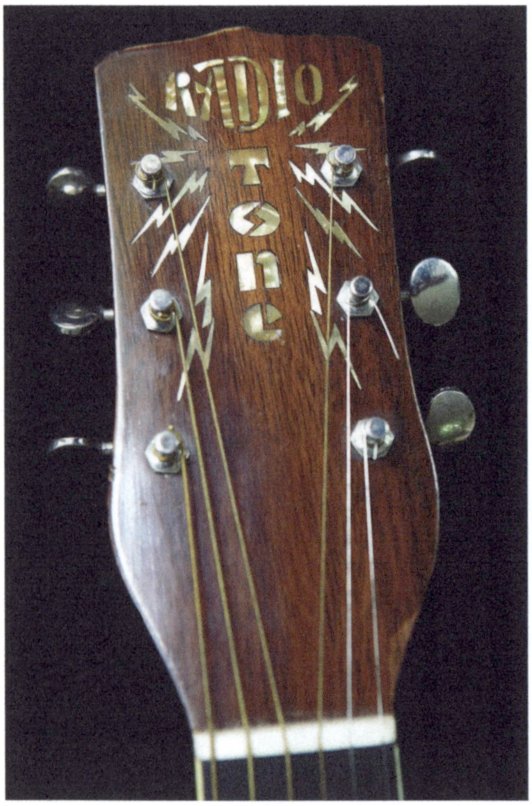

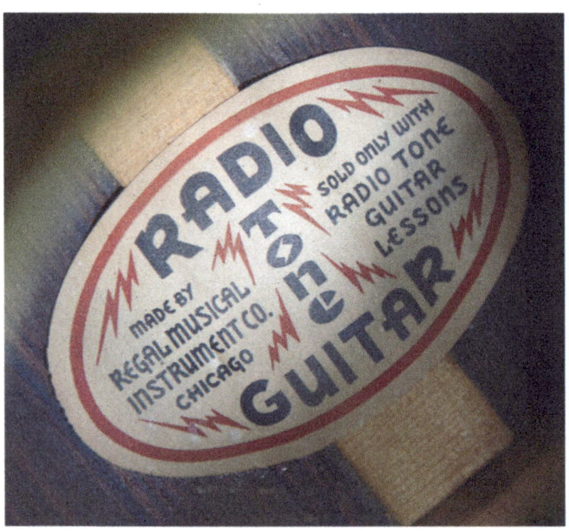

Another use of the Washburn body was on a high-grade "Radio Tone" guitar. Here, the body is sunburst and the headstock inlayed logo and lightning bolts/radio waves in pearl utilizes a related font to the Bacon instruments. Note the high end, individual tuners and art-deco fingerboard, also found on guitars made for the cast of WLS. Courtesy Randy Klimpert.

"Red" Foley, a pre-War star of the WLS Barndance heard over the Chicago airwaves, holds yet another example of a Washburn-bodied guitar with various other Regal parts, including the same fingerboard as the "Radio Tone" shown above. Photograph by "Theatrical/ Chicago," courtesy Richard Carlin.

Another performer with the same model (or same guitar) as pictured with "Red" Foley is "Lulu Belle" Wiseman. Before marrying Scotty Wiseman (pictured on the right with the banjo), "Lulu Belle" partnered with "Red" Foley, who may have passed the guitar onto her and/or made the connection with Regal. A better view of the guitar"s unusual curved headstock and medallion, which appears to have been adapted from an experimental archtop design, can be seen in this photograph. From the Illinois State Fair, possibly August 15, 1936, 1937 WLS Yearbook, courtesy Richard Carlin.

Same gal, same model of guitar, but in a natural finish. As this publicity photograph appeared in many publications, it's a bit hard to date it and the instrument. The earliest I've seen the photo is in 1943, but the date Scotty's model banjo was introduced (1937) might be closer to when the guitar was built.

(below) Close-up detail.

shown with, if not the same guitar, then the same model. Because the photo of Cooper, by then married to Scotty Wiseman, appears to be from the Illinois State Fair of 1936, the sunburst model must date from around that time. The second Regal guitar is identical except that it has a natural finish. It must be later because not only do Lulu Belle and Scotty look older and Scott Wiseman holds a newer banjo, but the publication date of the photograph are later as well. The guitar was probably made sometime in the late 1930s. Both guitars, while using Washburn/Radio Tone bodies, have the "Radio Tone" fingerboard along with a completely unusual headstock crowned with what looks to be a metal disc held on by two metal bands.

Crate

Summary

Instrument: Flattop guitar.

Model: "Crate."

Years Made: 1935-1936.

Brand(s): Regal, Montgomery Ward.

Quality: Low grade.

Special Features: Body made from packing crate.

Woods: Birch.

Measurements: N/A.

Logos Used: N/A.

Known Original Retail List Price: $2.95.

Before Lulu Belle began playing a high-end Regal, she posed with a home-made looking guitar for the WLS Family Album of 1935. Her instrument had a slotted, classical headstock and body imprinted with the message "Fragile, Handle With Care, From Regal Musical" as if it were assembled from a packing crate. Montgomery Ward offered the same instrument for sale in their spring/summer 1936 catalogue, although theirs had a solid headstock, painted top and soundhole binding and an ebonized fingerboard. "Easy to Hold," advertised Ward, "helps you to learn more rapidly, because you can give more attention to your playing. Lighter—makes playing less fatiguing." There is at least one surviving example that has a silkscreened vine on the lower top bout in white.

To show her rural roots, "Lulu Belle" dressed and acted "country" and initially appeared with this handmade-looking "packing crate" guitar. In reality, the instrument was a part of the Regal line. WLS Family Album, 1935.

This unidentified band from rural Virginia includes a Recording King "Jumbo" second from the right.

CLIFF CARLISLE

Country singer Cliff Carlisle with a Regal Recording King "Jumbo." From Hillbilly Hit Parade of 1945.

Jumbo

Summary

Instrument: Flattop guitar.

Model: "Jumbo," "Milord," "Inspiration."

Years Made: 1939-1951.

Brand(s): Regal, Recording King (1940-1944), "B&D," Herrick's (1941), Washburn (1937-1939).

Quality: Medium grade.

Special Features: Double "X" braced.

Woods: Spruce over mahogany, one example maple or birch, mahogany or poplar/basswood neck.

Measurements: 5" deep at end block, 15 5/8" lower bout, 11 5/8" upper bout, 1 ¾" width at nut, 25 ½" scale.

Logos Used: Recording King silkscreen on headstock, green headstock decal, "B&D" on "MOTS" headstock overlay or in pearl script, paper soundhole label "Custom Built," "Washburn" in pearl in headstock.

Known Original List Price: $48.00-$60.00 wholesale, $19.95-$24.95 retail.

After learning the ins and outs of solid headstock, fourteen fret to the large bodied guitars through their relationship with Washburn and Bacon, Regal made their final leap into the modern age by introducing their slope-shouldered dreadnaught "Jumbo" guitar in 1939. "Big Custom Built Bodies!" wrote Regal's copywriter in their 1939 catalogue. "Rich Quality! Powerful Tone! So Beautiful You Can Hardly Believe Their Low Price!" Obviously referencing Gibson's "J" line (Jumbo, J-35, J-45 etc), Regal's "Jumbo" was offered through Montgomery Ward under the "Recording King" brand, through the Regal catalogue, and also used for a few "one offs" for Bacon and others.

The "Jumbo" came with a solid headstock (slotted on the early Hawaiian models); rosewood fingerboard, rectangular bridge with two screws and headstock overlay (on the Recording Kings, black painted on the Regals); white celluloid bound top, fingerboard, soundhole and heelcap; twenty total frets (eighteen on one Hawaiian example); as well as a mahogany sunburst neck with a maple "truss rod" (switched to poplar in 1943 probably due to wartime shortages); and three-on-a-plate tuners with "valve" tuner covers. The pickguard was quite large and shaped like those used for some of the Regal-made Washburns from the same decade. The Regal versions of the "Jumbo" came in a natural finish with rectangular block fingerboard inlays, while the ones made for Ward were sunburst with large dots on the fingerboard and "strap hangers" at the headstock and endpin. Depending on their year of manufacture, affecting the availability of materials, some "Jumbos" had single or multi-piece tops and what appears to be single, multiple piece or veneered backs, not unlike what their counterparts at Gibson were doing in order to utilize whatever woods they could acquire at the time. The "Jumbo" came in both a twelve fret square neck model for Hawaiian lap playing and a fourteen fret round neck for regular guitar style.

The most interesting feature of the large bodied "Jumbo" was the use of two interlocking "X" braces to support the top (see diagram). Other companies, such as Harmony, also utilized this simple bracing system that saved time and materials.

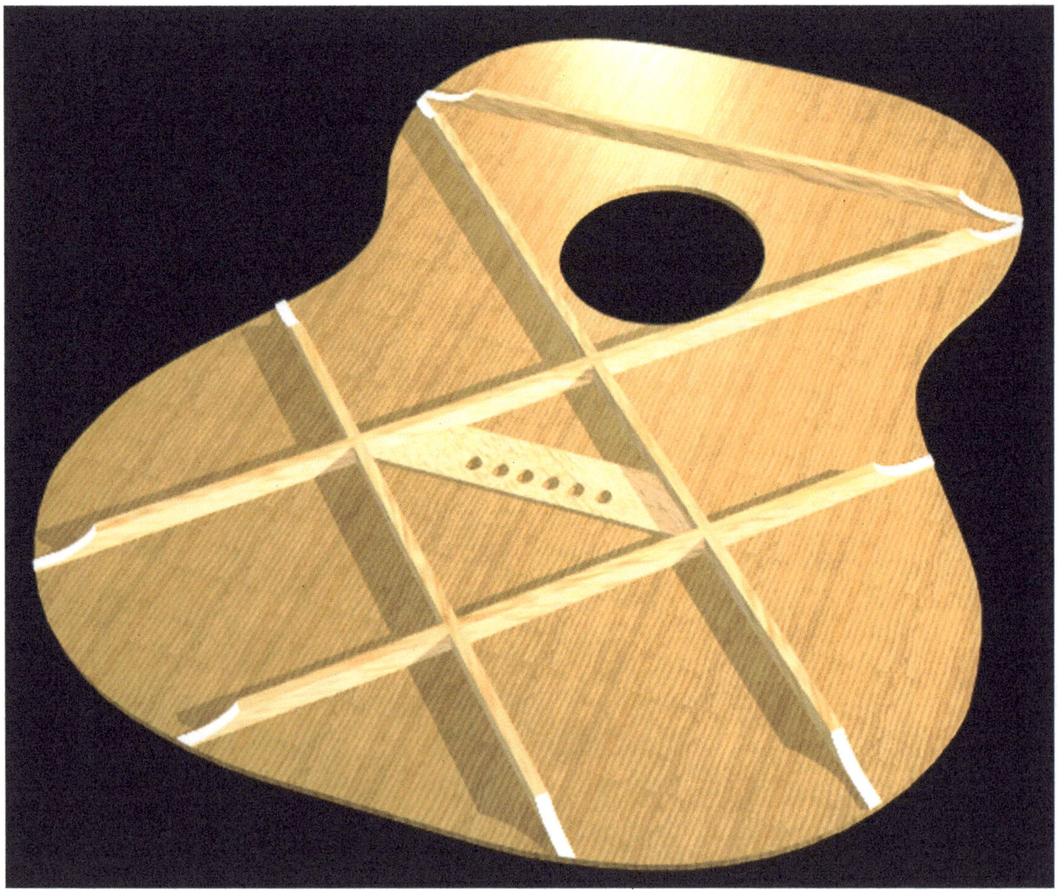

The "double X" bracing pattern used by Regal for their "Jumbo" guitar. This method of supporting the top saved time and materials and helped to stabilize the top of the guitar. Drawing by Aaron Morris.

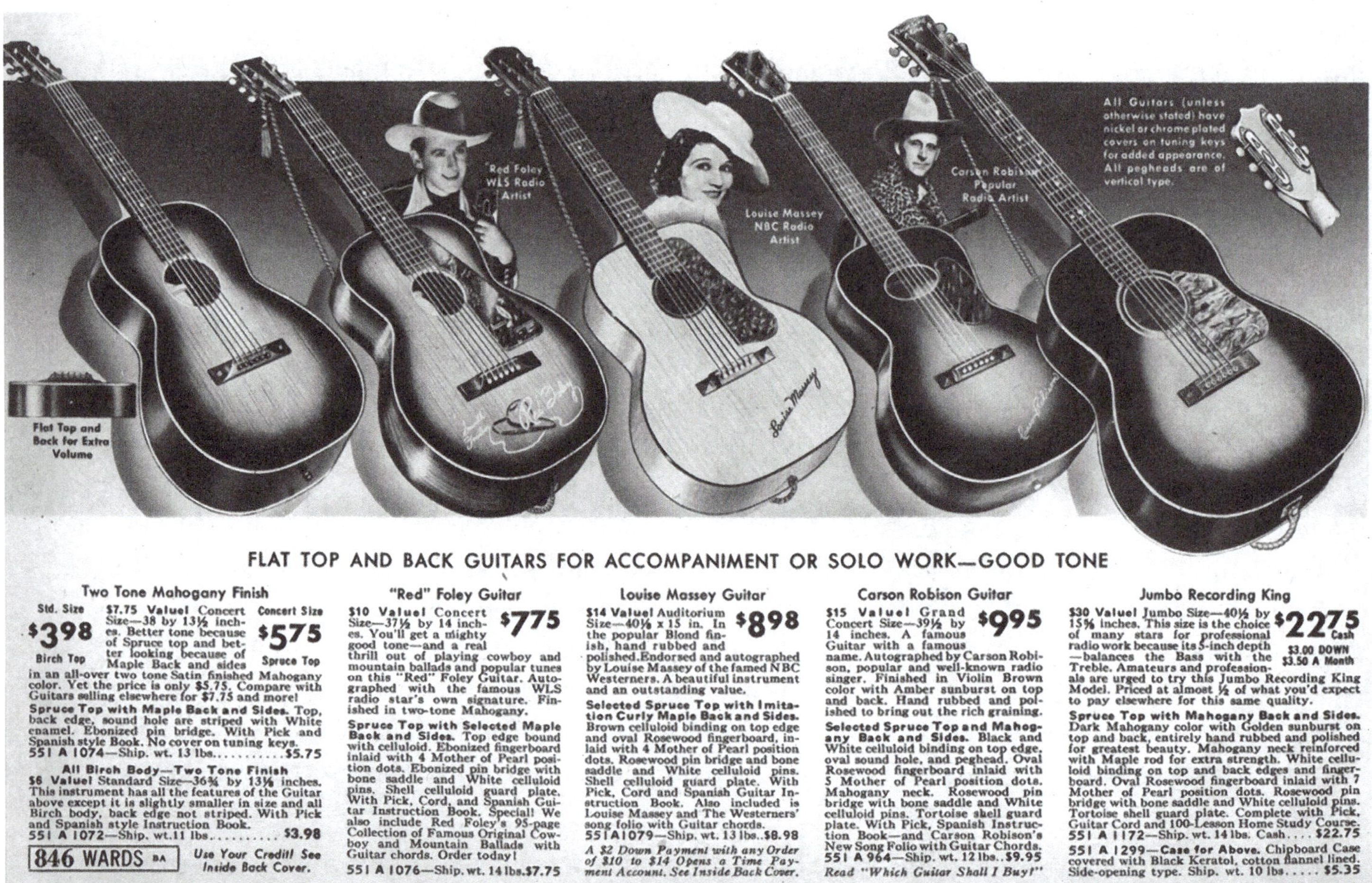

A line-up of Montgomery Ward guitars for the fall and winter of 1941, with the Regal Recording King "Jumbo" at the far right. Courtesy Gerry Clarke.

Inlay (right) by Joe Phetteplace, as used by Oahu and on the "Herrick Honolulu Artist." Courtesy Larry Phetteplace.

A possibly one-of-a-kind version of the "Jumbo" made, says the original owner, for Herrick's Music in Michigan. Note the fingerboard, which resembles those used by Regal for better quality Recording King archtops, and the headstock inlay, made by Joe Phetteplace (see photo above) and more commonly found on top-of-the-line Oahu guitars. Photographs/courtesy Mark Demaray.

Regal Recording King "Jumbo," as found with original soft shell case, braided strap and strap hangers.

Some close-ups details of a Regal "Jumbo" model in natural finish.

Regal "Milord" guitar, as shown in a 1951 Regal brochure.

By 1949, the Regal "Jumbo" had morphed into the "Milord." The "Milord" inlays, common to some other Regal models, have "Regal" in pearl with vertical rectangular blocks surrounding it on the headstock, along with triangular fingerboard inlays with a small rectangle in-between. Although there are differences in headstock and fingerboard inlays as well as in the soundhole rosette, the basic body shape stayed the same.

The Regal catalogue for 1951 (reproduced here) boasted that "Regal Milord Guitar is a big, he-man size instrument, so much in demand today for T.V. and radio solo work. Deep, booming bass with rich, brilliant treble is especially pronounced.

"YOU WILL BE PROUD TO FEATURE THIS REGAL MILORD GUITAR [their emphasis]. You will appreciate the finer craftsmanship."

"Doc" Hopkins was a Kentuckian who appeared on WLS in Chicago. Here he's shown with a Regal "Milord" guitar, the successor to the "Jumbo." From the 1949 WLS Yearbook, courtesy Richard Carlin.

Small Jumbo

Summary

Instrument: Flattop guitar.

Model: Small "Jumbo."

Years Made: 1937-1939

Brand(s): Regal, Playtime.

Quality: Mid-grade.

Special Features: None.

Woods: Spruce over birch or mahogany, poplar or maple neck.

Measurements: 25 1/2" scale, 15"-15 ½" lower bout, 11"-11 3/8" upper bout, 1 3/16" nut width, 4"-4 5/8" body depth at endpin.

Logos Used: Green headstock decal, "Regal" on headstock, "Playtime" silkscreened on headstock, "Recording King" silkscreened on headstock.

Known Original Wholesale List Price: $10.00-$45.00.

Close-ups of a "reduced size" version by Regal of the Recording King "Jumbo" made during World War II. Bridge is not original.

Two close-ups of "Playtime DeLuxe," made by Regal for sale by possibly Sears. The pickguard is as found on the "Jumbo," headstock logo is stenciled on, the back is veneered, but the fingerboard inlay is still pearl and abalone.

From 1937 onward, Regal also offered slightly smaller versions of their Gibson-like "Jumbo" guitar. The equivalent in size to a Martin 000 or OM, these guitars were sold under their own name by Regal, as Recording King for Montgomery Ward and as "Playtime" guitars possibly for Sears during World War II. All these guitars share some characteristics with the "Jumbo," although these have lateral-braced tops and most were meant to occupy the lower end of the price spectrum.

Milady

Summary

Instrument: Flattop guitar.

Model: "Milady."

Years Made: 1951.

Brand(s): Regal.

Quality: Mid-grade.

Special Features: "Ladies" size small guitar, short neck.

Woods: Spruce top, mahogany back and sides.

Measurements: "3/4" size, 11" by 15".

Logos Used: "Regal" inlaid into headstock.

Known Original Wholesale List Price: $40.00.

The companion to "Milord," the "Milady" model, offered in 1951, was advertised as designed specifically for women. Multiple triangles marked the third, fifth, seventh, tenth and twelfth frets of this twelve fret to the body, eighteen total fret fingerboard. The celluloid bound top was natural-finished spruce with a marquetry soundhole rosette, the standard Regal rectangular bridge was held down with two screws, and the tuners were three-on-a-plate standard for Regal's of that period.

"A breath-taking beauty of rare woods richly finished to bring out the natural glow and warmth of the wood itself." The "Milady" reduced size guitar, the companion to the "Super-Jumbo" "Milord" model. From a Regal mailing card.

Chapter Eight
Archtop Guitars

Roundhole: Carved Top

Summary

Instrument: Archtop guitar.

Model: Carved top with round soundhole.

Years Made: 1932-1937.

Brand(s): Regal.

Quality: High grade.

Special Features: Carved top fourteen fret slot head.

Woods: Spruce top, mahogany or curly maple back and sides, mahogany/walnut or mahogany neck.

Measurements: "Grand Concert" and "Auditorium" size.

Logos Used: Regal pearl script in headstock.

Known Original Retail List Price: $45.00.

Regal entered the archtop guitar market in a quest to provide a louder guitar for plectrum players. These guitars had tops carved from one piece of spruce along the lines of that found on violin family instruments. Gibson, applying violin carving techniques to mandolins and guitars almost since the beginning of their existence, had achieved success in the first half of the 1920s with the designs of Lloyd Loar. So, even though Regal was "late to the dance," they endeavored to catch up with other American guitar makers.

The Company's initial foray into archtops was a kind of a highbred, using a standard Regal neck with a slotted headstock on a carved top roundhole guitar. There were four models, available in both four and six string models. All used an ebony fingerboard which joined the body at the fourteenth fret and had twenty frets total, a floating bridge and hinged "trapeze" tailpiece and floating black pickguard. The two higher grade models had sides and back of curly maple, while the top version came with a carved maple back and gold plated hardware. The basic model was made in a "Grand Concert" size, while the three others were "Full Auditorium" sized.

The New REGAL GUITAR with CARVED Top

The New Regal Carved Top Guitar is the result of tireless and careful experiment. It embodies several greatly advanced ideas in Guitar construction and is recommended as being one of the very finest instruments made, and superior to many Guitars selling at double the price.

This Guitar produces a brilliant, powerful and enchanting tone, instantly the admiration of all who hear it, and is equally suitable for Hawaiian and Spanish playing, for orchestra work and solo playing.

Price $79.50

WHALEY ROYCE & CO., Limited - TORONTO, Ont.

(OVER)

Brochure used by Regal to introduce their new roundhole "Guitar with Carved Top."

The New REGAL GUITAR with CARVED Top

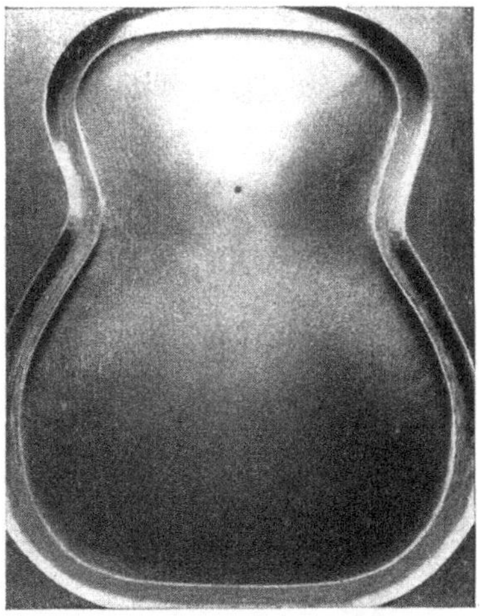

Front View of Top as carved out of vertical grain Spruce one inch (1") thick.

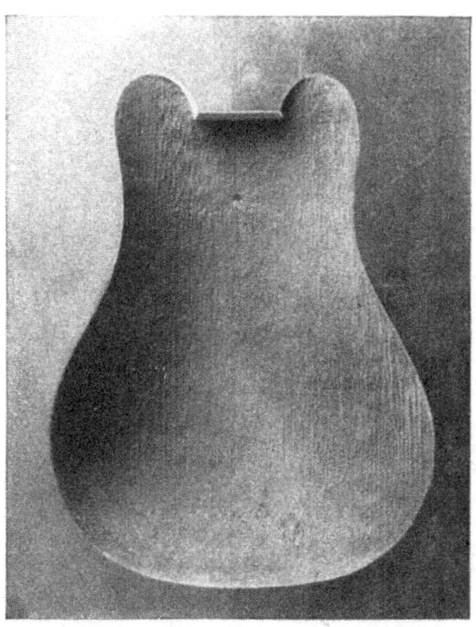

Back View of Top showing the same carefully gauged carving for the inside of the Guitar.

No. 1932.—Auditorium Size. Carved vertical grain Spruce top; selected Mahogany back and sides; Mahogany neck; genuine Ebony oval fingerboard with 20 frets, 14 of which are clear of the body. Black fibre guard plate, fine quality nickel patent heads, new style nickel tail-piece.
Finest materials, finest workmanship; hand-rubbed satin finish.......... **$79.50**

No. 1933.—Fine quality fancy leatherette case. Professional style, centre opening.......... **$17.50**

WHALEY ROYCE & CO., Limited - TORONTO, Ont.

(OVER)

Front view of a Regal-made B&J "Serenader" arched top twenty fret tenor guitar. The floating, contoured pickguard is as found on the "Custom Built" guitars. Photographs/courtesy Jake Murrow/Antebellum Instruments.

Roundhole: Pressed Top

Summary

Instrument: Archtop guitar.

Model: Pressed top with round soundhole.

Years Made: 1932-1937.

Brand(s): Regal, Tonk American, Artist DeLuxe, B&J.

Quality: Low grade.

Special Features: None.

Woods: Birch or spruce top, birch or mahogany back and sides.

Measurements: Various.

Logos Used: Regal green headstock decal, Regal medallion headstock decal logo, Regal on "MOTS" headstock overlay, Serenader headstock decal and paper soundhole label.

Known Original Wholesale List Price: $9.50-$18.00.

Along with their carved top roundholes, Regal introduced a low-priced line of "pressed" or bent-top archtops (i.e.: the tops were either forced into shape with bracing or "pressed" into shape in a machine, sometimes using thin multiple layers of wood to aid in the shaping process). These came in a variety of woods and sizes, but all had round soundholes, a floating bridge and pickguard, and tailpiece. Some came with fourteen frets to the body and twenty frets total, but, most only had twelve frets to the body and eighteen fret fingerboards.

"Le Domino Big Boy." Courtesy Retrofret Vintage Guitars.

Roundhole Pressed Top: Le Domino

Summary

Instrument: Pressed top with round soundhole.

Model: "Le Domino."

Years Made: 1934-1936.

Brand(s): Regal.

Quality: Moderate with high "cool" factor.

Special Features: Decalcomania dominos.

Woods: Spruce top, birch back and sides, basswood neck.

Measurements: 15 1/4" lower bout, 25 3/8" scale, 4" deep at end pin and 1 7/8" wide at the nut.

Logos Used: Regal paper soundhole label, "Le Domino" headstock decal or white silkscreen.

Known Original Wholesale List Price: $15.90.

The most famous of the pressed top Regal archtops was the "Le Domino Big Boy." Cut from the same cloth as the Oscar Schmidt-made Stella brand "Gambler" guitar, the "Le Domino Big Boy" came in "Auditorium Size," and was finished in a "Two-Tone Walnut Color." Its slotted headstock neck joined the body at the fourteenth fret, with twenty frets total. It came with a floating bridge and pickguard, a trapeze tailpiece, three-on-a-plate tuners and ebonized fingerboard. Top, back, soundhole and fingerboard were bound in white celluloid. Lateral top bracing helped to hold the arched top in shape (see Chapter Seven for information about other "Le Domino" models).

An unknown performer in a WLS Talent Show brought her "Le Domino Big Boy" along with her cowgirl garb. WLS Yearbook, 1937, courtesy Richard Carlin.

"F" Hole

As with their roundhole archtops, Regal was late to enter into "F" hole archtop market, waiting until 1935 to introduce their first models. Regal made way too many "F" holed archtops to describe them all here. And, like their roundholed archtops, many of them were low-end, bent or "pressed" top guitars. I'll try below to hit the highlights of Regal's foray into the carved top "jazz" guitar field.

F Hole: Bob Cat

Summary

Instrument: Archtop guitar.

Model: "F" hole.

Years Made: 1938-1939.

Brand(s): Regal.

Quality: High grade.

Special Features: Fancy headstock overlay.

Woods: Carved spruce top, curly mahogany back and sides, poplar or mahogany neck.

Measurements: 25 ½" scale, 1 and 11/16" fingerboard width at the nut, upper bout 11 5/8", lower bout 17 ¾", depth of body at the endpin 4".

Logos Used: Incised "Regal" in headstock overlay, Regal "Custom Built" paper soundhole label.

Known Original Wholesale List Price: $65.00.

In 1938, Regal introduced a high quality line of carved top archtops, including the "Bob Cat", "Esquire", "Prince", and the "Crown". The "Bob Cat" has made somewhat of a comeback, as it has been the "go to" guitar for Jimmie Vaughan and the Reverend Horton Heat. Another "Bob Cat" promoter is swing singer Carolyn Martin. Her husband Dave writes that:

"We had gone out to Albuquerque to attend the Western Music Association's convention, and, during that weekend, Carolyn got to spend a lot of time playing on some wonderful instruments, including our friend Suze Spencer Marshall's gorgeous 1951 Epiphone Emperor Regent. Coming back from the convention, Carolyn talked about how archtop guitars suited swing music so much better than dreadnaught shaped guitars. In any case, I got a call from our friend Steve Newman, a guitar tech in Memphis, who said, 'I

Carolyn Martin is happy to own a Regal "Bobcat" archtop guitar. Here's a view of the guitar, with a close-up of the layered headstock overlay (next page). Carolyn Martin portrait by Erick Anderson, guitar photographs by Dave Martin/courtesy Carolyn and Dave Martin.

think I've found a guitar for your wife.' He told me about the 'Bob Cat' and then sent it over for us to see. Carolyn was a little hesitant at first to buy another guitar, but after playing it for a few days, she fell in love with it.

"One interesting thing: the night it came in, Carolyn took it to her gig (she was still singing with the Time Jumpers then) to see what the archtop players in the band thought. Ranger Doug (from Riders in The Sky), Andy Reiss from the Time Jumpers and Suze Spenser Marshall, who happened to be in town that weekend, all said that (A) she needed to own the 'Bob Cat,' and (B), it needed heavier strings and the action needed to be raised to play swing rhythm.

"It's definitely a part of her style now. Though she has some other archtop guitars, the 'Bob Cat' is the one she takes out when she's singing swing, western swing or western music (three distinctly different genres, though with much overlap)."

Regal called Carolyn's "Bob Cat" "A fine toned Dance Orchestra Guitar with a neck that is easy and fast. Play without fatigue. Just note these features:

"Deep Super Auditorium Size, Carved Spruce Top, Curly Mahogany Band and Sides, Rosewood Finger Board, Adjustable Bridge, Beautifully Shaded and Polished to a Very High Luster, A Great Instrument for the finished player. Built For Today—Styled For Tomorrow."

The "Bob Cat" came with fourteen frets to the body and twenty frets total; a tortoise "lobster claw" floating pickguard bound in white; white bound top, back, heelcap, rosewood fingerboard and "F" holes; "W" shaped hinged tailpiece; and sunburst top, back and neck. Like the Regal Recording King's, the "Bob Cat" has valve covered tuners. And, unlike most Regal guitars, the "Bob Cat" has a serial number stamped into the back of the headstock (Carolyn's is number 115).

Post-War Regal "Esquire" archtop, with "Saturn" fingerboard and "Troubadour" headstock inlays. Courtesy Lark Street Guitars.

F Hole: Esquire

Summary

Instrument: Archtop guitar.

Model: "F" hole.

Years Made: 1938-1951.

Brand(s): Regal.

Quality: High grade.

Special Features: "Troubadour" figure inlaid in headstock, "violin" sides.

Woods: Carved spruce top; curly maple, mahogany, or rosewood (1951 model) back and sides; seven piece mahogany/walnut neck.

Measurements: 1 3/4" nut width, 24 5/8" scale, 3 1/2" deep at end pin, 15 1/2" lower bout, 11 and 1/4" upper bout (second version); 1 5/8" nut width, 24 ¾" scale, 3 3/8" deep at end pin, 15 ½" lower bout, 11 3/8" upper bout (combination version).

Logos Used: "Regal" in pearl on headstock.

Known Original Wholesale List Price: $125.00-$150.00.

There are at least three different versions of the "Esquire" produced by Regal:

The first has the characteristics of the other late 1930s guitars under discussion: a carved sunburst spruce top, celluloid-bound "F" holes, rosewood fingerboard, adjustable bridge and tailpiece, floating pickguard, fourteen frets to the body and twenty frets total. The "Esquire" version one came with maple back and violin-style sides, the "Troubadour" figure on the headstock, and chrome-plated metal parts.

Version two was a smaller guitar (measurements above) with post-War triangles and Saturns inlayed in the fingerboard, natural finish, mahogany sides and back, and seven piece mahogany/walnut neck (see photographs).

The third ""Esquire"" was premiered by Regal in 1951. It had rosewood back and sides, top and back bound in birch, gold plated hardware, triangle and square fingerboard inlays and the later-day headstock logo of "Regal" in pearl surrounded by vertical pearl triangles.

I have also seen a guitar with features from all three versions. The "Troubabour" neck of version two was wedded to the body of version three, with the sunburst spruce top and rosewood back bound in white celluloid, as is the seven piece neck and the raised "lobster claw" plastic tortoise pickguard. While this instrument lacks the full violin sides of the original "Esquire", Regal did make an attempt at emulating the top and back extensions with added pieces of wood.

The "Troubadour" figure utilized by Regal for the "Esquire", "Prince" and "Crown" guitars also shows up on banjos made by Slingerland and Washburn. Hubert Pleijsier, in his book on Washburn instruments, suggests that these were made for the multiple companies by an outside concern. Recent findings point to inlay artist Joe Phetteplace, who trained at Regal, as the supplier of those inlays (see photographs).

"Presenting The New 1951 Regal 'Esquire.'" This 1951 brochure shows off the "Esquire" archtop with "Saturn" inlays, "lobster claw" floating pickguard ala Bacon and large "Regal" headstock inlay.

F Hole: Prince

Summary

Instrument: Archtop guitar.

Model: "F" hole.

Years Made: 1938-1939, 1942-1943.

Brand(s): Regal, Recording King (1942-1943).

Quality: High grade.

Special Features: Big body.

Woods: Carved spruce top, curly mahogany or maple back and sides, mahogany neck.

Measurements: 18" lower bout, 25 3/8" scale, 1 and 11/16" nut width, 4 ¼" deep ("Super Auditorium").

Logos Used: "Regal" in pearl on headstock overlay.

Known Original List Price: $85.00 wholesale, $225.00 retail.

The Regal "Prince" was "royalty in waiting." Just one step below the top-of-the-line Regal archtops of the late 1930s, the "Prince" had many of the same features as the original "Esquire" model, with the addition of mahogany back and sides, black/white "zipper" binding on the top and back, bound pickguard and serial number stamped into the back of the headstock. In the 1940s, Regal made a version of the "Prince" for sale through the Montgomery Ward catalogue that came with mahogany or maple arched back and sides, a lower-grade tailpiece and "Recording King" in pearl replacing "Prince" below the Troubadour figure on the headstock. This was an unusually high grade instrument for Montgomery Ward to carry, as the majority of the Regal-made archtops they advertised sold for an eighth of the price.

As advertised by Regal, the ""Prince" was "Truly an Instrument for the Artist. Workmanship and finish to Please the Most Exacting Critics."

This unlabeled Regal archtop guitar appears to be a pre-War "Prince." Some of its features include the "Troubadour" headstock figure, "Jumbo" headstock shape, fancy floating pickguard, hinged "W" goldplated tailpiece, "zipper" binding, bound "F" holes and "violin" sides. Photographs by Ron Middlebrook.

Two versions of the "Troubadour" figure by Joe Phetteplace, as featured on the Regal "Esquire" and "Prince" archtops. Notice the generic "Troubadour" is slightly different then the "Prince." The reverse of the "Troubadour," as shown, features the handwritten annotation "4.25 plus 5c letter for engraving name." All courtesy Larry Phetteplace.

F Hole: Crown

Summary

Instrument: Archtop guitar.

Model: "F" hole.

Years Made: 1938-1939.

Brand(s): Regal.

Quality: High grade.

Special Features: Violin sides, gold plated metal parts.

Woods: Carved spruce top.

Measurements: 18 1/2" lower bout, 25 3/8" scale, 1 and 11/16" nut width.

Logos Used: "Regal" in pearl on headstock overlay.

Known Original Wholesale List Price: $250.00.

The "top of the line" Regal archtop whose name was (obviously) inspired by the Regal logo, this professional grade guitar was meant to take on all comers in its price range (which was the same as the high-end "B&D" archtops discussed below). The "Crown" was among the largest "jazz" guitars on the market, a twenty fret (fourteen to the body) behemoth with bound "F" holes, pearl around the top edge and on the floating pickguard, violin sides and gold plated tuners and tailpiece.

F Hole: Groton No. 2

Summary

Instrument: Archtop guitar.

Model: "F" hole.

Years Made: 1936-1939.

Brand(s): "B&D."

Quality: Medium grade.

Special Features: Floating "lobster claw" pickguard

Woods: Carved spruce top, mahogany back and sides, three-ply laminated neck.

Measurements: "Super Auditorium" 15 ¾" body width, 25 ½" scale, 3 ¼" body depth, 1 7/8" nut width.

Logos Used: "B&D" in white script in black plastic headstock overlay.

Known Original Wholesale List Price: $25.00.

During the second half of the 1930s, Regal made guitars and mandolins for the Bacon Banjo Company of Groton, Connecticut. The "Groton" brand was used for the lowest priced instruments in the line. The "Groton" No. 1 was a flattop, discussed and shown in Chapter Seven. Also shown in Chapter Seven is the archtop No. 2.

Utilizing the same neck as the "Groton" No. 1, the sunburst archtop body was bound top and back with white celluloid and had a twenty fret rosewood fingerboard that joined the body at the fourteenth fret.

F Hole: Ramona

Summary

Instrument: Archtop guitar.

Model: "F" hole.

Years Made: 1936-1939.

Brand(s): "B&D."

Quality: High grade.

Special Features: Carved rosewood back on high end model.

Woods: Spruce over mahogany or rosewood, three piece mahogany neck.

Measurements: "Super Auditorium:" 41" overall length, 15 3/16" at widest point, 4 1/4" body thickness at bridge. "Grand Auditorium:" 41 ½" overall length, 16" at widest part, 4 3/8" body thickness at bridge. A surviving model 3R is 16 ¾" at the lower bout, 4" deep at the end pin, scale length of 25 3/8" and nut width of 1 3/4".

Logos Used: "B&D" on tortoise plastic headstock overlay.

Known Original Wholesale List Price: $65.00-$100.00

While Bacon had the introductory-priced "Groton No. 2" model archtop, their quality "jazz" guitar line began with the "Ramona" fourteen fret to the body, twenty frets total models. This sunburst carved top and arched back guitar came in three models. The "No. 2, Super Auditorium size" and "No. 3, Grand Auditorium size" both had mahogany backs and sides. The "No. 3R" came with rosewood back and sides, and "zipper" binding. According to the experts at archtop.com, it is extremely difficult and expensive to carve an arched rosewood back as was used by Regal for the top Ramona model, making this a rare and unusual sounding instrument.

All the "Ramona" models came with white celluloid bound top, back and fingerboard; chrome plated hardware; white bound "lobster claw" floating pickguard; hinged trapeze-style tailpiece; rosewood fingerboard and adjustable rosewood bridge.

F Hole: Sultana

Summary

Instrument: Archtop guitar.

Model: "F" hole.

Years Made: 1936-1939.

Brand(s): "B&D."

Quality: High grade.

Special Features: Really big body, "violin" sides.

Woods: Spruce top, mahogany back and sides, seven piece mahogany neck.

Measurements: 18 1/8" at lower bout, 12 7/8" upper bout, 4" deep at end pin, 1 7/8" fingerboard width at nut, 25 ½" scale ("Coliseum" size).

Logos Used: "B&D" in pearl on headstock.

Known Original Wholesale List Price: $150.00-$325.00.

"B&D Sultana Grand" archtop guitar, as shown in the 1937 CMI catalogue. Courtesy the National Music Museum.

Four "B&D" archtops made by Regal for the Bacon Company of Groton, CT. The first two are two different "Ramona" models, the second page highlighting the fancier "Sultana I" (top) and "Sultana Grand" (bottom). From the CMI catalogue of 1937, courtesy The National Music Museum.

Sultana
Bacon
Sultana

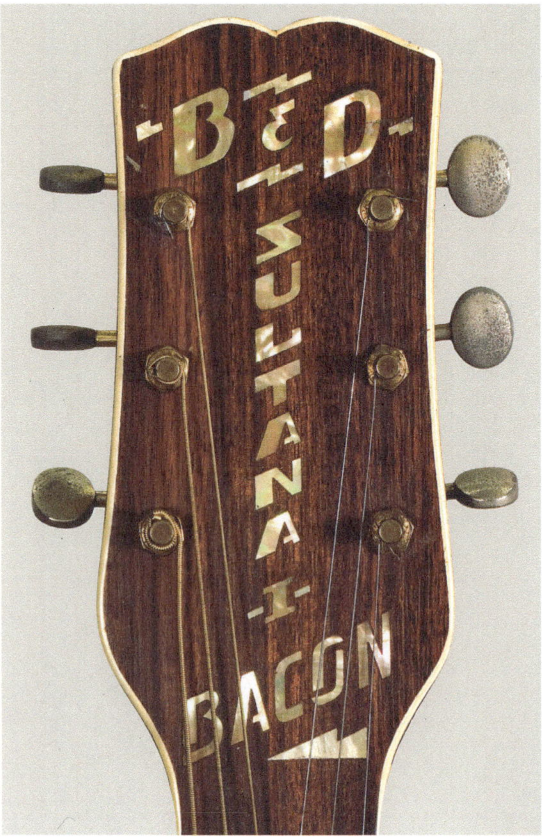

Here we have a Bacon "Sultana I" serial number 1159. Features include a "lobster claw" floating pickguard, "W" hinged engraved tailpiece, "Coliseum" size, individual tuners and "violin" sides. Courtesy the National Music Museum, the University of South Dakota, Bill Willroth, Sr., Photographer.

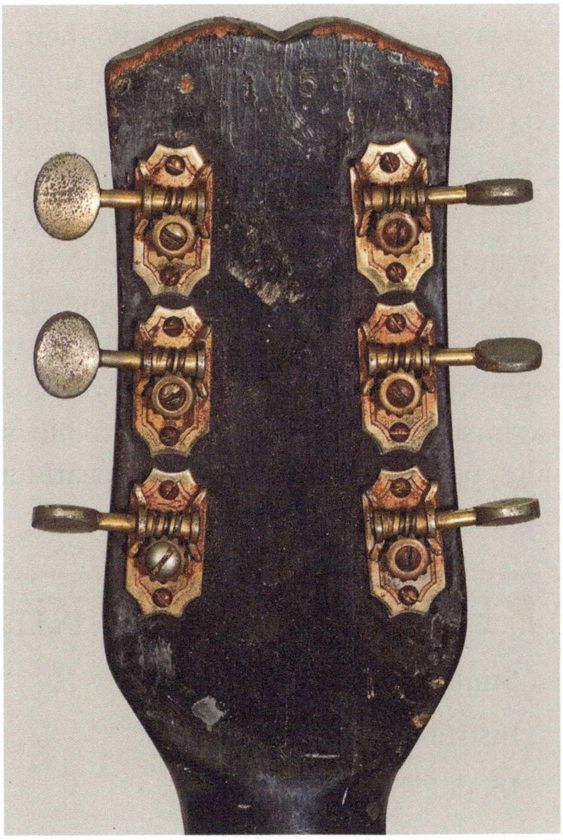

If you've never held one of the "Coliseum" size Bacon "Sultana" models, you're unaware of how big and how fancy an art deco jazz guitar can be. The "Sultana" "B&D" just blows all other guitars out of the water. As the copywriters told their distributors, "B&D Sultana guitars have enormous volume and carrying power with a tonal depth and richness comparable only to the longest concert sized pianos. No expense has been spared to make them the very finest guitars of the day."

So, what did you get for spending top dollar on one of these stunning archtops? The basic "Sultana I" had mahogany back and sides; white celluloid bound fingerboard, floating "lobster claw" pickguard, top and back; sunburst carved spruce top; fourteen frets to the body, twenty total fret fingerboard; art deco tailpiece with "Sultana" and "Bacon" engraved on the cross pieces; gold plated hardware; pearl headstock and fingerboard inlay; and a four digit serial number embossed into the back of the peghead. The "Sultana II" came with curly maple back and sides, and additional "zipper" binding and "scrimshaw" engraved fingerboard block inlays. The "Sultana Grand" adds bird's-eye maple back and sides, pearl bound top and back, pearl tuner buttons, white bound "F" holes, and floating pickguard engraved with an "Eastern" scene.

F Hole: Recording King

Summary

Instrument: Archtop guitar.

Model: "F" hole.

Years Made: 1940-1943.

Brand(s): Regal, Recording King.

Quality: Low to high grade.

Special Features: None.

Woods: Carved spruce top; curly maple back and sides; five piece maple neck, mahogany neck with maple rod, or poplar neck.

Measurements: Upper bout 11 5/16", lower bout 15 ¾", body depth at endpin 3 7/16"; 41 ½" by 16" ("Grand Auditorium"), 11 and 1/2" upper bout, 16 1/2" lower bout, 4" deep at edge, 41"-42" total length ("Super Auditorium").

Logos Used: "Recording King" silkscreened on headstock in white.

Known Original Retail List Price: $18.95-$32.95.

The "Recording King" brand acoustic archtops that Regal made for Montgomery Ward during the first half of the 1940s were typical of the low-end Regal-made guitars during that time. In fact, many came with the same neck topped with the white "Recording King" headstock logo and three-on-a-plate tuners with "valve" covers. "Zipper" binding wasn't uncommon, fingerboards and adjustable bridges were made of rosewood, tops and backs were bound in white celluloid and some had carved spruce tops. One "Super Auditorium" example priced on Montgomery Ward's higher end that survives has a five piece maple sunburst ala "Jumbo" neck, metal tuner buttons, strap hangers at the headstock and built into the Kluson tailpiece, carved spruce sunburst top, one piece arched sunburst veneered maple back and sides, triple bound rosewood fingerboard with fancy inlays, white bound tortoise plastic pickguard, white bound top, white bound back and "F" holes, "Recording King" silkscreened on the headstock and inlaid vertical bars below the logo.

WHICH GUITAR SHALL I BUY?

Buy a Flat Top and Back Guitar if you plan to use your instrument for Spanish style solo playing or for Hawaiian style playing of any kind. Tone is mellow and full. A very popular type, the Flat Top comes in various sizes: ¾, Standard, Concert, Grand Concert, Auditorium and Jumbo. The Jumbo Model, because of its larger, deeper body, produces the deeper, more powerful tone needed for professional appearances or for radio work.

Buy a Fully Arched Top and Back Guitar if you are interested in voice accompaniment or orchestra work. It is made in the two larger sizes, Auditorium and Grand Auditorium, and produces a rich, sparkling tone with more than normal carrying power. Can be used for Spanish style playing only.

The finest fully arched Guitars have carved tops and are for professional orchestra work or for advanced players who want the very highest quality Guitar. This type has the added richness and brilliance demanded by top-notch players.

Buy An Amplifying Guitar if you desire an instrument particularly adapted to the plaintive ballad type singing done in the hill and range country. It is also ideal for stage use as its patented cone construction gives increased volume and sustained tone. Comes only in Grand Concert size and designed for Spanish style playing. For Hawaiian playing, order additional Hawaiian outfit 51 A 2960 on page 852.

Which Woods Are Best? The least expensive Guitars have all Birch bodies and a reasonably good tone. Wards better Guitars have tops of fine grained Spruce, for clear, rich, resonant tone. Backs and sides are of Maple or Mahogany. The best Guitars have tops of choice Eastern Spruce and backs and sides of richly flamed Curly Maple, the finest woods money can buy.

Other Important Features Include:

Binding: Low priced Guitars do not have bound edges but are sometimes striped with colored paint or enamel. More expensive Guitars have one or more of the following parts bound with inlaid celluloid to prevent cracking: sound holes, fingerboard, top and back edges, pegheads.

Fingerboard: Low priced Guitars have ebonized fingerboards. Better Guitars have fingerboards of beautifully fashioned Rosewood for greater ease in playing.

Position Markers: Guitars low in price have only a few inlaid dots, others have more as price increases. The finest instruments have large Mother of Pearl block inlays for markers.

Patent Heads: Hold the pegs to the head and are of ordinary Steel, Brass, Nickel or Chrome plate and Gold Plate. Steel is used on the lowest priced; Gold on the finest.

Guard Plates: Tortoise shell celluloid is more attractive, of better quality and far more expensive than plain celluloid. Consequently, guard plates of this material are used only on Wards more costly instruments.

All Wards Guitars are Fully Guaranteed. The tone and beauty of each is in accordance with its price—the more you wish to pay, the finer, more excellent the instrument you receive. Yet be assured, whether you pay $3.98 or $55.00, you save from 15% to 40% when you buy your Guitar at Wards. Buy the best Guitar you can afford—And use Wards Time Payment Plan. See Inside Back Cover for Terms and Full Information.

FULLY ARCHED CARVED TOP RECORDING KING GUITARS BY NATIONALLY KNOWN MAKERS

"Regal" Recording King — **$19.95** Cash — $2.50 DOWN — $3.00 A Month

$42.50 Value! Grand Auditorium Size—41½ by 16 inches. If you plan to do professional orchestra work, this Guitar will give you more than satisfactory service. Excellent tone and good playing quality at a very low price. Check the following features!

Carved Spruce Top with Northern Maple Back and Sides. Finished in Dark Red Mahogany color with Amber sunburst effect on top and back, hand rubbed and polished to a glossy finish. Attractive checked Black and White celluloid binding on top edge; White celluloid bound back edge. Oval Rosewood fingerboard inlaid with 6 Mother of Pearl position dots. Adjustable Rosewood bridge. Celluloid shell guard plate. Nickel plated hinged type tailpiece. Complete with Pick, Guitar Cord and 100-Lesson Home Study Course.

551 A 1165—Ship. wt. 13 lbs. . . . **$19.95**

551 A 1393—Case for Above Guitar. Chipboard Case covered with Black Keratol, cotton flannel lined. Side-opening type. Ship. wt. 11 lbs. **$5.35**

Wards Guarantee Satisfaction! Read about Money-Back Guarantee on Pg. 1165.

"Regal" Recording King — **$29.95** Cash — $3 DOWN — $4 A Month

$60 Value! Grand Auditorium Size—42 by 16½ inches. This instrument is slightly larger than the Guitar at the left and is of better quality; more expensive woods and many additional refinements gives this instrument greater beauty and finer tone.

Carved Selected Spruce Top with Curly Maple Back and Sides. Finished in Brown Mahogany color with Golden sunburst on top and back, carefully hand rubbed and beautifully polished. Top and back edges are bound with 3 (White-Black-White) layers of celluloid. White celluloid binding on fingerboard, shell guard plate and 2 Violin style "F" holes. Oval Rosewood fingerboard is inlaid with 8 Mother of Pearl position markers. Neck reinforced with a Maple rod—adds strength and resists warping. Adjustable Rosewood bridge. Chrome plated hinged type tailpiece. Individual patent heads. Complete with Pick, Guitar Cord and 100-Lesson Home Study Course.

551 A 1080—Ship. wt. 13 lbs. . . . **$29.95**

For Case for Above Guitar Order 551 A 1402 or 551 A 1396 Listed at Right.

Protect Your Guitar while storing or while in transit! Order a Guitar Case for your instrument from these pages or from a wider selection on Page 853.

$45.00 Cash — With Chromium Plated Metal Parts

Recording King — Kay Kraft's Finest Guitar

$55.00 Cash — With Gold Plated Metal Parts

Kay Kraft Master Size—42 by 17¼ inches, 5 inches deep. Full resonant bass tone and greater volume. We know of no Guitar sold anywhere for less than $75 that is its equal in tone, construction or beauty!

Choicest Woods were selected and graded from many pieces of the very best quality to assure absolute uniformity in matching. Carved Eastern Spruce for the top and rich Curly Maple for the back and sides. 5-ply Curly Maple neck reinforced with a *steel rod* for extra strength and to resist warping. Smooth finished Oval Rosewood fingerboard, adjustable bridge.

Beautifully Finished in natural Blond or Violin Brown color. Brown-White celluloid inlay over Brown shell celluloid binding on top, back edges. Brown shell celluloid bound fingerboard, peghead, Violin style "F" holes. Mother of Pearl block inlays on fingerboard, Rosewood veneered peghead. Brown plastic guard plate. Hand-rubbed, polished to a beautiful glossy luster. Hinged type tailpiece. Individual patent heads. With Pick, Guitar Cord and 100-Lesson Home Study Course. Ship. wt. each 14 lbs.

Ⓐ **551 A 1163—Blond.** Chrome plated metal parts. **$45.00**

Ⓐ **551 A 1164—Blond.** Gold Plated metal parts. $75 value. **$55.00**

Ⓑ **551 A 970—Violin Brown Color.** Same as 551 A 1163 but with White-Black inlay over White binding. **$45.00**

Ⓑ **551 A 971—Violin Brown Color.** Same as 551 A 1164 but with White-Black inlay over White binding. **$55.00**

551 A 1402—Case for above Guitars and 551 A 1080 at left. Hardwood body covered with crocodile-grained, artificial leather. Duvetyn lined. Ship. wt. 12 lbs. **$9.98**

551 A 1396—Case. Like above but Curly Plush lined . . **15.95**

"Which Guitar Shall I Buy?" Remo Biondi, guitarist with Gene Krupa, can help you to choose! The two Recording King archtops of the left are Regal-made for Montgomery Ward. Fall/Winter, 1941 catalogue, courtesy Gerry Clarke.

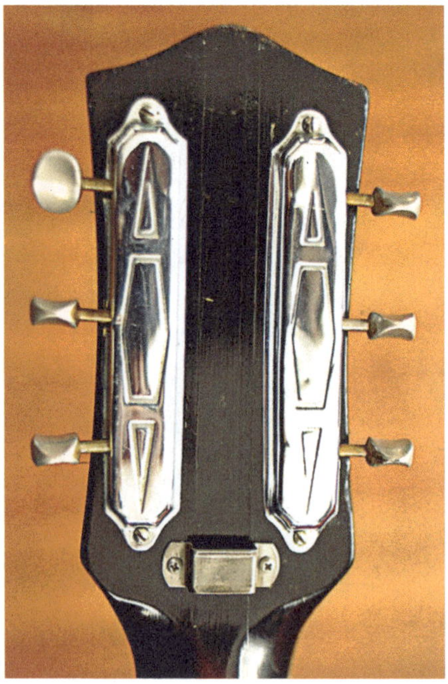

Regal Recording King carved top archtop guitar, made for Montgomery Ward circa 1940-1945. Notice the five piece neck in the headstock close-up. Photographs by Mark Zimin.

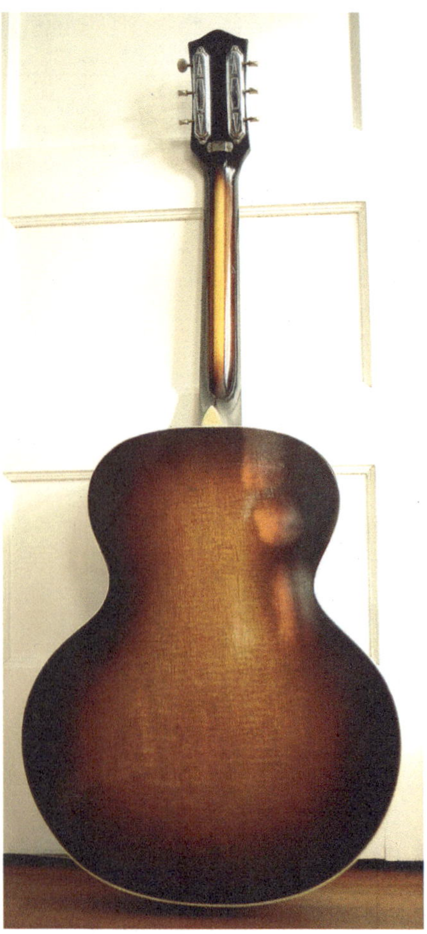

Chapter Nine

"Four Strings, No Waiting": Ukuleles

The ukulele, the littlest of four stringed instruments in the plectrum family, captured the hearts and minds of Americans following performances of Hawaiian musicians at the Pan Pacific Exposition held during 1915 in San Francisco. Two years later, the uke made its first appearance in the Montgomery Ward catalogue. However, it took until the 1920s before the ukulele caught on with the mainland public.

Regal Musical Instrument made their first ukuleles as early as 1924. Over the next fifty years, Regal made a lot of ukes. I mean, a lot of ukes. Often, they were commissioned to manufacture designs owned by their distributors, or had pictorial themes applied at outsourced firms. Unfortunately, since they made the same models (and, sometimes, during the same years) for the same wholesalers as Harmony, Kay and others, it can sometimes hard to distinguish the Regal-made instruments from those built by other companies.

Wendell Hall Red Head

Summary

Instrument: Ukulele.

Model: Wendell Hall "Red Head."

Years Made: 1924-1926.

Brand(s): Regal.

Quality: Medium.

Special Features: Red painted tuners and headstock.

Woods: Imitation koa, koa, "African" mahogany, poplar/basswood neck.

Measurements: 20 ½-21" overall length, 5" upper bout, 6"-6 1/2" lower bout, 2 3/8-2 3/4" deep at the end block, 13"-13 1/4" scale, 1 and ¼"-1 3/8" nut width.

Logos Used: Regal paper soundhole label, Wendell Hall headstock label.

Known Original List Price: Retail $4.35, wholesale $4.50-$9.00.

Wendell Hall, "The Red Headed Music Maker from Dixieland," was born in St. George, Kansas. After early work as a song plugger for Forster Music in St. Louis, Hall had a hit record with "It Ain't Gonna Rain No Mo'." A WEAF radio program sponsored by Eveready batteries followed, along with the addition by Eveready of a red stripe ("red head") to their batteries made to power radio receivers. The next year, Regal introduced their Wendell Hall signature ukulele at the Illinois Products Exposition in Chicago.

Regal-made a number of versions of the "Red Head" uke: one of imitation koa, one of imitation koa with marquetry around the top and soundhole and one of real koa with marquetry decoration and celluloid pegs. There was also a mahogany "Red Head." Two different headstock labels were used, both with a headshot of Hall along with his signature. Some had red painted wooden violin tuning pegs and black celluloid soundhole binding. All were twelve frets to the body and had no fingerboard (i.e.: the frets were set into the neck).

"The Ukulele Room" at the Guitar and Amp Center, Harrisonburg, VA. Collection of Warren Dovell.

Wendell Hall, "The Red Headed Music Maker," with a top-of-the-line Regal tiple, photographed in Chicago around 1935.

Two "Red Heads" (ukuleles, that is) are better then one. With two different headstock logos, of course. Collection of Warren Dovell.

PROGRESSIVE MUSICAL INSTRUMENT CORPORATION

"REGAL" Ukulele No. 6 as pictured above. Finest mahogany body with hand-shaped mahogany neck; sound hole and both edges inlaid with varicolored block inlay and bound with black celluloid; wood pegs replaced with patent pegs. A very good looking instrument with superior tone qualities.

Style Number 6 *Price $6.00*

"REGAL" Ukulele No. 3 as pictured above. Birch back, top and sides; hardwood neck accurately fretted; ebonized extension finger board; wood pegs replaced with patent pegs; sound hole, top and back edges bound with white celluloid; entire instrument stained dark mahogany color; satin finish.

Style Number 3 *Price $4.20*

Mail Your Orders to 319 Sixth Avenue, New York, N. Y.

A pair of Regal ukuleles as offered in the PMI catalogue of circa 1928. Two versions of the "No. 6" on the right are shown from the collection of Randy Klimpert. Catalogue image courtesy The National Music Museum.

Marquetry Mahogany/Koa

Summary

Instrument: Ukulele.

Model: Marquetry uke.

Years Made: 1928

Brand(s): Regal.

Quality: Medium grade.

Special Features: Marquetry.

Woods: Mahogany body, mahogany or poplar/basswood neck.

Measurements: Scale is 13 1/4″-14 ¾″, lower bout width 6 ¼″-7 and 9/16″, nut width is 1 and ½″ and length is 21″-23″.

Logos Used: Paper soundhole label.

Known Original Wholesale List Price: $6.00.

This twelve fret ukulele is a budget version of the white bound mahogany uke below. The model came with black binding and marquetry around the top, back and soundhole, with marquetry up the neck and headstock on some versions.

TBCO Sterling

Summary

Instrument: Ukulele.

Model: Mahogany uke.

Years Made: 1928.

Brand(s): Regal, Sterling.

Quality: Good.

Special Features: Curved fingerboard extension, marquetry.

Woods: Mahogany.

Measurements: N/A.

Logos Used: Paper soundhole label, Sterling headstock decal, T. B. Co. soundhole stamp.

Known Original Wholesale List Price: $12.00.

This is one of Regal's nicer ukuleles, with a black celluloid bound top, back, and soundhole; black and white celluloid around the fingerboard and headstock; and marquetry around top, back and soundhole, as well as down the middle of the fingerboard. Bridge is made of mahogany, and tuners are friction pegs with black or white celluloid buttons. Twelve frets to the body, plus three partial frets over the top completes this instrument. The T. B. (Tonk Bros) Co. version has a soundhole stamp that reads "Hawaiian Ukulele Made by T. B. Co (see photograph)."

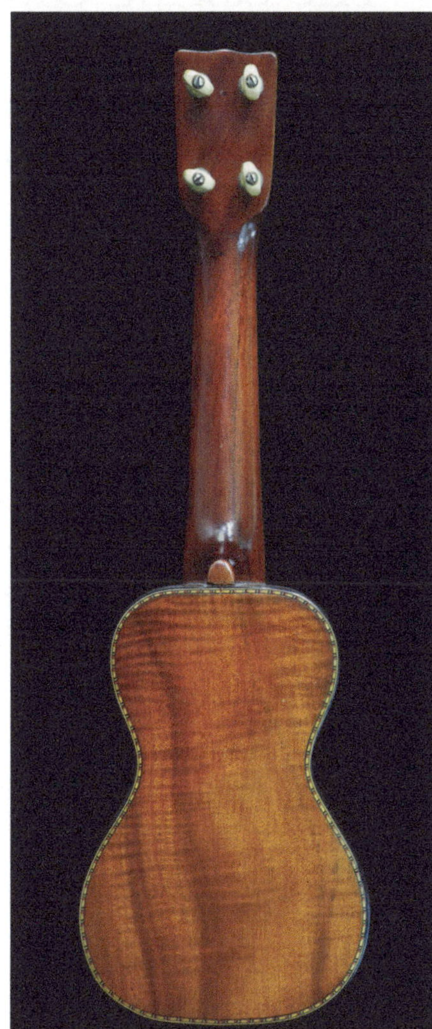

Four images of another marquetry uke, this one branded on the headstock decal and stamped within the soundhole "TB [Tonk Bros.] Co." "Sterling" was a Tonk Bros. house brand. Courtesy Randy Klimpert.

White Bound Mahogany

Summary

Instrument: Ukulele.

Model: Superior.

Years Made: 1928.

Brand(s): Regal.

Quality: High quality.

Special Features: None.

Woods: Mahogany.

Measurements: N/A.

Logos Used: Paper soundhole label, Regal pearl headstock medallion.

Known Original Wholesale List Price: $24.00.

This top-of-the-line Regal ukulele for 1928 featured a figured mahogany body and neck; a white celluloid bound top, back, fingerboard and soundhole; fine lines around top, back and soundhole; rosewood headstock overlay and pearl dots at five, seven and ten; as well as a twelve fret fingerboard with a "V" extension fingerboard.

HA HA The Laffing Uke

Summary

Instrument: Ukulele.

Model: "HA HA The Laffing Uke."

Years Made: 1928.

Brand(s): Regal.

Quality: Low grade.

Special Features: Painted "blackface minstrel" figure on face.

Woods: Birch with poplar/basswood neck.

Measurements: N/A.

Logos Used: Paper soundhole label, "HA HA The Laffing Uke" headstock decal.

Known Original Wholesale List Price: $5.00.

Talk about politically incorrect. "HA HA The Laffing Uke" featured a faux koawood finish with a blackface minstrel figure painted onto the face of the instrument. To top it off, the multi-colored minstrel's mouth is the uke's soundhole. Need we say more?

PROGRESSIVE MUSICAL INSTRUMENT CORPORATION

"REGAL SUPERIOR" Ukulele No. 10 as pictured above. Finest fiddle-back mahogany body with solid mahogany neck; raised extension rosewood finger board with pearl position figures; sound hole and both edges inlaid with fine veneer lines; sound hole and finger board bound with white celluloid; both edges bound with especially wide band of white celluloid; with rounded edges; bone nut; neck and bridge hand shaped with well rounded edges and corners; best patent pegs; exceptionally well finished.

Style Number 10 *Price $24.00*

"REGAL" Ukulele No. 8 as pictured above. Figured mahogany body with solid mahogany neck and raised extension mahogany finger board; colored block inlaying around sound hole, both edges, on sides at top and back and down center of head and finger board; sound hole and both edges bound with black celluloid; finger board is bound with white and black celluloid; fine mahogany bridge with beveled ends; patent tuning pegs; hand-rubbed to a dull satin finish.

Style Number 8 *Price $12.00*

Mail Your Orders to 319 Sixth Avenue, New York, N. Y.

Another pair of Regal ukuleles as offered in the PMI catalogue of circa 1928. The "No. 8" is same as the marquetry Tonk Bros. uke just prior and the "No. 10" follows this image. Catalogue image courtesy The National Music Museum.

The Progressive catalogue "No. 10" in four close-up views. Courtesy Randy Klimpert.

"HA-HA The Laffing Uke." Courtesy Warren Dovell.

Custom Built

Summary

Instrument: Ukulele.

Model: Custom Built.

Years Made: 1931-1937.

Brand(s): Regal.

Quality: Medium grade.

Special Features: None.

Woods: Mahogany.

Measurements: N/A.

Logos Used: Paper soundhole label, Regal green headstock decal (1937).

Known Original Wholesale List Price: $7.50-10.00.

Little is known about the Regal "Custom Built" ukuleles. Only a few catalogues identify them as "Custom" and I've yet to see one in person. These all mahogany instruments came with rosewood extension fingerboards of twelve frets, Grover tuning pegs, soundhole binding on the No. 1 and black/white celluloid top, back and soundhole binding on the No. 2.

Tonk American

Summary

Instrument: Ukulele.

Model: Tonk American.

Years Made: 1930.

Brand(s): Tonk.

Quality: Medium grade.

Special Features: Extended fingerboard over top of soundhole.

Woods: Natural spruce top, dark stained birch back and sides.

Measurements: Concert Size: 21 7/8" body length, 6 5/8" lower bout, 5 1/8" upper bout, 2 ¼" deep.

Logos Used: "Tonk American" headstock decal.

Known Original Wholesale List Price: $9.00.

White celluloid bound ebonized maple fingerboard, top and bottom with fine lines accentuate this ukulele made by Regal for the Tonk Bros. distributors. Two different fingerboards were used, one with fifteen frets total and a squared bottom, and a second with seventeen frets and a pointed bottom. Either way, this uke gave you a lot more frets and, therefore, a greater musical range.

Another Tonk Bros. ukulele made by Regal, this one labeled "Tonk-American." Courtesy Randy Klimpert.

Mapeliene/Scroll Stencil/Whoopee

Summary

Instrument: Tenor ukulele.

Model: "Mapeliene," "Scroll Stencil" and "Whoopee."

Years Made: 1930-1934.

Brand(s): Regal, Sterling, Norwood.

Quality: Low grade.

Special Features: "Scroll" silkscreened on top in various colors.

Woods: Birch, maple or mahogany.

Measurements: Tenor size.

Logos Used: Regal medallion headstock decal.

Known Original Wholesale List Price: $4.00-8.00.

Regal utilized a "scroll" painted top pattern for a related family of ukuleles, including the "Mapeliene" and the "Whoopee." The "Mapeliene" family of six string flattop guitar, tenor guitar, mandolin and ukulele, all were finished in, you guessed it, "natural maple color and graining." The "Mapeliene" (or "White Beauty") instruments also came with silver/black vinyl fingerboards. The "Whoopee" added the word "Whoopee" in flames above the soundhole to a green stenciled scroll-decorated top and came with a pointed fingerboard extension. Other "Scroll Stencil" models had the more rounded Regal headstock shape, a fifteen fret extended fingerboard, binding and marquetry around the top and soundhole, and blue "MOTS" fingerboard and headstock overlays or a cherry red "mahogany" finish. But, "beware" as Harmony was also known to use the scroll silkscreen on its ukes as well.

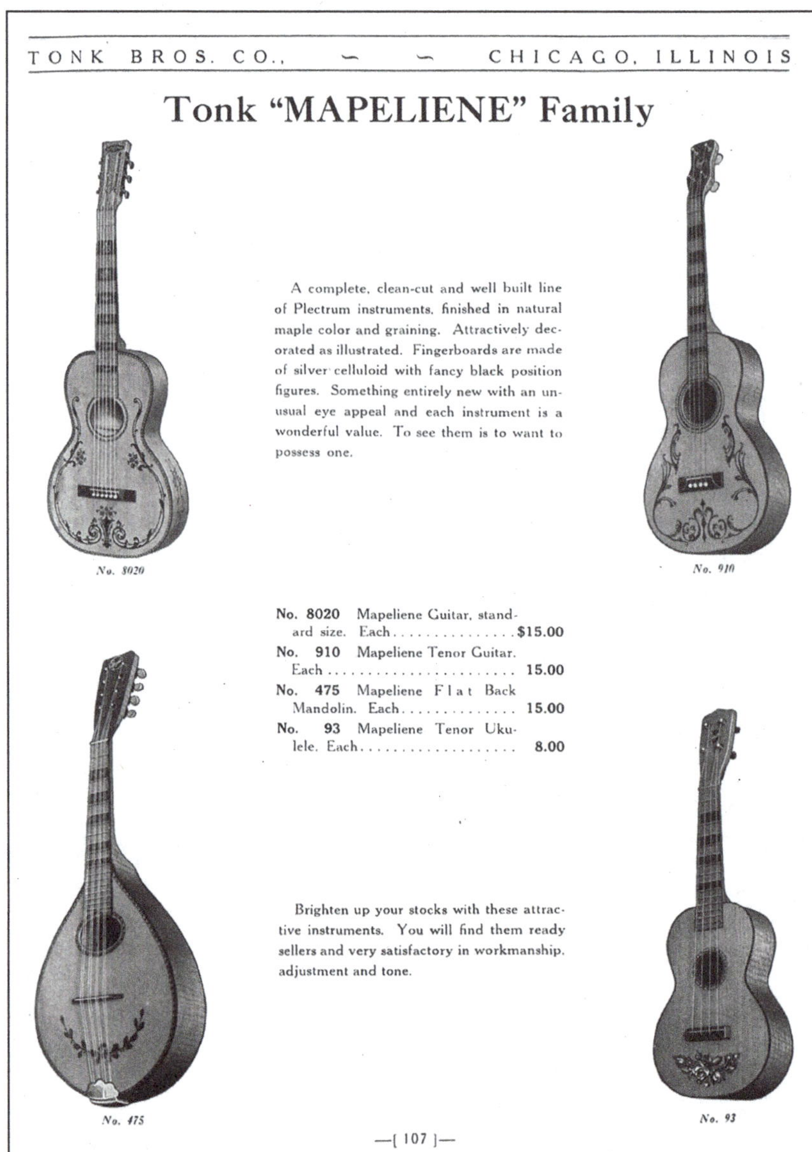

TONK BROS. CO., — — CHICAGO, ILLINOIS

Tonk "MAPELIENE" Family

A complete, clean-cut and well built line of Plectrum instruments, finished in natural maple color and graining. Attractively decorated as illustrated. Fingerboards are made of silver celluloid with fancy black position figures. Something entirely new with an unusual eye appeal and each instrument is a wonderful value. To see them is to want to possess one.

No. 8020

No. 910

No. 8020 Mapeliene Guitar, standard size. Each $15.00

No. 910 Mapeliene Tenor Guitar. Each 15.00

No. 475 Mapeliene Flat Back Mandolin. Each 15.00

No. 93 Mapeliene Tenor Ukulele. Each 8.00

Brighten up your stocks with these attractive instruments. You will find them ready sellers and very satisfactory in workmanship, adjustment and tone.

No. 475

—[107]—

No. 93

The "Tonk 'Mapeliene' Family" of guitar, tenor guitar, mandolin and ukulele. From Tonk Bros. wholesale catalogue of 1930. Courtesy Elderly Instruments.

The "Whoopee" ukulele. Photograph/courtesy Thomas Walsh.

"Scroll Stencil," another version of the "Whoopee." Courtesy Thomas Walsh.

Egyptian

Summary

Instrument: Concert ukulele.

Model: "Egyptian."

Years Made: 1930.

Brand(s): Regal.

Quality: Low grade construction, high grade decoration.

Special Features: Egyptian decalcomania.

Woods: Birch with hardwood neck.

Measurements: Concert ukulele, 1 and ¼" inch width at nut, 13 ¼" scale.

Logos Used: None.

Known Original Wholesale List Price: $4.00-$4.20.

The mystery of this ukulele is not just in the pyramid featured on its face. Evidently, J. R. Stewart originated this design, which was taken over by Regal when Stewart bit the dust and the Tonk Bros. acquired Stewart's assets in 1930. Tonk catalogues show both obviously Regal-made versions alongside "Egyptian" ukuleles of a lower price and different construction details. The known Regal "Egyptian" ukes have a "deep Maroon or Olive Green color" finished body, top, back and soundhole bound in either wood or white celluloid and "patent" friction tuning pegs. Decals of a Pharaoh's head (on the "head" stock and around the rosette) and Pyramids (between the soundhole and the bridge) complete the design. The Regal-made "Egyptian" ukuleles feature a rounded headstock shape, while the supposed Stewart's have a "swoop (angled)" peghead.

The "Egyptian" ukulele, Photographs by Dave Matchette, courtesy Elderly Instruments.

Art Moderne

Summary

Instrument: Concert size.

Model: "Art Moderne."

Years Made: 1929-1939.

Brand(s): Regal, B&J Serenader, Varsity.

Quality: Low grade.

Special Features: "V" shaped stencil on face.

Woods: Birch, "hardwood" neck.

Measurements: Concert size.

Logos Used: Green headstock decal.

Known Original Wholesale List Price: $2.70-$4.20.

The "Art Moderne" ukulele was touted as "A Ukulele with Ornamentation in [a] Futuristic Design." The common feature between the various models was a stenciled top design dominated by several large "V" shapes. Most featured "MOTS"-covered fingerboards and single point headstocks, friction "patent" pegs, a pointed fingerboard extension, and a black and "aluminum" finish, although some came in a brown "walnut" stain. Like the "Mapeliene" instruments, the "Art Moderne" design was shared between various types of stringed instruments and utilized by at least Regal and Harmony (during the first half of the 1930s) for a variety of wholesale distributors.

A version of the "V" decorated "Art Moderne" ukulele. Courtesy Warren Dovell.

FOA

Summary

Instrument: Ukulele.

Model: "FOA."

Years Made: 1931-1935.

Brand(s): Regal, Artex, Blue Bird.

Quality: Low grade.

Special Features: "Pearlette" fingerboard, "FOA" faux koa finish.

Woods: Basswood/poplar neck.

Measurements: "Regular" size.

Logos Used: Paper soundhole label, medallion headstock decal (1931-1935), Artex headstock decal, Blue Bird headstock decal.

Known Original Wholesale List Price: $3.30-$3.80.

The "FOA" ukulele featured a painted body made to resemble koa, flamed mahogany, "fiddle graining," or "snakewood," depending on which catalogue description you read. It came on most versions with a snazzy inlaid fingerboard extension, twelve frets to the body, "patent" friction pegs, a rosette of celluloid rings, and colored wood or marquetry binding.

Green Lacquer

Summary

Instrument: Tenor ukulele.

Model: "Green Lacquer."

Years Made: 1932-1936.

Brand(s): Regal.

Quality: Low grade.

Special Features: None.

Woods: Probably birch.

Measurements: 21" long, 6 3/4" lower bout, and 2 1/4" deep at the endpin.

Logos Used: Medallion headstock decal.

Known Original Wholesale List Price: $4.00.

There are several versions of this tenor ukulele with a green lacquer finish. Most have "MOTS" fingerboards either in white "pearlette" or in blue with white accents, various decalcomanias below the bridge, and the same inlaid fingerboard extension found on the "Foa" ukulele above. Some were also bound with "red edging."

Bluebird brand "Foa" uke in three close-ups. Courtesy Warren Dovell.

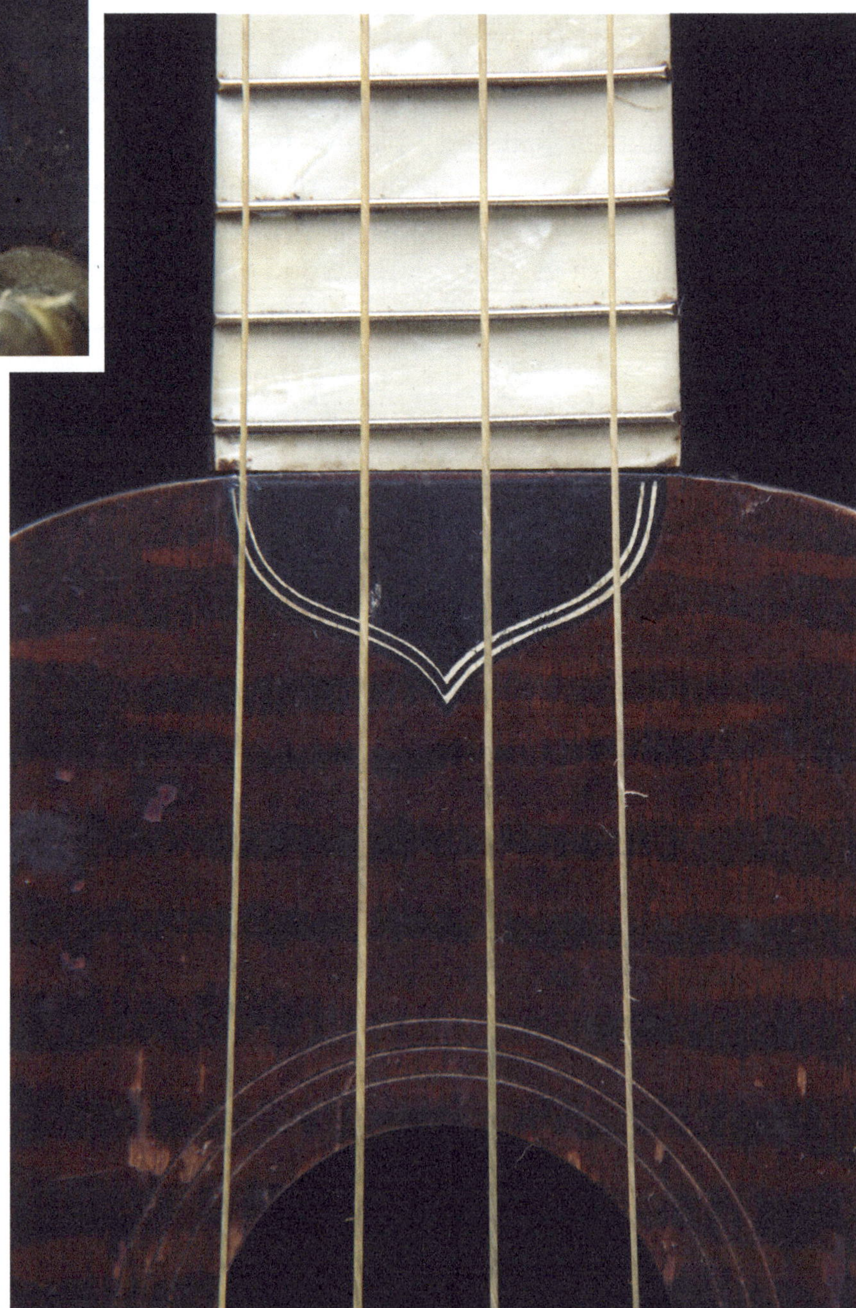

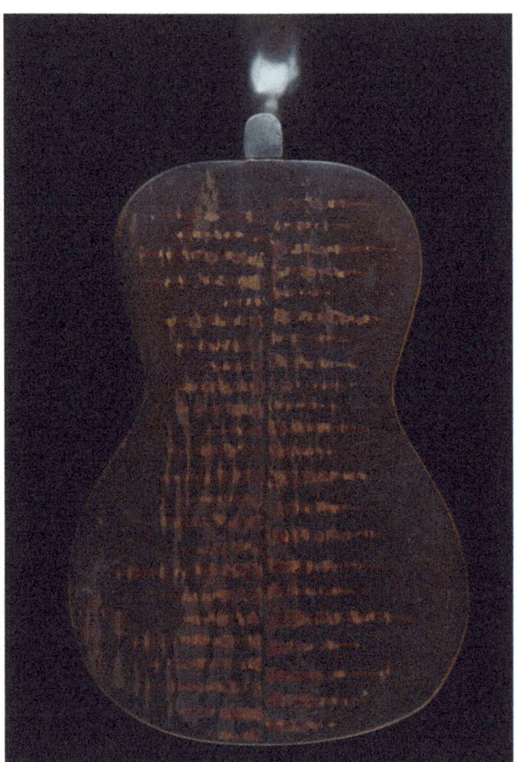

"Green Lacquer" ukulele with "pearlette" fingerboard, decalcomania below the bridge and medallion headstock decal logo. Courtesy Warren Dovell.

"Crystaline" finish ukulele, by Regal (full front) and Stella (back close-up). Regal photograph/courtesy Thomas Walsh, Stella photographed by Dave Matchette, courtesy Elderly Instruments.

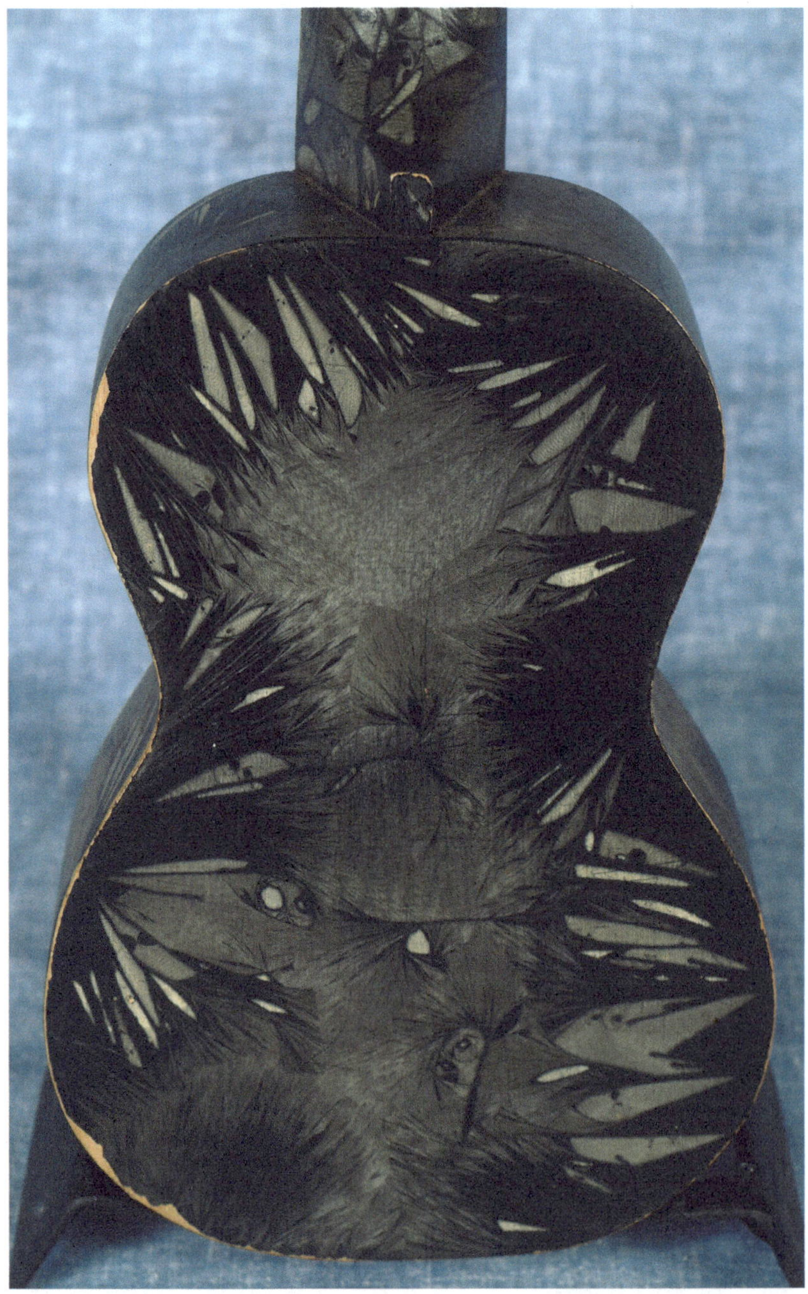

Crystaline

Summary

Instrument: Soprano? and Tenor ukulele.

Model: Crystaline finish.

Years Made: 1932.

Brand(s): Regal.

Quality: Low grade.

Special Features: "Crystaline" finish.

Woods: Birch.

Measurements: Various sizes.

Logos Used: Medallion headstock decal.

Known Original List Price: $2.00-$3.50 wholesale, $1.00 retail.

Here is ANOTHER finish applied to both Harmony and Regal-made instruments and utilized, in addition to ukuleles, for mandolins, six strings and tenor guitars during the same period. The "Crystaline" came in red, brown, blue, "gunmetal" (gray) and black, although green seems to have been the most popular finish. One example has a red "burst" in the middle of the top, back, neck and fingerboard. Other features include an incised three ring rosette.

Le Domino

Summary

Instrument: Ukulele.

Model: "Le Domino."

Years Made: "Unknown."

Brand(s): Le Domino.

Quality: Low grade.

Special Features: Domino decalcomania.

Woods: Spruce top, poplar neck.

Measurements: Unknown.

Logos Used: "Le Domino" headstock stencil.

Known Original List Price: Unknown.

There are two different "Le Domino" designs used for ukuleles marketed by Regal. First, the J. R. Stewart brown/black finish with domino decalcomania utilized both by Stewart before 1930 and by Regal after Stewart's bankruptcy that year. Regal adapted this finish for their "Big Boy" archtop guitar (see Chapter Eight for "Le Domino" roundhole archtops) and also appear to have sold a backlog of Stewart-made ukes, with the J. R. Stewart logo on the headstock, as late as 1936. At some point, Regal-made the "Le Domino" pictured here, in a natural finish with "Le Domino" stenciled on the headstock, and fingerboard inlays and dominos below the bridge in decalcomania.

Second version of the "Le Domino" design. Courtesy Warren Dovell.

Red Dragon

Summary

Instrument: Ukulele.

Model: "Red Dragon."

Years Made: 1935.

Brand(s): Regal.

Quality: Low grade, but what a looker!

Special Features: Dragon decalcomania.

Woods: Probably birch.

Measurements: "Regulation" size.

Logos Used: Paper soundhole label.

Known Original Wholesale List Price: $3.00.

"Finished in deep black ebony shaded to ivory in the center, ornamented with 'Red Dragon' decalcomania; white striping around top edge."--Grossman Catalogue Supplement, 1935.

Clown

Summary

Instrument: Ukulele.

Model: "Clown."

Years Made: 1937-1949.

Brand(s): Regal.

Quality: Low grade.

Special Features: Clown silkscreen around soundhole in brown or white, natural or mahogany finish.

Woods: Birch with possibly pine neck.

Measurements: "Standard size."

Logos Used: Green headstock decal, Regal blue/multi-colored headstock decal.

Known Original Wholesale List Price: $2.30-$4.75.

"Red Dragon" design ukulele, front and headstock. Courtesy Warren Dovell.

From the Regal catalogue, Five Regal ukuleles for 1939, including a "Clown" second from the left and an "Art Moderne" second from the right.

Nautical

Summary

Instrument: "Standard" and "Concert" ukulele.

Model: "Nautical."

Years Made: 1938-1952.

Brand(s): Regal.

Quality: Low grade

Special Features: Nautical design in white over brown, green or red tops with matching painted bodies, fingerboards, bridges and headstocks.

Woods: Birch?

Measurements: 20 ¾" by 6 ¾" "Standard," and "Concert" size.

Logos Used: Some version of Regal headstock decal.

Known Original List Price: $2.50-$4.00 wholesale, $2.69-$4.98 retail.

Red Burst

Summary

Instrument: Ukulele.

Model: "Red Burst."

Years Made: 1939.

Brand(s): Regal, Bluebird.

Quality: Low grade.

Special Features: Black body with red top sunburst with white painted top and soundhole binding.

Woods: Probably birch.

Measurements: "Standard" size.

Logos Used: Some version of headstock decal, "Bluebird" (house brand of The Sorkin Music House in Philadelphia) stenciled in white on headstock.

Known Original Wholesale List Price: $2.50.

"Nautical" ukulele duo, courtesy Warren Dovell.

Bigger Profits For You With Regal Fast Selling Ukuleles

No. 1939 Ukulele Assortment — All different — Packed twelve to the carton.

Bright, cheerful colors, highly decorated with beautiful stencil designs. Retail at **$2.50** each.

You will find these the fastest selling Ukuleles you ever handled. Just the thing for week-end sales.

Price **$2.50** each — 12 to the carton.

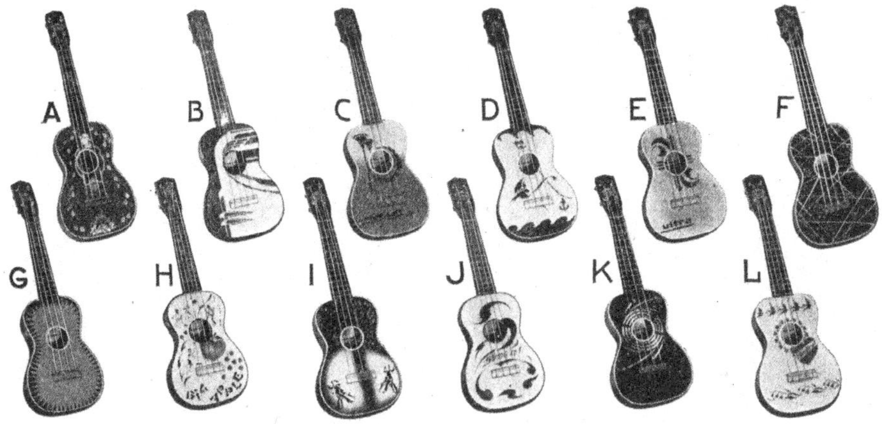

An assortment of "painted" Regal ukuleles, including (A) "Boy Scout," (B) "Art Deco," (C) "Good Luck," (D) "Nautical," (E) "Ultra," (G) "Red Burst" and (H) "Big Apple." From the 1939 Regal catalogue.

No. 2000 Ukulele Assortment mounted on beautiful display stand as pictured. Put them right in the window. Concert size, beautifully colored and artistically decorated.

A big Ukulele and a big value.

Six Ukuleles mounted as pictured.

$4.00 each or **$23.00** for six mounted. Order this assortment now!

[33]

Six more ukuleles from the 1939 Regal catalogue, from left to right, "Art Deco," "Sweetheart," "Good Luck," "Nautical," "Boy Scout" and "Big Apple."

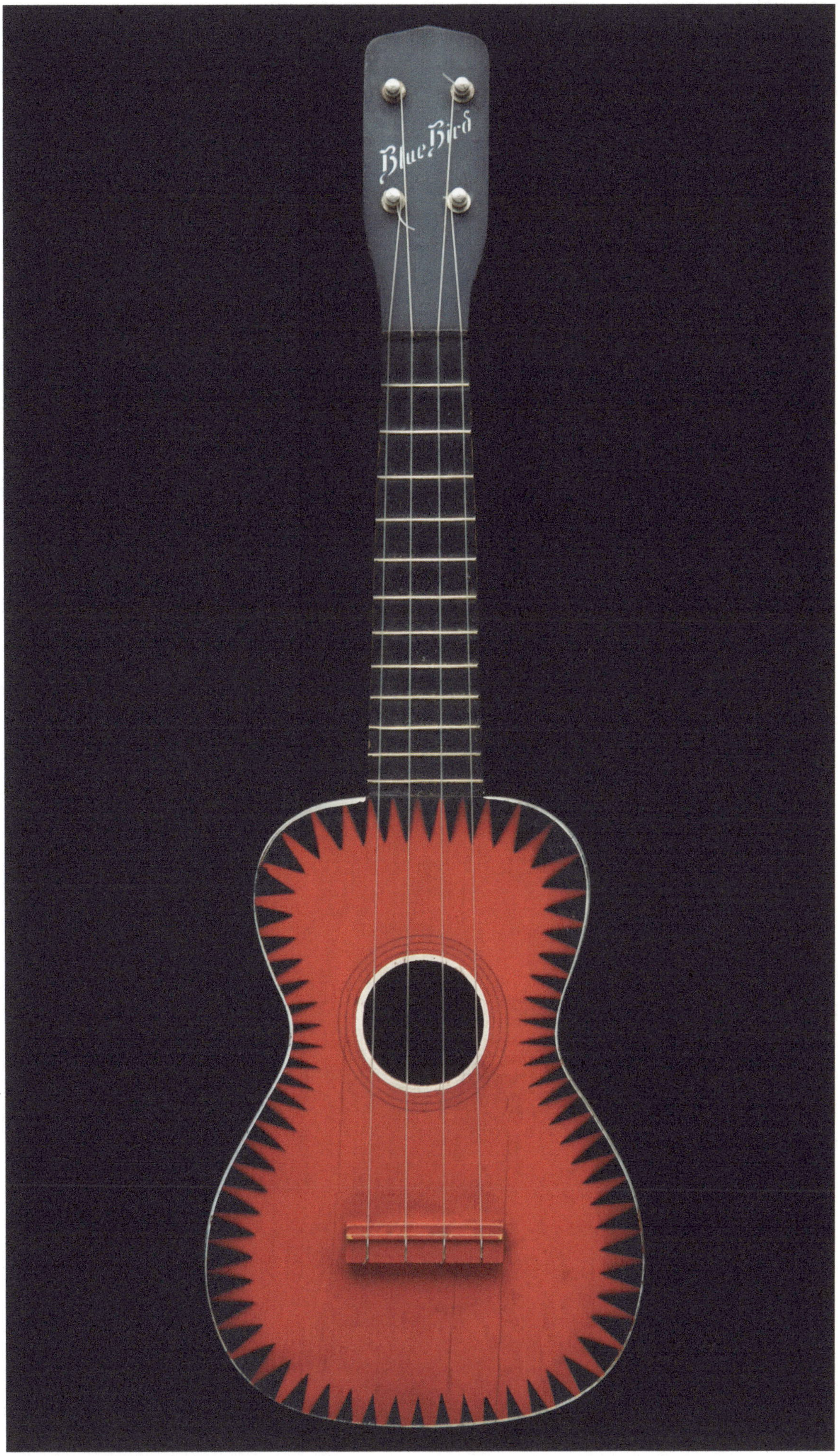

"Red Burst" ukulele, courtesy Warren Dovell.

Boy Scout

Summary

Instrument: Ukulele.

Model: "Boy Scout."

Years Made: 1939.

Brand(s): Regal, Bluebird.

Quality: Low grade.

Special Features: Grey-brown painted body with white screened with blue and red accented bear tracks, Boy Scout head (above soundhole), American flat shield (below soundhole) and campfire (below bridge). Painted white top and soundhole binding.

Woods: Probably birch.

Measurements: "Standard" and "Concert" size.

Logos Used: Some version of headstock decal, "Bluebird" stenciled in white on headstock.

Known Original Wholesale List Price: $2.50-$4.00.

Sweetheart

Summary

Instrument: Ukulele.

Model: "Sweetheart."

Years Made: 1939.

Brand(s): Regal.

Quality: Low grade.

Special Features: Brown painted back, sides and fingerboard, pink painted top and bridge with silkscreened bluebirds across the top bout and bluebells across the lower bout along with red hearts for the rosette and a large red heart with "Sweetheart" printed within it for the pickguard. Painted white top and soundhole binding.

Woods: Probably birch.

Measurements: "Standard" and "Concert" size.

Logos Used: Green headstock decal.

Known Original Wholesale List Price: $2.50-$4.00.

"Boy Scout" ukulele, courtesy Warren Dovell.

Ultra

Summary

Instrument: Ukulele.

Model: "Ultra."

Years Made: 1939.

Brand(s): Regal.

Quality: Low grade.

Special Features: As with the "Sweetheart": brown painted back, sides and neck; white painted top with silkscreened brown soundhole rosette; dancing figure on the lower bout and the word "Ultra" below the bridge. Red fingerboard.

Woods: Probably birch.

Measurements: "Standard" and "Concert" size.

Logos Used: Blue/multicolored headstock decal.

Known Original Wholesale List Price: $2.50-$4.00.

Good Luck

Summary

Instrument: Ukulele.

Model: "Good Luck."

Years Made: 1939.

Brand(s): Regal.

Quality: Low grade.

Special Features: Green painted back?, sides, neck, and fingerboard; yellow painted upper bout and red painted lower bout top with black screened flowers; soundhole rope or feathers binding and "Good Luck" below bridge.

Woods: Probably birch.

Measurements: "Standard" and "Concert" size.

Logos Used: Green headstock decal.

Known Original Wholesale List Price: $2.50-$4.00.

"Good Luck" model uke, photograph/courtesy Thomas Walsh.

Wendell Hall Master Crown Ukulele

Summary

Instrument: Tenor ukulele.

Model: Wendell Hall Master "Crown" Ukulele.

Years Made: 1939

Brand(s): Regal.

Quality: Medium grade.

Special Features: Regal "Crown" soundhole shape, curved fingerboard extension with fifteen frets, white bound top and back with black fine line.

Woods: Natural spruce top, mahogany neck, birch or mahogany back and sides.

Measurements: "Tenor" ukulele.

Logos Used: "Wendell Hall Master Ukulele" headstock decal.

Known Original Wholesale List Price: $9.00.

Victory

Summary

Instrument: Ukulele.

Model: "Victory."

Years Made: 1942-1943.

Brand(s): Regal.

Quality: Low grade.

Special Features: Wartime themed decoration.

Woods: Birch body and neck.

Measurements: "Standard" size: overall length is 20 7/8", 6 ¾" wide at lower bout, 2 3/8" in depth at the end block, scale length is 13".

Logos Used: Green headstock decal, blue/multicolored headstock decal.

Known Original Retail List Price: $1.79-$2.50.

Possibly the pinnacle of the Regal painted ukuleles was the "Victory". Conceived in the days following the attack on Pearl Harbor and aimed at inspiring patriotic strumming (and sales), the "Victory" has a blue painted body with a red "V" design and red lower fingerboard, along with white silkscreened "V"s, warplanes and American Bald Eagle. And, in keeping with war-time restrictions, Regal utilized the "non-critical materials" of wooden pegs and maple (!) frets.

A "Wendell Hall Master Ukulele," with a Regal "logo" crown-shaped soundhole. Courtesy Warren Dovell.

"Victory" ukulele, courtesy Warren Dovell.

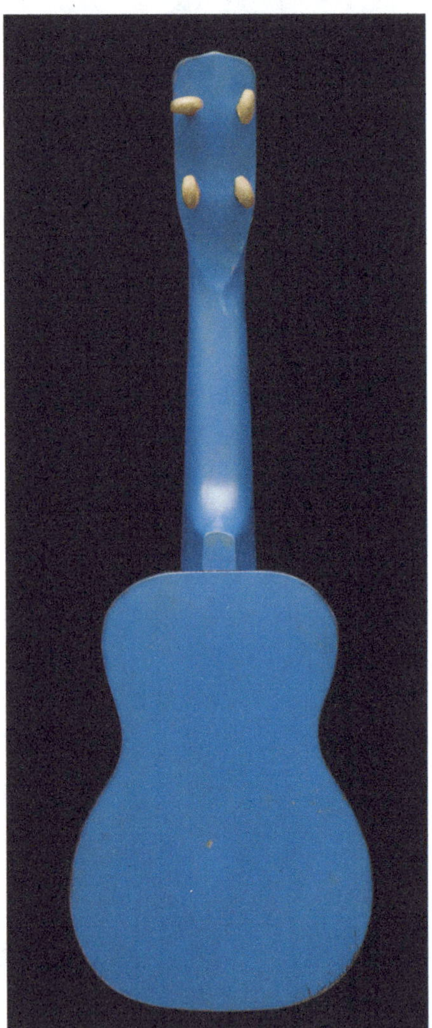

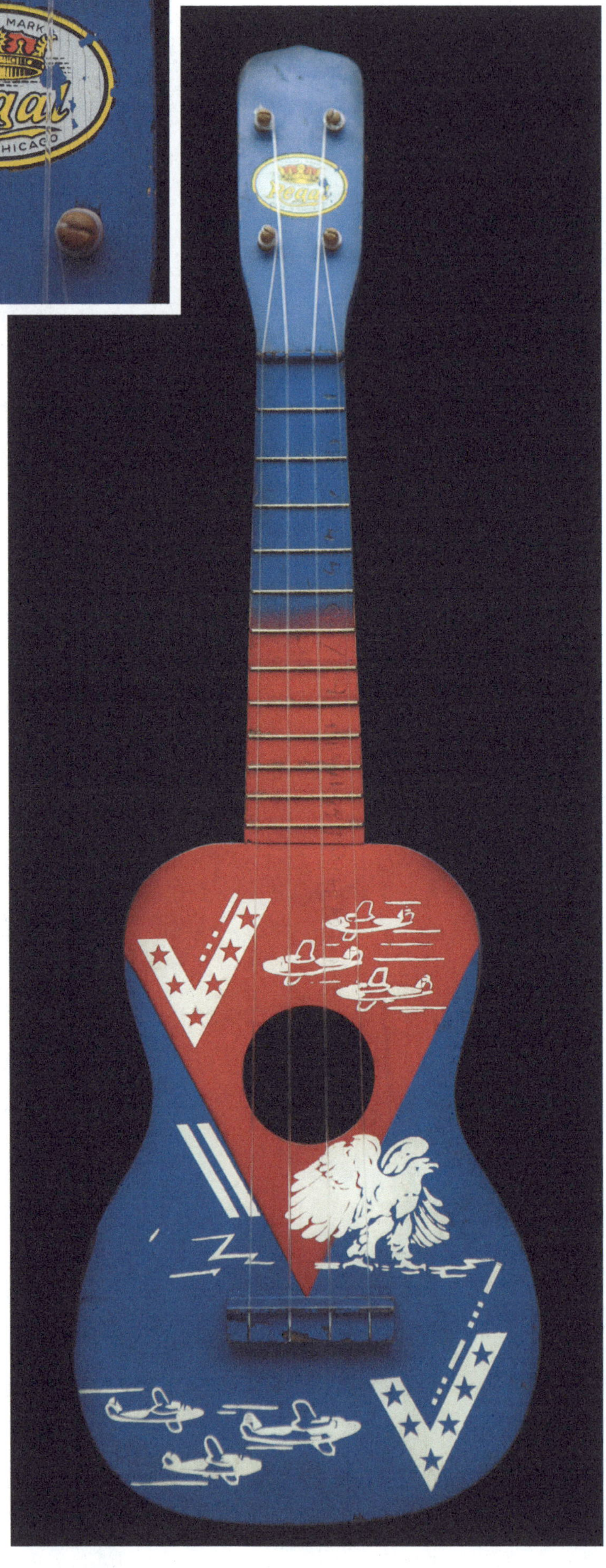

TV-Tee Vee/TeeViola

Summary

Instrument: "Concert," Tenor and Baritone ukulele.

Model: Wendell Hall "TV-Tee Vee/TeeViola."

Years Made: 1949-1951.

Brand(s): Regal.

Quality: Medium grade.

Special Features: Triangular-shaped soundhole on earlier models, "smile" bridge on later models.

Woods: Natural spruce top, mahogany or birch back and sides.

Measurements: Concert size: 14 3/4" scale, 7 1/2" lower bout, 2 1/4" body depth;

Tenor size: 17" scale, 9" lower bout, 6 ½" inch upper bout, 3" body depth, 26 ¾" overall length, 1 3/8" nut width.

Logos Used: Blue/multi-colored headstock logo.

Known Original Wholesale List Price: $10.95-$29.00.

Regal's relationship with Wendell Hall continued into the 1950s, when the popularity of the new television medium, which featured a ukulele strumming Arthur Godfrey, may have inspired Regal to revive their Hall brand. In addition to the details listed in the summary above, the instrument featured "Wendell Hall, TV" (earlier) or "TeeViola" (later) stenciled in white over a dark painted headstock overlay, bound soundhole, and rosewood fingerboard with "V" extension and no additional frets (earlier) or straight extended fingerboard with eighteen total frets (later models). The "TeeViola" had individual Kluson guitar tuners with white buttons, and the "smile" bridge also used by Regal for Washburn instruments appears on the "TeeViola" ukuleles in rosewood. All "TV/TeeViola" ukes had dark finished back, sides and necks. A version of the "TV" also turned up without the "Wendell Hall" designation in a brown sunburst.

"Wendell Hall TV" and "TeeViola," both pages with multiple views, courtesy Warren Dovell.

Regal
Wendell Hall
TEEVIOLA

Wendell Hall
TEEVIOLA

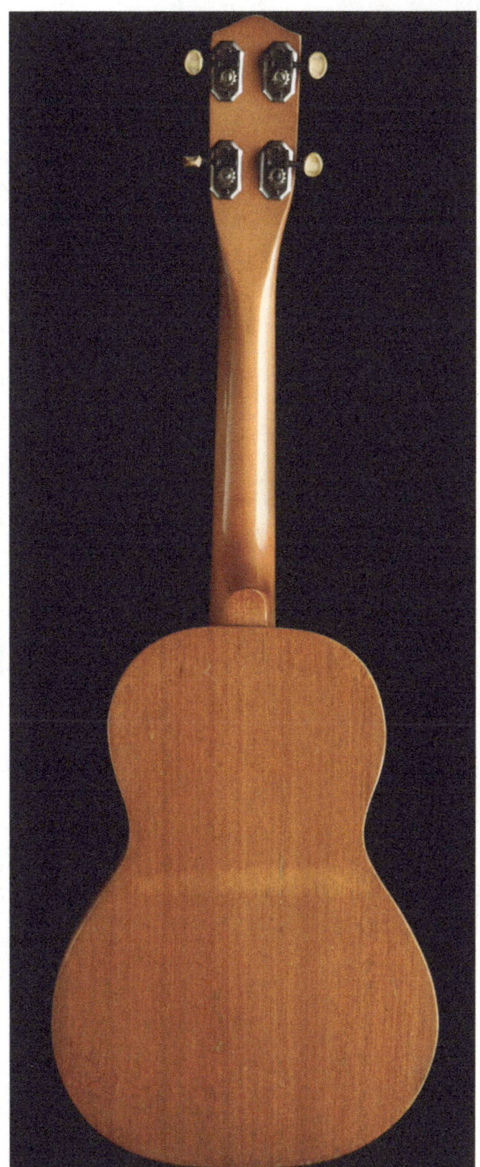

"Panda" uke (notice the bamboo frets), courtesy Warren Dovell.

Panda

Summary

Instrument: Ukulele.

Model: "Panda."

Years Made: Unknown.

Brand(s): Regal.

Quality: Low grade.

Special Features: White painted neck and body with five different panda characters silkscreened on front in black; painted black top, back and soundhole binding; bamboo frets. Probably based on children's book from the time when this model was manufactured.

Woods: Probably birch.

Measurements: "Standard" ukulele.

Logos Used: Green headstock decal.

Known Original List Price: Unknown.

Jungle

Summary

Instrument: Ukulele.

Model: "Jungle."

Years Made: Unknown.

Brand(s): Unknown.

Quality: Low grade.

Special Features: Covered in fake leopard fur, painted fingerboard dots, friction pegs with white buttons, 12 fret fingerboard.

Woods: Birch body, poplar neck.

Measurements: 13" scale, 1 5/16" nut width.

Logos Used: "Jungle Uke" horizontally in green lettering over a leopard head in yellow decal on headstock.

Known Original List Price: Unknown.

"Jungle Uke" is covered in fake fur. Photograph by Dave Matchette, courtesy Elderly Instruments.

F Hole

Summary

Instrument: Ukulele.

Model: "F" Hole.

Years Made: Unknown.

Brand(s): Regal.

Quality: Medium grade.

Special Features: Curved fingerboard extension with fifteen frets total, "F" holes in top bout, two point mandolin-shaped body.

Woods: Natural spruce top, mahogany neck

Measurements: Unknown.

Logos Used: Medallion headstock decal.

Known Original Wholesale List Price: Unknown.

Tiple and Taropatch: Tiple

On the heels of exploding interest in the ukulele came other Hawaiian-derived instruments. By 1925, Regal had entered the tiple and taropatch market. As described by copywriters for the Tonk Bros. in their 1930 tiple catalogue listing:

"This wonderful little instrument has a Guitar-shaped body about 12 inches long and the length of the neck is approximately 16 inches, making a total of 28 inches over all. The Tiple will appeal immediately to the advanced Ukulele player. The Tiple is strung with 10 steel strings. The F# and D set consist of three strings with one string tuned an octave lower. The A and B sets consist of two strings with one string on the A set tuned an octave lower. This scheme of tuning brings harmony that blends remarkably."

In 1939, Regal totted the tiple to their ukulele customers:

"Don't Overlook the Possibilities of the Tiple—Every Ukulele Player Is A Prospective Buyer.

"The Tiple is played just like the Ukulele and everyone has ever strummed a Ukulele would be happy to know just how much music they can get out of the Tiple. Tell your Ukulele players about it and you will be surprised over the number you will sell."

By the way, some folks pronounce this instrument's name "tip-ul" and other say "tip-le".

Nuff said!

"F" hole ukulele, courtesy Randy Klimpert.

PROGRESSIVE MUSICAL INSTRUMENT CORPORATION

"REGAL" Tiple as pictured above. It is about the size of a one-half size Guitar, strung with ten steel strings and tuned the same as a Ukulele or Taropatch; back and sides of mahogany; fine spruce top; hardwood neck; sound hole and top edge inlaid with colored block inlaying; both edges and sound hole bound with black celluloid; hand-rubbed to a satin finish.

Style Number 40 *Price $21.00*

"REGAL" Taro Patch No. 31 as pictured above. Finest mahogany body with hand-shaped mahogany neck; accurately scaled and fretted: sound hole and top edge bound with wide band of white celluloid; natural mahogany color, hand-rubbed to satin like finish. Wood pegs replaced with patent pegs. Good quality strings.

Style Number 31 *Price $12.00*

Mail Your Orders to 319 Sixth Avenue, New York, N. Y.

Regal Taro Patch and Tiple, as pictured in the PMI catalogue circa 1928. Courtesy The National Music Museum.

Schultz No. 2350

Summary

Instrument: Tiple.

Model: Schultz No. 2350.

Years Made: 1928-1949.

Brand(s): Regal, Bluebird, Datanta.

Quality: Low grade.

Special Features: None.

Woods: Birch body, maple neck.

Measurements: 8 ¾-9" at lower bout, 6 ½-3/4" at upper bout, 3-3 3/32" deep, scale measures 17", nut measures 1 and ½".

Logos Used: Medallion headstock decal (1928-1937), green headstock decal (1937-1949).

Known Original Wholesale List Price: $10.00-$16.00.

Regal's entry-level tiple came with a "mahogany-shaded" all birch body, bound top and sometimes back in white celluloid or paint; white bound or painted soundhole; twelve frets to the body eighteen frets total; a "double-decker" rectangular bridge; mahogany-finish neck; "ebonized" maple bridge, heelcap and fingerboard; and five-on-a-plate tuners. Some versions had "MOTS" "pearlette" fingerboards, pickguards and headstock overlays, and some late 1930s instruments are described in catalogues as having a plastic tortoiseshell pickguard.

Grossman No. 3475

Summary

Instrument: Tiple.

Model: Grossman No. 3475

Years Made: 1928-1949.

Brand(s): Regal, Bluebird, Datanta.

Quality: Low grade.

Special Features: Upgraded version of Schultz No. 2350 added wood marquetry top and soundhole binding, along with a rosewood headstock overlay and fingerboard, and black binding on late 1930s models. "MOTS" "pearlette" or the vinyl fingerboards found on other Regal instruments (some models).

Woods: Natural spruce top, birch back and sides, basswood/poplar neck.

Measurements: 8 ¾-9" at lower bout, 6 ½-3/4" at upper bout, 3-3 3/32" deep, scale measures 17", nut measures 1 and ½".

Logos Used: Medallion headstock decal (1928-1937), green headstock decal (1937-1949), paper soundhole label.

Known Original Wholesale List Price: $11.00-14.50.

Schultz No. 2351

Summary

Instrument: Tiple.

Model: Schultz No. 2351

Years Made: 1926-1949.

Brand(s): Regal, The Vernon.

Quality: High grade.

Special Features: None.

Woods: Natural spruce top, mahogany back and sides, "hardwood" poplar/basswood or mahogany neck.

Measurements: 8 ¾-9" at lower bout, 6 ½-3/4" at upper bout, 3-3 3/32" deep, scale measures 17", nut measures 1 and ½".

Logos Used: Paper soundhole label, medallion headstock decal (1928-1935), green headstock decal (1935-1949), blue/multi-colored headstock decal, "The Vernon" black on white celluloid plate attached to headstock.

Known Original Wholesale List Price: $16.00-$22.00.

Regal's top-of-the-line tiple adds a mahogany back and sides to the natural spruce top. Top, back, heelcap and soundhole are bound in black or white celluloid, top and soundhole also bound in colored wood marquetry, with tortoise binding or a sunburst neck on some models.

Schultz No. 2352

Summary

Instrument: Tiple

Model: Schultz No. 2352 "Junior Tiple."

Years Made: 1928.

Brand(s): Regal.

Quality: Low grade.

Special Features: ½ size instrument tuned in octaves, oval soundhole, "tulip" shaped headstock.

Woods: Birch body bound front and back in white celluloid.

Measurements: "Slightly larger than a concert size ukulele," length 22 ½", upper bout 5 3/8", lower bout 7 ½".

Logos Used: Medallion headstock logo, paper soundhole label.

Known Original Wholesale List Price: $9.00.

Tiple and Taropatch: Taropatch

Summary

Instrument: Taropatch.

Model: Taropatch.

Years Made: 1925-1928.

Brand(s): Regal.

Quality: Ok.

Special Features: A ukulele with double course strings tuned in unisons.

Woods: Mahogany body, "hardwood" or mahogany neck, soundhole and top bound in colored marquetry and black or white celluloid, wooden or patent friction pegs.

Measurements: Body size between a concert and tenor size ukulele.

Logos Used: Paper soundhole label.

Known Original Wholesale List Price: $12.00.

⚜ Chapter Ten ⚜

"Octofone," "Hawyofone" and "Basso Guitar"

"Octofone"

Frank Kordick was an inveterate tinkerer, particularly adept at coming up with "improvements" for existing instruments and music related paraphernalia. In many cases, the cure was worse then the disease! Such was the case with Kordick's patented tuning device for the ukulele. This bulky metal "contrivance" fit over the strings, in the process making all four the same note and, therefore, making tuning much simpler. And all for the low cost of just seventy-five cents! In early 1927, Regal introduced a new spray instrument "finish" that Kordick developed, building a special fireproof room on the factory's second floor to facilitate its use.

However, Frank Kordick's most outstanding accomplishment in his attempt at creating new products for the working musician had to have been the "Octofone." Introduced in January of 1928, the "Octofone" (so named because it was "eight instruments in one" and also had eight strings that could be tuned in octaves) was aimed at the booming market of four string plectrum instrument players. According to Regal, this four double-coursed long neck mandocello-like contrivance could be tuned and played like a tenor guitar, banjo, ukulele or mandolin, therefore allowing musicians to "double" on a lower pitched instrument without a change in fingering, "and get the best tone qualities of each!" Regal put all their advertising muscle behind the "Octofone", placing it in the hands of professional musicians, promoting it in the pages of Popular Mechanics, and arranging for radio recitals featuring the instrument. Besides selling through Regal's regular wholesale network, the Company sold the "Octofone" through Montgomery Ward in 1931 and 1932.

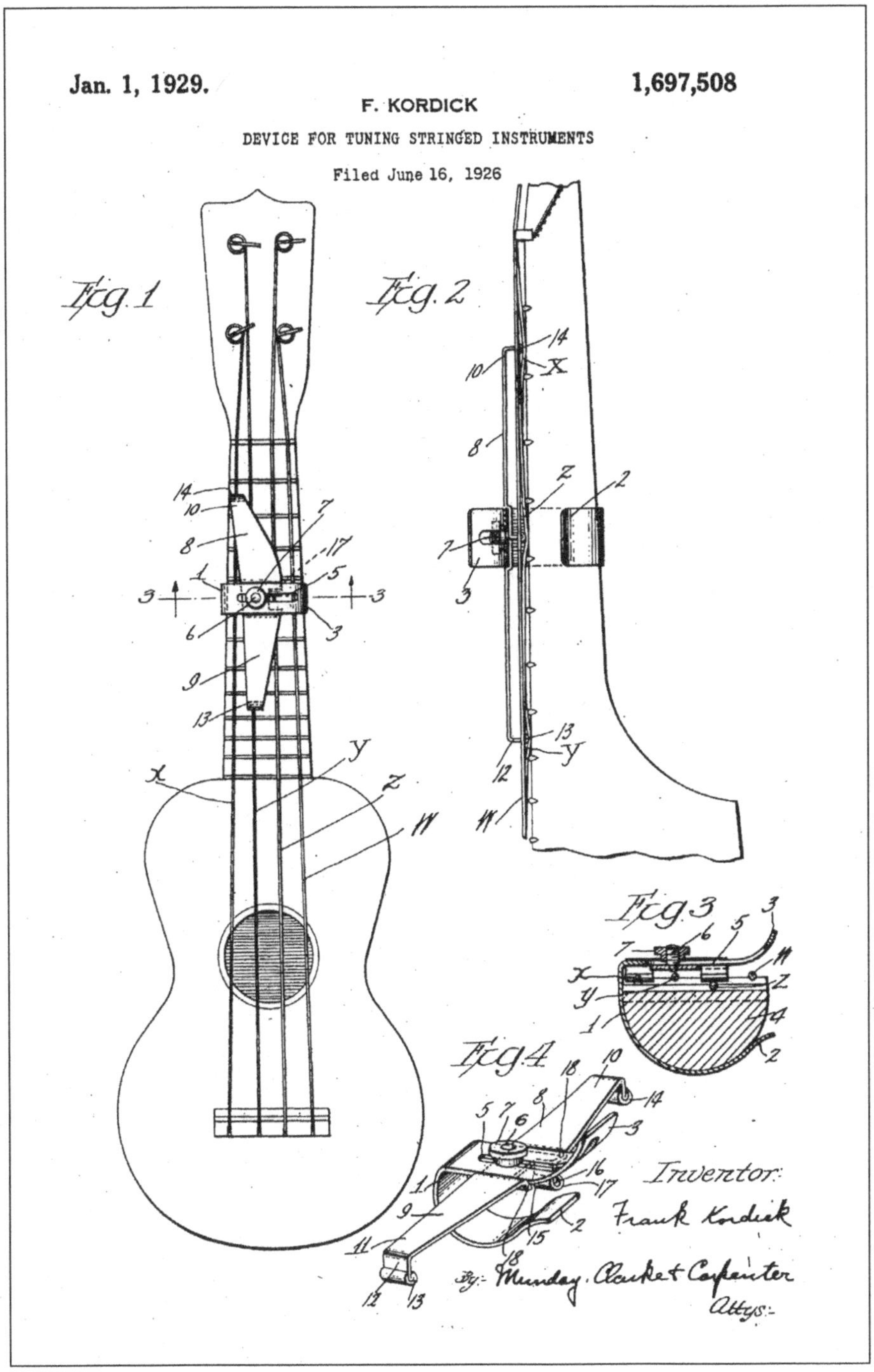

Patent drawing, "F. Kordick, Device for Tuning Stringed Instruments, Filed June 26, 1926."

Octofone

Summary

Instrument: "Octofone."

Model: "Octofone."

Years Made: 1928-1949 (birch), 1928-1939 (mahogany).

Brand(s): Regal.

Quality: Low to medium grade.

Special Features: Long-necked eight-string, unusual body shape.

Woods: Natural spruce over birch or mahogany, "hardwood" (poplar/basswood) or mahogany neck.

Measurements: Overall length is 33 1/2", 10 5/8"-10 11/16" width, 3"-3 1/8" in depth at the end block, scale length is 21" (standard for the tenor banjo), width of nut is 1 3/8".

Logos Used: Oval "Octofone" headstock decal, "PAT. APLD. FOR" on early models, Regal oval paper soundhole label.

Known Original List Price: $9.85-$13.85 retail, $15.00-$25.50 wholesale (birch); $30.00 wholesale (mahogany).

Regal made two versions of the "Octofone," the No. 1 with birch back and sides and the No. 7 with mahogany back, sides and neck. Both came with twelve frets to the body and a total of nineteen frets, a floating bridge, ebonized fingerboard, tulip shaped headstock, four-on-a-plate square ended tuners with top gears and Bell Brand tailpiece.

The No. 1 had an ebonized bridge; back, sides and neck finished to resemble mahogany; top and back bound in black celluloid (plus white celluloid around the back on some models beginning around 1930); and a soundhole rosette of colored wood marquetry blocks and fine lines. In 1938, the finish (or the descriptive wording) changed from "mahogany" to "imitation walnut." The No. 7 added colored marquetry top binding, a pearl trimmed bridge, and white celluloid binding on the top, back and soundhole. It was discontinued in 1939.

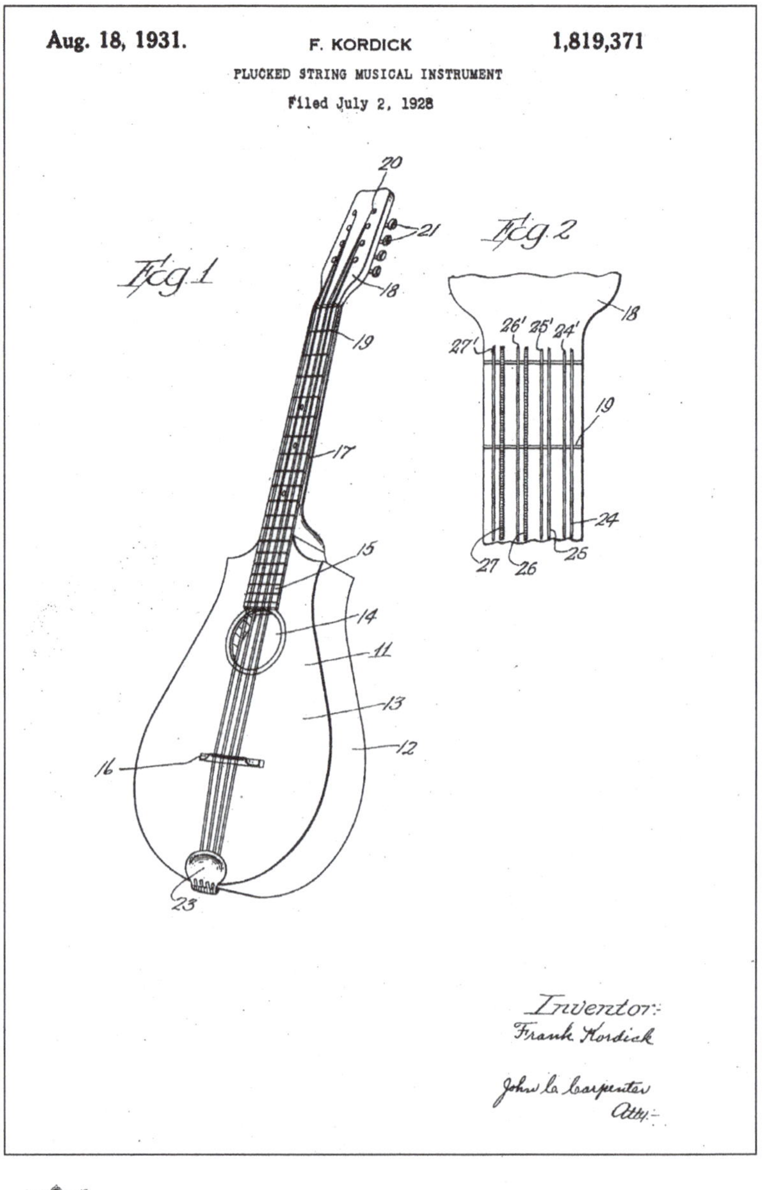

Patent drawing by Frank Kordick from July 2, 1928 for the "Octofone."

Octofone with Tenor Guitar Neck

Summary

Instrument: "Octofone."

Model: With Tenor Guitar Neck.

Years Made: 1928-1933.

Brand(s): Regal.

Quality: Low to mid-grade.

Special Features: Four string replaces eight string neck, adds "MOTS" "pearlette" fingerboard and headstock overlay, and changes to curved headstock shape ala Oahu faux painted guitar (see Chapter Seven).

Woods: Natural spruce over "rosewood" finished birch, "hardwood" (maple) neck.

Measurements: Overall length is 33 1/2", 10 5/8"-10 11/16" width, 3"-3 1/8" in depth at the end block, scale length is 21", width of nut is 1 3/8".

Logos Used: Regal medallion headstock decal, oval paper soundhole label.

Known Original Wholesale List Price: $15.00 (birch), $30.00 (mahogany).

Regal also utilized the "Octofone" body for a model of tenor guitar. Additionally, some "Octofone" four string necks ended up on regular guitar bodies.

Banjoists!

Take Those Soft Passages On The Octofone

BANJOISTS get sweet and harmonious tonal combinations when using Regal's new OCTOFONE as a doubling instrument. The OCTOFONE can be tuned as a Tenor Guitar, Tenor Banjo, Ukelele, Mandola, Mando 'Cello, and similar instruments, and get the best tone qualities of each!

Think of the advantages possessed by the owner of the OCTOFONE. He has a doubling instrument for solos and soft passages. Not only that, but he has a **new style** instrument, that can be tuned in **eight** different ways. Lastly, he has an instrument, out only a few months, that already exceeds the tenor guitar in popularity.

The instrument is shown below, played by George B. Menden, of Maurie Sherman's All Star College Inn Orchestra. His unsolicited testimony appears also.

George B. Menden, Banjoist, who doubles on the Octofone in Maurie Sherman's All Star College Inn Orchestra, Hotel Sherman, Chicago.

George B. Menden writes:
"Have been using my new Octofone for all my regular orchestra - recording and broadcasting work and have been receiving many compliments on its tone quality, especially over the air.
"It seems to be every banjo player's aim to double these days, and I like to recommend the Octofone as an ideal 'double instrument.' "

MADE BY

Regal Musical Instrument Co.

Grand at Sawyer

CHICAGO, ILL.

M. E. 5

Regal Musical Instrument Co.
Grand at Sawyer
Chicago, Ill.

Gentlemen: Please send me complete information about the Octofone.

Name ....

Address ....

Dealer's Name ....

George B. Menden demonstrates the "Octofone" in a Regal advertisement from June of 1928. Musical Enterprise, courtesy The National Music Museum.

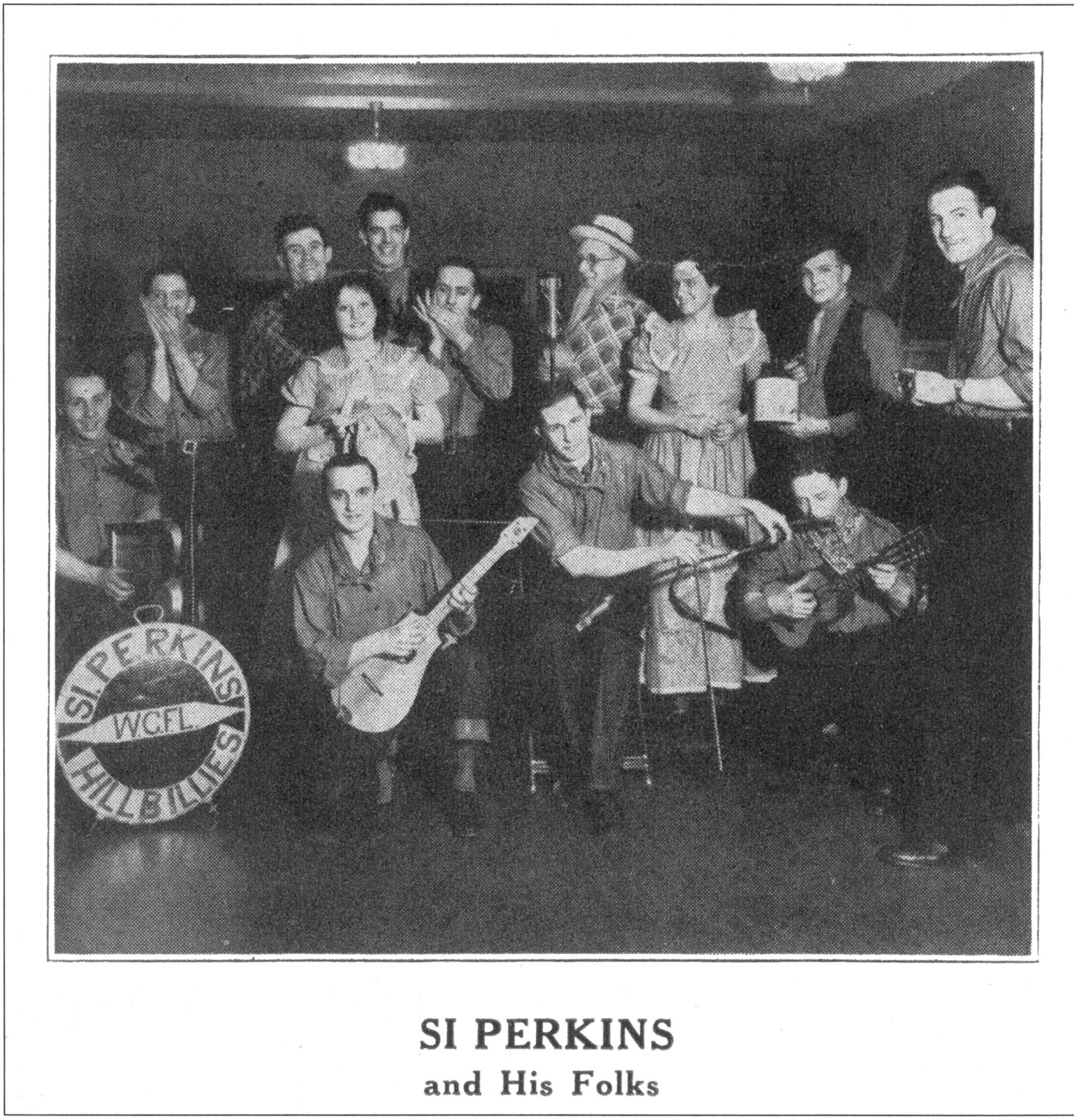

Si Perkins and His Folks, as they appeared on WCFL (Chicago Federation of Labor) radio station in 1935. Besides the "Octofone" with a tenor guitar neck, the tiple far right in the front may be a Regal product as well. From the sheet music cover for "The Bronk That Wouldn't Bust."

WE'RE POSITIVELY SENTIMENTAL ABOUT THE OCTOFONE!

It's our "baby" and your golden opportunity to cash in on a new market.

The Octofone—a Regal Creation. It is made especially for Ukulele players. It enables them to play a really advanced instrument without changing their technique. If they can strum a Ukulele, they can play the Octofone.

It is strung with eight strings tuned in octaves and produces a very pleasing and harmonious tone.

With each instrument we include free a very fine instruction book which any Ukulele player will readily understand.

The Octofone is a remarkable sales stimulator and you should have it on display.

The Regal Octofone is made in two grades.

No. 1325—Octofone in imitation walnut....**$15.00**

No. 1326—Octofone in genuine mahogany **30.00**

Challenge Case to fit.......... **4.50**

This handsome display card free with your order for either model.

[32]

"We're Positively Sentimental About the Octofone!" Regal catalogue, 1939.

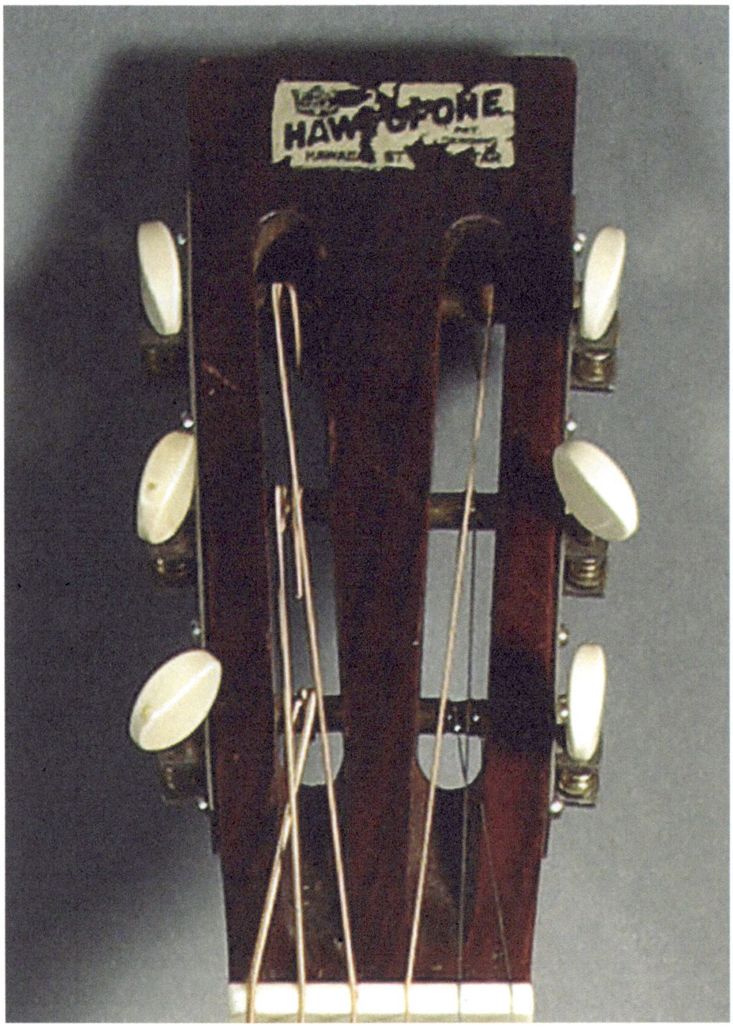

Combine "Hawaiian Guitar" with "Octofone" and you get the "Hawyofone." Here's the "higher grade" version made from mahogany. Photograph/courtesy Spruce Tree Music.

Hawyofone

Summary

Instrument: Hawaiian guitar.

Model: "Hawyofone."

Years Made: 1930-1938.

Brand(s): Regal, Sterling.

Quality: Low grade.

Special Features: Vaguely Weissenborn body style.

Woods: Birch or mahogany, "hardwood" neck.

Measurements: N/A.

Logos Used: "Hawyofone" headstock decal, "Regal" script headstock logo.

Known Original Wholesale List Price: $13.50-21.00.

No surprise that Regal made this wacky Hawaiian guitar, nor of the bizarre spelling of the model name combining the first part of "Hawaii" (as "Hawy") with the second part of "Octofone." This instrument came in two models, the lower being birch bound in black celluloid with a wood marquetry rosette, a "gun metal pearlette" "MOTS" fingerboard and pickguard, along with an ebonized bridge. The higher version was made of mahogany bound with black and white wood purfling (see photograph). There's not much else to say about this instrument, except that the shape was supposed to facilitate holding the guitar more comfortably in one's lap.

Basso Guitar

Instrument: Bass Guitar.

Model: "Basso Guitar."

Years Made: 1937-1939.

Brand(s): Regal.

Quality: Compared to what?

Special Features: Really big four string guitar played like a bass.

Woods: Possibly spruce over mahogany.

Measurements: 65" high from top to bottom with another 10" obtainable with the adjustable end pin, 23 ¾" across bout.

Logos Used: Oval paper sound hole label, Regal green headstock decal logo.

Known Original List Price: $67.50-$75.00 wholesale, $55.00 retail.

Just when you thought you'd seen it all, Regal (and President Frank Kordick) delivered the "coup de gras" in the form of the "Basso Guitar." Not a guitar, but, not quite a string bass, the "Basso Guitar" was a sight to behold indeed. Standing upright, it featured a slotted headstock; black/brown sunburst top, back and neck; floating bridge and tailpiece; with a rosewood fingerboard of fourteen frets to the body and twenty frets total. Regal laid on the hyperbole when it boasted:

"The biggest guitar in the world. The realization of the bass player's dream. . . because it is just what the dance orchestra man or string band bass player has been looking for.

"This beautiful instrument combines the volume and resonance of the double bass with the brilliant tonal qualities of the finest guitar! Strings and tuning are the same as the double bass. To be picked, plucked or slapped. It cannot be bowed. Frets lie flush with finger boards as guide for guitar players, making notes easier to find. . . and tones naturally come out in truer value.

"The BassoGuitar is a big NOVELTY number. Made for guitar players desiring 'bass background' . . . for string groups . . . for small dance bands. It is strongly constructed, though light, making it well suited for road work.

"Novelty value of the BassoGuitar is very important. It is bound to be the talk of any night club, tavern or stringed group. . . . because it is the biggest guitar in the world. It is a 'Natural' for the small guitar groups using the double bass.

"The BassoGuitar is strongly built, so that it can stand up under the strain of constant travel."

The Highlanders bluegrass band also utilized a "Basso Guitar." Courtesy Tom Mylet.

Regal BASSOGUITAR

bove: Del Mar's Franciscans, Salt Lake City, Utah
elow: King's Jesters, Chicago

The biggest guitar in the world. Stands 65" high from head to bottom with another 10" obtainable by adjustable end pin.

This beautiful instrument combines the volume and resonance of the double bass with the brilliant tonal quality of the finest guitar! To be picked, plucked or slapped; frets lie flush with finger boards as guide for guitar players.

The Bassoguitar is a big NOVELTY number. Made for guitar players desiring "bass background" . . . for string groups . . . for small dance bands. It is strongly constructed, though light, making it well suited for road work.

Wurlitzer's Strummer's Club, Piqua, O.

Regal "Basso Guitar," Regal catalogue, 1937. Courtesy The National Music Museum.

A Regal Timeline

1800's

February, 1878: Indianapolis, Indiana, Emil Wulschner opens his first music store.

1891: Indianapolis, Indiana, name change to "Wulschner & Son."

Circa 1895: Indianapolis, Indiana, Wulschner begins using the name "Regal" and the "crown" trademark to brand guitars, mandolins and banjos.

Circa 1898: Indianapolis, Indiana, John Keyes joins Wulschner firm to supervise the opening of separate manufacturing facility.

September, 1898: Indianapolis, Indiana, Wulschner opens factory on South Capitol Avenue.

1900's

April 8, 1900: Emil Wulschner dies, company incorporated as "Wulschner Music Company."

May, 1900: Indianapolis, Indiana, Regal Manufacturing Company established, headed by Wulschner's wife Flora, stepson Alex Stewart and William Ludlow.

April-August, 1901: Indianapolis, Indiana, Regal Manufacturing separated from the Wulschner Music Company and sold to a group of local investors. John Keyes stays with Regal to run the day-to-day business.

Circa fall, 1903: John Keyes leaves Regal.

February, 1904: Indianapolis, Indiana, Regal Manufacturing Company goes out of business.

November, 1904: Lyon & Healy of Chicago purchases remaining assets of the Regal Manufacturing Company, including the trade name, completed instruments, parts and raw materials.

November, 1906: Chicago, Illinois, Lyon & Healy renews the registration of the Regal trademark.

February, 1908: Chicago, Illinois, the Regal Musical Instrument Company incorporated as a separate entity from Lyon & Healy, headed by former L&H employees Frank Kordick/president, Anton Nelson/treasurer, Herman Schlitt/secretary and Marselius Danielson.

Circa 1911: Chicago, Illinois, Regal moves into its own factory building at 3211 West Grand Avenue.

Summer, 1917: Chicago, Illinois, Regal factory expanded.

Circa June, 1921: Chicago, Illinois, Albert Hunter joins Regal management.

1927: Chicago, Illinois, Anton Nelson leaves Regal, Albert Hunter assumes his duties.

1929: Chicago, Illinois, transfer of Regal trademark from Lyon & Healy completed.

1938: Chicago, Illinois, Regal begins selling directly to retail dealers, forsaking the network of wholesalers.

November 16, 1940: Chicago, Illinois, Regal president Frank Kordick dies. Al Hunter assumes the leadership role at Regal, aided by Herman Schlitt and his son Arthur.

November 28, 1955: Chicago, Illinois, the Regal Musical Instrument Company is liquidated, with the trademark passing to Harmony.

Circa 1955-1960s: Harmony uses leftover Regal parts and trade name on various instruments, including a line of acoustic guitars made for Fender.

1987-present: San Francisco, California, Saga Musical Instruments begins use of the Regal name and trademark for a line of resophonic instruments.

Regal Labels

Regal Advertisements

At least some of these bowl back mandolins were made by Regal. Montgomery Ward catalogue, spring/summer, 1922. Courtesy the Chicago History Museum.

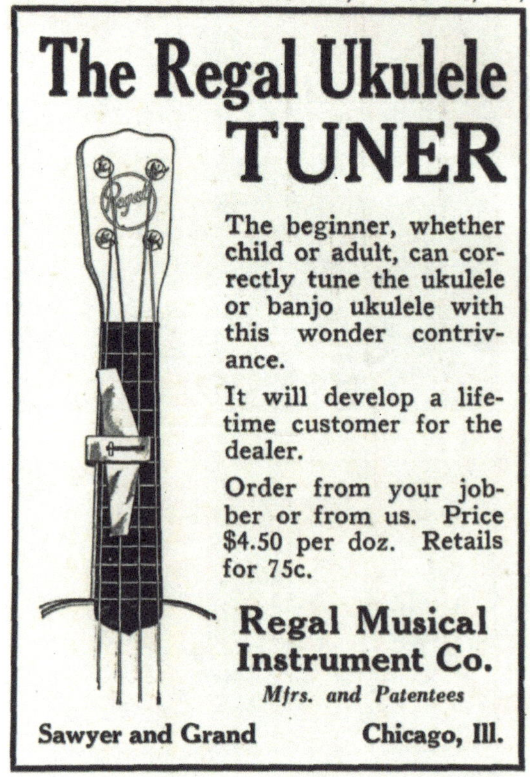

The Music Trade Review, December 11, 1926. Courtesy of Dan Del Fiorentino, Museum of Making Music.

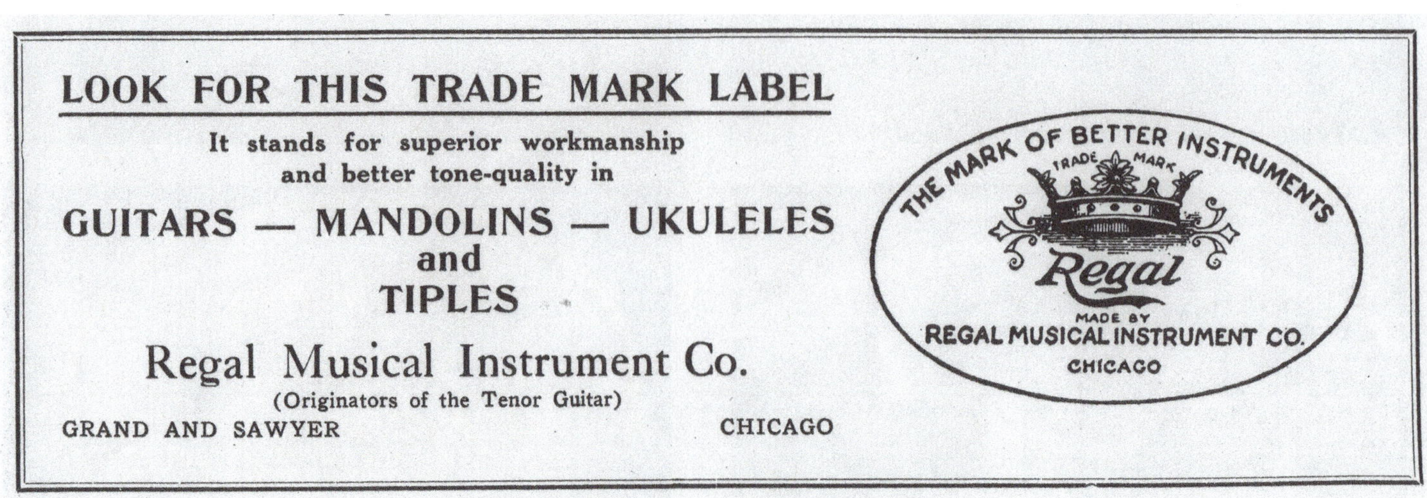

Frets magazine, July 1926.

The Music Trade Review, December 1930. Courtesy of Dan Del Fiorentino, Museum of Making Music.

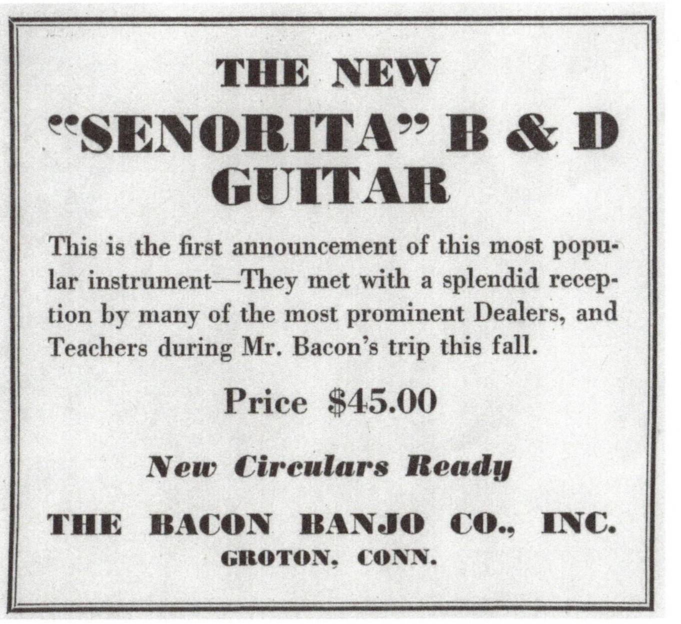

Metronome, December 11, 1926.

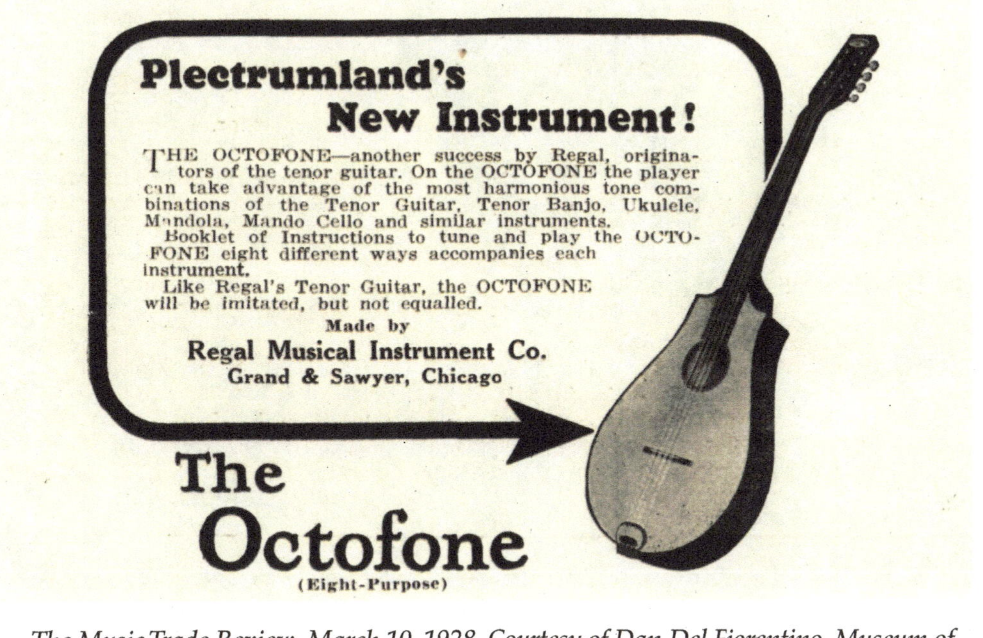

The Music Trade Review, March 10, 1928. Courtesy of Dan Del Fiorentino, Museum of Making Music.

Junior cowboy Gordon Gamm can't wait to show off this Regal guitar to his Aunt Ruth. Circa 1950.

More Great Books from Centerstream...

COWBOY GUITARS

by Steve Evans and Ron Middlebrook
foreword by Roy Rogers, Jr.

Back in the good old days, all of America was infatuated with the singing cowboys of movies and radio. This huge interest led to the production of "cowboy guitars." This fun, fact-filled book is an outstanding roundup of these wonderful instruments.

00000281 Softcover (232 pages) $35.00
00000303 Hardcover (234 pages) $55.00

SPANN'S GUIDE TO GIBSON
1902-1941

by Joe Spann

This detailed look at the inner workings of the famous musical instrument manufacturer of Kalamazoo, Michigan before World War II. For the first time, Gibson fans can learn about the employees who built the instruments, exactly where the raw materials came from, the identity of parts vendors, and how the production was carried out. The book explains Gibson's per-World War II factory order number (FON) and serial number systems, and corrects long-standing chronological errors. Previously unknown information about every aspect of the operation is covered in-depth. Noted historian Joe Spann gathered firsthand info from per-war employees, and had access to major Gibson collections around the world. Long time Gibson experts, as well as casual collectors, will find this volume an indispensable addition to their reference shelf.

00001525 302 pages $39.99

THE GIBSON 175
Its History and Its Players

by Adrian Ingram

Debuting in 1949 and in continuous production ever since, the ES-175 is one of the most versatile and famous guitars in music history. The first Gibson electric to feature a Florentine cutaway, the ES-175 was also one of the first Electric Spanish guitars to be fitted with P.A.F. humbuckers and is prized for its playability, craftsmanship, and full rich tone. Written by noted author/guitarist Adrian Ingram, contents include: the complete history of the 175, The Players, a beautiful ES-175 Color Gallery, Chronology, Shipping Totals, and more. This book is a must for every guitar player and enthusiast or collector.

00001134 .... $24.95

THE GIBSON 335
Its History and Its Players

by Adrian Ingram

Gibson's first "semi-acoustic" the ES-335, which was neither totally solid nor fully acoustic, is the guitar of choice used by many famous guitarists such as Andy Summers, Elvin Bishop, Lee Ritenour, Jay Graydon, Robben Ford, Freddie King, John McLaughin, Jimmy Page, Chuck Berry, Tony Mottola, Johnny Rivers, Jack Wilkins, Bono, Grant Green, Eric Clapton, Stevie Ray Vaughan, Alvin Lee, B.B. King, Emily Remler, Otis Rush, Pete Townshend, John Lee Hooker, and Larry Carlton. This book includes the complete history of the 335, the players, a beautiful color section, chronology, shipping totals and more. A must-have for every 335 player and guitar enthusiast or collector!

00000353 120 pages $29.95

THE GIBSON L5

by Adrian Ingram

Introduced in 1922, the Gibson L5 is the precursor of the modern archtop guitar. This book takes a look at its history and most famous players, from its creation, through the Norlin years, to its standing today as the world's most popular jazz guitar. Includes a 16-page full color photo section.

00000216 112 pages $29.95

GRETSCH – THE GUITARS OF THE FRED GRETSCH COMPANY

by Jay Scott

This comprehensive manual uncovers the history of Gretsch guitars through 32 pages of color photos, hundreds of black & white photos, and forewords by Fred Gretsch, George Harrison, Randy Bachman, Brian Setzer, and Duane Eddy. It covers each model in depth, including patent numbers and drawings for collectors.

00000142 286 pages $35.00

THE HISTORY & ARTISTRY OF NATIONAL RESONATOR INSTRUMENTS

by Bob Brozman

This book is a history book, source book and owner's manual for players and fans that covers the facts and figures necessary for serious collectors. In addition to many black and white historical photos, there is a 32-page color section, and appendixes with serial numbers for all instruments, a company chronology, and a Hawaiian Artist Discography.

00000154 296 pages $35.00

CENTERSTREAM®

P.O. Box 17878 - Anaheim Hills, CA 92817
(714) 779-9390 www.centerstream-usa.com

More Great Books from Centerstream...

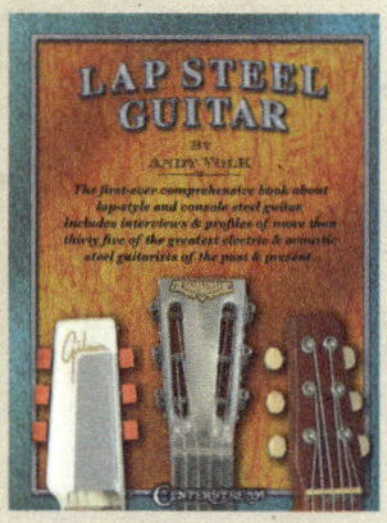

LAP STEEL GUITAR
by Andy Volk

This first-ever comprehensive book about lap-steel and console steel guitars includes: interviews and profiles of more than 35 of the greatest electric and acoustic steel guitarists of the past and present, representing most forms of music played in the world today. Also includes resources for guitars, amplifiers, accessories, instructional materials, steel guitar tunings; and much more.

00000320 336 pages $35.00

THE LARSONS' CREATIONS – CENTENNIAL EDITION
Guitars & Mandolins

by Robert Carl Hartman

This book is an account of two brothers who were premier producers of stringed instruments in the early part of this century. Swedish immigrant cabinet makers Carl and August Larson made instruments under the brand names of Maurer, Prairie State, Euphonon, W.J. Dyer & Bro., Wm. C. Stahl, and under their own name, and their highly collectible creations are considered today to be some of the finest ever made. This volume includes 16 pages of full-color photos, classic advertisements and catalogs, and a CD featuring guitarist Muriel Anderson playing 11 songs on 11 Larson instruments.

00001043 Hardcover Book/CD Pack $65.00
00001042 Softcover Book/CD Pack $45.00

MAKING AN ARCHTOP GUITAR
by Robert Benedetto

The definitive work on the design and construction of an acoustic archtop guitar by one of the most talented luthiers of the twentieth century. Benedetto shows all aspects of construction, even through marketing your finished work. Includes a list of suppliers; a list of serial numbers for Benedetto guitars; full-color plates; photos from the author's personal scrapbook; and fold-out templates.

00000174 260 pages $39.95

MUSIC MAN: 1978 TO 1982 (AND THEN SOME!)
The Other Side of the Story

by Frank W/M Green

Legendary for their construction and longevity, Music Man amps have earned the trust and respect of musicians worldwide. The company was the brainchild of industry vets Leo Fender, Forrest White, and Tom Walker. This book examines the latter – the company's "genius chief pilot/navigator" – particularly during the productive epoch from 1978 to 1982.

00001100 .... $24.95

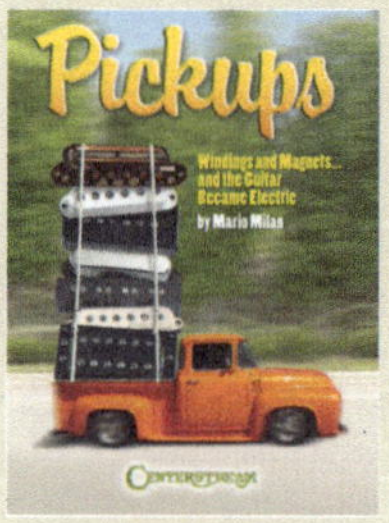

PICKUPS, WINDINGS AND MAGNETS
... And the Guitar Became Electric

by Mario Milan

Guitar collectors rejoice! The first book to examine pickups in detail is here! Covers everything from the first experiments to classic models conceived for Rickenbacker, Gibson, Fender, Gretsch, Danelectro, Epiphone, and others, with an overview of Japanese and European manufacturers. Includes a 32-page color section of the most popular models and rarities, a timeline, info on building pickups and technical specs, and biographical notes on George Beauchamp, Leo Fender, Seth Lover, Larry DiMarzio, and Seymour Duncan.

00001026 .... $29.95

RICKENBACKER
by Richard Smith

A complete and illustrated history of the development of Rickenbacker instruments from 1931 to the present, complete with information and full-color photos of the many Rickenbacker artists.

00000098 256 pages $35.00

WASHBURN PREWAR INSTRUMENT STYLES
Guitars, Mandolins, Banjos and Ukuleles 1883-1940

By Hubert Pleijsier

The vintage guitar collecting market continues to grow. This book is the first of its kind to report on pre-war Washburn guitars, mandolins, banjos and ukuleles. It contains detailed information about more than 450 instrument styles, serial numbering schemes and estimated production totals. A gorgeous 32-page color photo section of the most collectibles will make this book a "must" for players and collectors alike.

00001176 272 pages $45.00

RING THE BANJAR!
The Banjo in America from Folklore to Factory

by Robert Lloyd Webb

This is a second edition of a publication originally published to coincide with an exhibition of the same name at the Massachusetts Institute of Technology Museum. Includes information on the banjo's enduring popularity, the banjo makers of Boston, instruments from the exhibition, a glossary and bibliography of the banjo, and more.

00000087 102 pages $24.95

CENTERSTREAM®

P.O. Box 17878 - Anaheim Hills, CA 92817
(714) 779-9390 www.centerstream-usa.com